Praise for *The Six Disciplines of Breakthrough Learning*

"ATD is proud to co-publish this edition of *The Six Disciplines*. The content of the book is organized well, with case studies, illustrations, and other call-outs along the way that help readers understand the essence of the 6Ds. Practitioners in talent development will benefit from the practical knowledge and tools the authors share with the industry."

—Courtney Vital Kriebs, senior director, Education, Association for Talent Development (ATD)

"Every time I picked up *The Six Disciplines*, it caused me to stop, think, and rethink how I could take a more disciplined and purposeful approach to designing high-impact learning for results. A treasure trove for learning professionals who want to shift focus to performance rather than learning per se, to produce greater value from their efforts, and be valued as business partners."

—Serene Sim, head/principal learning designer, Learning Design and Technology Unit, Capability and People Development, Civil Service College, Singapore

"Roy, Andy, and Cal have done it again! They continue to raise the bar on what we as learning leaders should expect from ourselves and our function. I adopted the 6Ds methodology years ago, so was pleased to introduce the process and unleash its power more recently here at Keurig Green Mountain. Prepare to gain some great insights and success stories from this book."

—Jayne Johnson, vice president, Talent, Learning and Organization Development, Keurig Green Mountain, Burlington, Vermont, USA

"*The Six Disciplines of Breakthrough Learning* has become the hottest phrase in the T+D field in China. There are even more tools, best practices, and successful cases in the third edition. This book is a roadmap for harnessing synergy of training and business results in organizations."

—Yubo Fu, vice chief editor, Publishing House of Electronics Industry, Beijing, China

"A lot of training and development books teach technical concepts that just happen to be in a business context. The authors of this book have instead applied business concepts to teach pragmatic techniques in training—an important juxtaposition which makes all the difference in adding real value to organizations. This book should be in every training and development professional's personal toolkit. Brilliant!"

—Jennifer Hersom, senior vice president, Executive Leadership Development, Bank of America, Chicago, Illinois, USA

"In the last three years, the 6Ds have changed the face of learning for us and it is now a mandated process for all our learning interventions. The 6Ds go a long way in building the learning professionals' capability and enhancing the credibility of the function as a real business partner. This new edition felt like a fresh read and has deepened my commitment to 6Ds."

—Hemalakshmi Raju, learning leader, Tata Motors Ltd, Mumbai, Maharashtra, India

"The 6Ds framework is foundational for anyone concerned with delivering learning that drives results. The authors continue to work on learning transfer and the third edition contains their latest insights and additional practical tools."

—Bob Sachs, vice president, National Learning and Development, Kaiser Permanente, Oakland, California, USA

"*The Six Disciplines* is the roadmap to change behavior that impacts performance. Whether you are a business person who has an interest in developing others, or an experienced talent development professional, the 6D process will help you keep your focus exactly where it needs to be: on improving business performance."

—Connie Chartrand, global head, Talent Development, Morgan Stanley, New York, New York, USA

"Easy to read, and more importantly, easy to implement, the 6Ds is without doubt the most comprehensive guide on 'how to' create real business results from learning. Thank you, Roy, Andy, and Cal, for inspiring us to create even better outcomes."

—Emma Weber, chief executive officer, Lever–Transfer of Learning, Sydney, Australia

"I am delighted to see the third edition of *The Six Disciplines* is yet a further improvement on the previous editions. Combined with the wisdom of the methodology are truly practical guidance and tools that assist learning professionals in its application. This book provides value at all levels of a learning organization."

—Cheryl Lightfoot, director, Learning and Development, Merck & Co., Inc., Upper Gwynedd, Pennsylvania, USA

"This book should be the primary source of inspiration by any training professional whose aim is to convert a single training event into a learning and development experience, promoting efficient and long-lasting knowledge transfer. By demonstrating that learning is far beyond training and leads to human capital development, Pollock, Jefferson, and Wick set the training area in the position of a strategic business partner—not solely a supporting HR function."

—Grzegorz Plezia, learning and development consultant, Warsaw, Poland

"While there are many books on instructional design, this is all about process optimization! The authors build a compelling case to rigorously view ALL aspects of training as contributors to increased business performance. The third edition is as refreshing and thought-provoking to read as the previous ones and adds a new dimension in terms of hands-on practical tools. But here is my warning: after reading this book, you will have a hard time finding any excuse not to incorporate those principles into your daily practices."

—Marcus Assenmacher, senior director, Curriculum Development, Global Commercial Operations, Pfizer, Munich, Germany.

"I highly recommend the 6Ds method to anyone wanting to improve their training and information retention processes. This approach has been essential in helping my team standardize our technology training and increase its effectiveness. As a result of the 6Ds implementation in our organization, we have centralized our training methodology and implemented processes to streamline deployments and drive business performance."

—Shawn Thomas, director, Technology Learning Solutions, Bristol Myers Squibb, Plainsboro, New Jersey, USA

"A must-read for all trainers, *The Six Disciplines of Breakthrough Learning* offers an innovative new approach and practical advice on achieving impactful results through training."

—Julian Blaydes, general manager, The Royale Chulan Damansara Hotel, Petaling Jaya, Selangor, Malaysia

"*The Six Disciplines of Breakthrough Learning* should be mandatory reading for everyone who works in the learning and human development field. It is a very valuable resource and will definitely improve business outcomes. The authors have written an important guide that helped us design high-impact learning programs that delivered great value to our organization and learners."

—Sérgio Krivtzoff, project manager, Telefónica Learning Services, São Paulo, Brazil

"The third edition of *The Six Disciplines* is even better than the ones before. It offers learning professionals new step-by-step, comprehensive guides, tools, and approaches for ensuring optimal learning. By integrating logic modeling, this edition helps L&D departments achieve even better results of greater value. It rolls the Planning Wheel one step further and considers a broader range of factors that play an important role in learning effectiveness. I feel sincerely that no other book in the literature offers greater value."

—Cenk Tasanyurek, managing partner, PSQ International, Dubai, United Arab Emirates

THE SIX DISCIPLINES OF BREAKTHROUGH LEARNING

How to Turn Training and Development into Business Results

THIRD EDITION

Roy V. H. Pollock
Andrew McK. Jefferson
Calhoun W. Wick

WILEY

Cover image: Ris Fleming-Allen
Cover design: Wiley
Authors' photographs: Terence Roberts

Published by John Wiley & Sons, Inc., Hoboken, New Jersey

Published simultaneously in Canada

For general information about our other products and services, please contact our Customer Care Department within the United States at (800) 762-2974, outside the United States at (317) 572-3993 or fax (317) 572-4002.

Wiley publishes in a variety of print and electronic formats and by print-on-demand. Some material included with standard print versions of this book may not be included in e-books or in print-on-demand. If this book refers to media such as a CD or DVD that is not included in the version you purchased, you may download this material at http://booksupport.wiley.com. For more information about Wiley products, visit www.wiley.com.

Library of Congress Cataloging-in-Publication Data has been applied for and is on file with the Library of Congress.
ISBN 978-1-118-64799-8 (hbk)
ISBN 978-1-11-867744-5 (ebk)
ISBN 978-1-118-67717-9 (ebk)

Printed in the United States of America

10 9 8 7 6 5 4 3 2

CONTENTS

To our families, for encouraging us to pursue our dreams; to our clients, for allowing us to join them in their pursuit of excellence; and to our colleagues in learning and development, for their commitment to helping others achieve their full potential.

FOREWORD

Conrado Schlochauer, Principal
AfferoLab, Sao Paulo, Brazil

I remember vividly the first time I heard about the 6Ds. It was during a congress in Florida. Jayne Johnson, the then director, Leadership Education, for GE Global Learning Crotonville, was speaking. She was explaining how her company was really connecting corporate learning to business results. She mentioned *The Six Disciplines of Breakthrough Learning* several times during her presentation.

That was in early April of 2010. If you are a geeky early adopter like me, that date will mean something to you. The first iPad had just been released and I had managed to obtain one. I became so curious about the *Six Disciplines* that I bought the book *during* Jayne's speech, testing my new device at the same time. I started reading it immediately after her presentation.

I realized that I had finally found a method that reflects exactly what I believe about the right role for Learning and Development in the corporate world; one that agreed with my more than twenty years of experience in this field as a partner in Latin America's largest training company. I used all my free time during the breaks, at night, and on my flight back to Brazil reading, re-reading, and making notes.

As soon as I arrived back at my office, I did two things: The first was to buy copies of the book for my team, tell them to read it, and start organizing small working sessions to plan how we would integrate *The Six Disciplines* into our work with our clients.

The second one was to call the authors and start a conversation. It was (and continues to be) a good one. Andy, Roy, and Cal are not only some of the brightest professionals in the training industry, but they are also wonderfully open to new people, new insights, and new approaches. I considered myself lucky to be able to share time and best practices with all of them. We continue to discuss ideas and concepts for making learning and development even more effective and valuable.

In the five years since I downloaded my first copy of *The Six Disciplines*, I have seen its influence grow all over the world. My colleagues and I have introduced the 6Ds with great success throughout Latin America. The ATD (formerly ASTD) has started paying a lot more attention to learning transfer, and Roy, Andy, and Cal have taught workshops for corporate learning professionals on six continents, in person, and over the Internet.

This new edition of *The Six Disciplines* illustrates how the method continues to mature and evolve. The authors are practitioners as well as scholars; they listen to and work with real training people during their workshops, speeches, webinars, and consulting. The third edition incorporates new research insights as well as the best ideas and approaches that they have discussed with clients and students. It also reflects the learnings from the forty-some case studies in the excellent *Field Guide to the 6Ds* published in 2014.

I am confident that this third edition of *The Six Disciplines* will help us, as adult learning professionals, be even more proficient at a time when our field is being challenged as never before in the business world.

Here is how I think the 6Ds will change the way you think about corporate learning.

- *The 6Ds shifts the dialogue from HR-speak to business language.* When you start a learning project by structuring an Outcomes Planning Wheel with D1: Define the Business Outcomes in mind, it is almost impossible to go back to our former dialect, in which the logistics of training were more important than the business needs. It has been amazing to see line managers start using expressions like "complete experience," "learning transfer," and "new finish line."
- *The 6Ds makes us treat adult learners like adult learners.* I earned my Ph.D. in learning psychology researching adult learners. So it is very frustrating for me to see how few programs really use and apply andragogy principles and adult learning tools. In a straightforward and practical way, the third discipline—Deliver for Application—promotes experience sharing and real-world application. We don't need to continually

teach new content to adult professionals. There is enough content and knowledge already. We must help adult learners by offering curatorship and discussion on how and why they will apply this new learning to improve their performance.

- *The 6Ds challenges the corporate learning industry to rethink its approach.* We all know that there is a lot (and I mean a *lot*) of opportunity for improvement of our current *modus operandi.* Corporate training programs still produce far too much "learning scrap"—training that is never applied. We need to rethink our processes, our structures, and our systems, in order to realize the full benefits that Learning and Development can and should provide. For instance, the competences required to clearly define business outcomes are different from the ones we have in our departments now. Likewise, professionally managing learning transfer for maximum impact will require a change in the way a T&D department is built. Implementing the 6Ds in your Learning Organization will take significant effort. We have been doing things the way we are doing them for a long time, and change is hard. But I can say—based on my personal experience working with many different organizations—that the transformation in the way that learning is viewed and valued will be well worth the work.

- *The 6Ds provides a framework to organize, understand, and apply new concepts in corporate learning.* Every day, we hear about "new" concepts questioning the role of the formal learning initiatives in the corporate world. My personal view—based on my research and experience in the corporate and adult learning fields—is that if you understand the 6Ds in a conceptual way, you will understand that informal learning, social learning, 70-20-10, and so forth, are simply aspects of the complete learning experience (D2). In other words, the preparation, learning transfer, and achievement phases are rich opportunities for learning informally and socially; they are where the 70-20 learning happens.

When I speak about *The Six Disciplines,* I always like to point out the simplicity and the generosity of the model that Andy, Roy, and Cal have offered to the corporate learning field. Simple, because as I have often heard them say: "The 6Ds are common sense, even though they are not common practice." They didn't try to reinvent the wheel and they didn't overcomplicate it. Yet the approach is still rich in both depth and novelty. This third edition includes many recently released books and research studies. Indeed, the references include an excellent list of important reads for any corporate learning professional.

By generosity, I am referring to the way that the authors write all their books with the intention of helping you to *implement* the 6Ds in your organization. They include real "how-to" advice. All you have to do is read this book and you can start the process. Participating in a workshop will provide additional insight; plus, you can find more help in their other books and guides. If you have any questions, there is a LinkedIn group for 6Ds enthusiasts. For me, this reflects their real commitment to changing and improving our field.

During my Ph.D. program, I studied lifelong learning. Over the last forty years, many organizations (for example, UNESCO, European Union, OCDE) have discussed how to help literate adults keep learning in a rapidly changing society. Nevertheless, there has not been a lot of real action. I believe that we in corporate learning have an important leadership role to play. When we improve the quality and meaning of corporate learning, we are the ones who are implementing important, concrete, and structured actions related to lifelong learning.

By taking the disciplined 6Ds approach, we not only help companies increase their productivity and profitability, but we also help individuals become better professionals and learners and, as a consequence, we help society as a whole.

INTRODUCTION: THE SIX Ds

"Managed well, the learning function can become an indispensable, strategic partner with a significant impact on an organization's goals."

—David Vance

Two FACTS OF MODERN BUSINESS are irrefutable: (1) the pace of change is accelerating and (2) competition is ever more global and intense. In today's environment, "the organization's ability to learn faster (and possibly better) than the competition becomes its most sustainable competitive advantage" (de Geus, 2002, p. 157).

This book is dedicated to our conviction that corporate learning initiatives are vital, add real value, and help create competitive advantage. At the same time, we are convinced that such initiatives can and should add much greater value than they do today. *The Six Disciplines* describes a process and principles for extracting greater returns from the investments organizations make in learning and from the efforts of learning professionals.

Learning happens all the time—at work and elsewhere, planned and organically. Corporate training departments exist to help ensure that employees learn mission-critical skills at the right time and place so that the organization achieves its objectives.

> Learning can and should add even more value than it does today.

Indeed, "the *only* reason learning functions exist is to drive business outcomes" (Smith, 2010, p. 10).

Unfortunately, relatively few corporate learning functions achieve David Vance's vision of "indispensable, strategic partner with a significant impact" (Vance, 2010). To the contrary, numerous studies suggest that training and development is not highly valued by business managers. A survey conducted by the Corporate Leadership Council of the Executive Board, for example, found that "more than 50 percent of line managers believe that shutting down the L&D function would have no impact on employee performance" (Corporate Executive Board, 2009). Clearly, something is amiss between learning's potential and its current perception.

Fifteen years ago we started on a quest to understand why most learning initiatives fail to realize their full potential for strategic contribution. Our goal was to develop methods and tools that would allow them to do so. Since then we have worked with hundreds of organizations, large and small, in many industries around the world. We have been part of breakthrough learning initiatives that delivered results of undeniable value and that helped propel their organizations to a higher level of performance. Unfortunately, we have also observed many well-intentioned training initiatives flounder, producing little in the way of meaningful results.

When we compared the differences between these two extremes, we discovered that there is no "magic bullet"—no one, simple fix that transforms corporate learning from a peripheral function into a strategic imperative. We discovered instead that effective learning initiatives are the result of a disciplined and systematic process executed with passion, excellence, and a commitment to continuous improvement.

We distilled the practices that drive high-impact learning into six disciplines, which we described in *The Six Disciplines of Breakthrough Learning* (Wick, Pollock, Jefferson, & Flanagan, 2006) and updated in a second edition four years later (Wick, Pollock, & Jefferson, 2010). We chose a name that started with a "D" for each discipline to make them easier to remember and apply. They have subsequently become known as the 6Ds® (Figure I.1).

Many organizations throughout the world have adopted the *Six Disciplines* as the organizing principles for their training and development efforts. The 6Ds have proven to be a powerful and enduring approach to defining, designing, delivering, and assessing corporate learning. This third edition of *The Six Disciplines of Breakthrough Learning* has been extensively revised to incorporate new insights, research, and best practices. It includes the checklists we developed for the 6Ds Workshops (Pollock, Jefferson, & Wick, 2013) and *The Field Guide to the 6Ds* (Pollock, Jefferson, & Wick, 2014). We have added "practical application" tips throughout the text to help you translate research and theory into practice.

FIGURE I.1.   THE 6DS THAT TURN LEARNING INTO
BUSINESS RESULTS

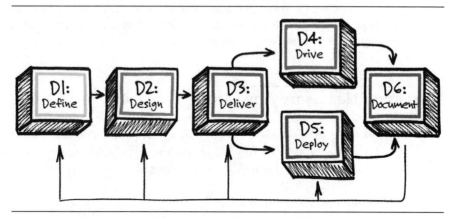

A WORD ABOUT TERMINOLOGY

We need to say a bit at this point about terminology.

This book is about optimizing the planned learning that organizations, typically companies, provide for their employees. The 6Ds principles, however, also apply to not-for-profit enterprises and government agencies. For simplicity, we use the term "business," "company," or "corporate" to refer to the sponsoring organization and ask the reader to substitute another term if appropriate. A knowledgeable and competent workforce is essential for any organization, whether or not it is expected to produce a profit. Indeed, given the generally more limited resources of not-for-profit organizations, their need for efficiency and effectiveness is even greater.

We will often use the word "training" to refer to an intentional effort to teach people how to do something, since the term is still widely used and understood. Trying to replace every instance of "training" with "learning" would have created some awkward and potentially confusing prose. By "training" we mean purposeful efforts to teach people how to perform job roles in which the requisite skills are well understood—for example, sales, customer service, supervision, safe work practices, and so forth. Our use of "training" does not pre-suppose any particular methodology or technology; we intend it to include the whole spectrum of purposeful learning—from e-learning to classrooms, structured to social, mobile to mentoring.

Education, in contrast, we define as preparing people to deal with novel challenges in which the best path forward is unknown (and often unknowable) in advance. As such, education tends to focus much more on the application of principles and theories rather than specific skills. Development, as in "learning and development" or "training and development," has a longitudinal aspect. That is, development entails a series of training, educational, and experiential opportunities *over time* to help individuals achieve their full potential.

The 6Ds are designed to maximize the business value of the intentional learning opportunities provided for employees—regardless of when or where those occur, through what medium, or by what method.

Is Training Necessary Any More?

Based on interviews of successful managers, Lombardo and Eichinger formulated the 70/20/10 model, according to which: "Lessons learned by successful and effective managers are roughly

- 70 percent from tough jobs
- 20 percent from people (mostly the boss)
- 10 percent from courses and reading" (Lombardo & Eichinger, 1996)

McCall, Lombardo, and Morrison (1988) went further, pointing out that "Only a minute part of a manager's time is spent in the classroom, suggesting that it's the other 99.9 percent of the time that the bulk of development takes place." That kind of observation, combined with today's technology-enabled information access, have led some to question whether it still makes sense to invest in training at all, or to suggest that "only 10 percent of learning and development's budget, time, and resources should be spent on one-off learning sessions that equip employees with new skills" (Robertson, 2014).

First, it should be pointed out that the 70/20/10 "rule" was derived from studies that focused on executive success, rather than the full range of jobs and job skills. The ratios would almost certainly be different for other roles such as sales, technical support, quality assurance, or research.

Second, the ratio is a broad generalization based on retrospective personal reflections. The hypothesis is impossible to test; there is no way that the relative contribution of all the different sources of learning could be measured accurately across a whole career.

Third, even if the percentages could be determined, they are likely to be misleading since they do not take into account the *criticality* of the learning. A small percentage does not necessarily mean unimportant or dispensable. For example, learning to read consumed only a minute fraction of the total time you have spent learning in your life—almost certainly less that 1 percent—but it has been absolutely essential for everything else.

Thus, 70/20/10 is a broad generalization, not a prescription for the ideal ratio. That most learning takes place outside of training initiatives should come as a surprise to no one;

> Most learning takes place outside of training initiatives.

it is where most people spend the vast majority of their time. Nor does 70/20/10 diminish the value of the right training at the right time for the right people. Even the original study noted that "formal coursework, however, was sometimes included by executives as an event that made a significant difference to them" (McCall, Lombardo, & Morrison, 1988, p. 180). The 70/20/10 ratio actually suggests that formal training is efficient; it supposedly contributes 10 percent to success, although the average employee spends about thirty hours a year in training—less than 2 percent of his or her time at work (ASTD, 2013).

What the model does do is serve to remind workplace learning professionals that people are learning all the time. Unless the training, coaching, culture, and performance management systems are all in alignment, corporate-sponsored learning initiatives are unlikely to have much effect.

Case in Point I.1
Training Is More Important Than Ever

Vikram Bector is the chief talent officer for Reliance Industries, Ltd., the largest private sector company in India. He has also served as chief talent officer for Tata Motors, where he helped establish the Tata Motors Academy, and as chief learning officer for Deloitte, India.

"The need for training has never been greater," Vikram told us, "especially in high-growth markets like India, China, and Brazil. Young managers are being buoyed along by the rapidly rising tide of growth. They are often promoted without adequate training or experience for their new roles. In many cases, they don't know what they don't know. That increases their risk of failure, which hurts their careers, the people who work for them, and the organization as a whole.

"We are also seeing more and more young people coming into the workforce who are not adequately prepared to succeed in business. Although they are often university-educated and tech-savvy, they are not industry-ready. Many lack the background knowledge, work habits, and social skills their employers need. Businesses and universities must work together more closely to ensure that graduates are ready for their first jobs and beyond.

"It's not just the employees who aren't ready; many businesses aren't either. They have not kept pace with the changing business climate and economy. Organizations need to look at changing the nature of work, re-create it, and remodel it to suit the needs and learning styles of the next generation. Talented individuals want engaging work and stretch assignments, mentorship, and the ability to learn, grow, and do different things. Too many companies still create mundane and repetitive jobs and then are surprised when their best talent leaves. They need to understand that 'great talent wants to work for great organizations and clients.'

"Training is a core business function that is vital to the success of the enterprise as a whole. It is not just another HR process. It needs to be closely aligned to the business strategy, and it needs to be managed like a business—with clear objectives, sound processes, and meaningful measures of success.

"The widespread use of technology and unlimited information available on the Internet is not an adequate substitute for training that teaches people how to lead, manage, satisfy customers, and otherwise perform their jobs. For many jobs, we need to reinstitute more of an apprentice model in which younger employees are observed and mentored on the job by those who have already mastered the discipline. There is really no substitute for such experience.

"I don't see the need for training decreasing. I am convinced that the most successful companies will be those who use training as a core element of their business strategy and deliver the right training to the right people when they need it."

The importance of incidental learning notwithstanding, planned and structured learning is still vital in organizations (see Case in Point I.1). Professionally planned and executed learning initiatives are essential to ensure:

- *Consistency*—making sure that all associates are taught the same approach and that these are consistent with company values and policies as well as legal, regulatory, and safety requirements.
- *Efficiency*—done well, training groups of employees is more efficient than training each individually or letting them discover everything they need to know on their own. A planned program of learning can be especially important for making new employees productive quickly with company- and job-specific knowledge and skills.
- *Quality*—knowledge of instructional design and access to subject matter experts enables workplace learning professionals to design higher quality and more effective interventions than relying solely on informal learning. "Without intentional support, informal learning can be unruly and therefore costly. Unconsciously, incompetent people often help others become the same" (Gottfredson & Mosher, 2011, p. 11).

- *Awareness*—people don't know what they don't know. So even if information is available, they may not know they need it. Salespeople need to learn new products; operators may be unaware of the dangers of certain actions; managers may need 360-degree feedback to help them identify blind spots.

Companies invest in training and development to improve performance (Figure I.2) in areas key to their success and competitiveness. The value of a training department, therefore, is determined by the effectiveness and efficiency with which it contributes to better performance, not the number of initiatives, kinds of training it provides, or technology it employs. Workplace learning professionals need to shift their focus from delivering training to delivering improved performance. Fred Harburg said it well: "We are not in the business of providing classes, learning tools, or even learning itself. We are in the business of facilitating improved business results" (Harburg, 2004, p. 21).

> We are in the business of facilitating improved business results.

Once workplace learning professionals accept that their mandate is to deliver performance improvement, rather than training per se, they

FIGURE I.2. THE PURPOSE OF TRAINING IS TO IMPROVE PERFORMANCE

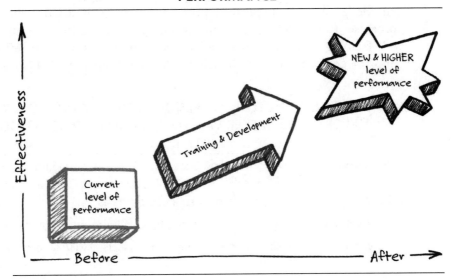

embrace a broader spectrum of methods, media, and approaches, which includes *not training* when the goal can be achieved more effectively in other ways.

When Is Training the Answer?

This book is about maximizing the value of performance improvement efforts that involve learning and development. That is not to say, however, that training is the only path to performance improvement or necessarily the best path. Indeed, the misuse of training as an improvement strategy wastes significant time, money, and effort and contributes to the relatively poor perception of training by business leaders. The first question that should be asked about any request for training is whether training is a necessary or appropriate solution.

On-the-job performance is influenced by factors at three levels: the worker, the work, and the workplace (Addison, Haig, & Kearney, 2009, p. 6). All three are themselves influenced by the political and business climate (the world) in which the organization operates. The key elements of each level are given in Table I.1.

What this means is that job performance is always the result of the interaction between individual capabilities and environmental influences. Substandard performance can result from an impediment at any level, or any combination of levels. For example, a worker might have the necessary knowledge and skills to perform proficiently, but be thwarted by inefficient processes (the work) or by counterproductive policies (the workplace).

Training initiatives (planned learning interventions) are efforts to improve performance by enhancing individuals' capabilities. That assumes

TABLE I.1. THE FOUR LEVELS OF FACTORS THAT IMPACT PERFORMANCE (AFTER VAN TIEM, MOSELEY, & DESSINGER, 2012, p. 6).

The Worker	Individuals' knowledge and skills, capacity, motivation, and expectations
The Work	Work flow, processes, and procedures
The Workplace	Organization, resources, tools, culture, mission, and values
The World	Political and economic climate; societal values, norms, and culture

that the impediment to performance is at the individual worker level. Training is an appropriate and potentially effective response *if, and only if,* a lack of skills or knowledge is the root cause of the gap between actual and desired performance.

As Table I.1 illustrates, however, there are many other systemic factors that contribute (positively or negatively) to performance. "We often find that a project brought to us as a Worker/Individual Level problem, such as, 'These people need train-

> Job performance is the result of interaction between individual capabilities and environmental influences.

ing,' … has to be solved at the Workplace/Organization Level" (Addison, Haig, & Kearney, 2009, p. 56). If the real issues are at the work or the workplace level, then trying to improve the worker is a waste of time and money and a source of frustration for all concerned.

The problem is that many managers see training as the solution to every sort of performance challenge, even when the real issues lie elsewhere (Pollock, 2013). Learning professionals in our 6Ds Workshops estimate that 20 to 50 percent of the training they do is doomed to failure because the real issue is not a lack of skills or knowledge among those being trained. Mager and Pipe (1997) suggested that the key question to ask when trying to decide whether training is an appropriate response is: "If their lives depended on it, would they be able to perform adequately?" (Figure I.3). If they can, then it is a problem of "Will I?," not "Can I?" That's important to know because "If a genuine lack of skill is not the problem, then you can forget training as a potential solution" (Mager & Pipe, 1997, p. 93).

FIGURE I.3.   THE KEY QUESTION IN DECIDING WHETHER OR NOT TRAINING WILL HELP IMPROVE PERFORMANCE

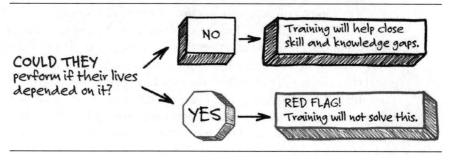

Whenever Mark Thompson, president and chief engagement officer of McKinley Solutions, is asked to provide a specific course, he says, "Sure, that could help." But then he asks to meet over a cup of coffee to discuss in greater depth the issue the client is trying to solve. He says that 30 to 40 percent of the time, the discussion leads to quite a different solution. "So, for example, we were asked to come in to do a professional development course. On further investigation, though, we learned that what the company needed most was for leaders to improve their ability to inspire trust by being more transparent. Rather than a generic program, we proposed instead 360-degree feedback review sessions with targeted skill-building and coaching. What we delivered was a true performance improvement solution; had we simply taken the order for what was asked—an off-the-shelf leadership program—it would have been far less effective."

The point is that the first and most important decision that needs to be made is whether or not training is an appropriate solution. If it is the wrong solution, then it won't work, no matter how well it is designed and executed. Use the flow chart (Exhibit I.2) to help you identify the real issues. If a lack of skills or knowledge contributes to the performance gap, then use the 6Ds to design, deliver, and document the results of a planned learning intervention. If the real issue is in the environment, processes, or performance management system, help management address the real issues and don't waste resources on training (Jaenke, 2013).

Learning and the Moment of Truth

Regardless of how employees learn new skills—in a live class, virtually, through a simulation, on the job from a co-worker or manager, or any number of other ways—that learning only adds value if it is applied appropriately at the "moment of truth." The moment of truth occurs when an employee has the opportunity to apply the new knowledge and skill in the course of his or her work. Employees have two choices (Figure I.4): complete the task in the new way they just learned, or continue to perform as before (same old way), which might be to do nothing at all.

If they choose to perform in the new (and presumably better) manner, then the learning creates value. If they persist (or revert) to performing in the way that they had previously, then the learning is of no value, performance won't improve, and the investment in learning was a waste of time and resources (see Learning Scrap below).

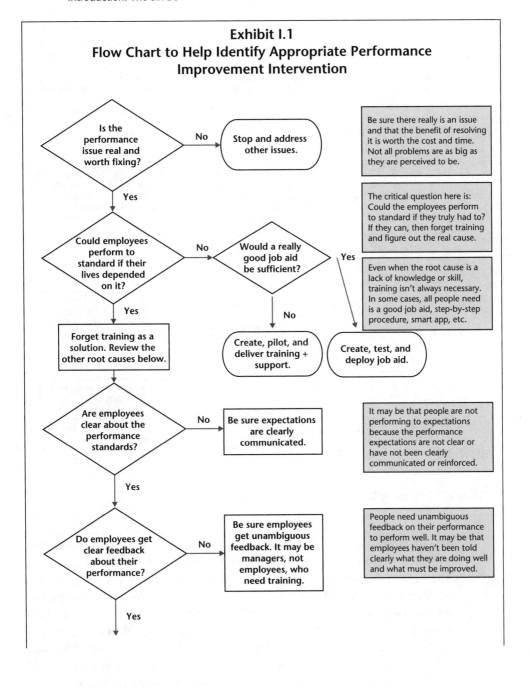

Exhibit I.1
Flow Chart to Help Identify Appropriate Performance Improvement Intervention

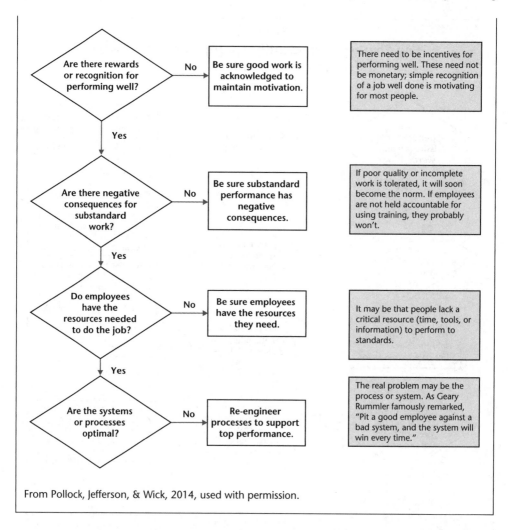

Are there rewards or recognition for performing well? — **No** → Be sure good work is acknowledged to maintain motivation.

There need to be incentives for performing well. These need not be monetary; simple recognition of a job well done is motivating for most people.

Are there negative consequences for substandard work? — **No** → Be sure substandard performance has negative consequences.

If poor quality or incomplete work is tolerated, it will soon become the norm. If employees are not held accountable for using training, they probably won't.

Do employees have the resources needed to do the job? — **No** → Be sure employees have the resources they need.

It may be that people lack a critical resource (time, tools, or information) to perform to standards.

Are the systems or processes optimal? — **No** → Re-engineer processes to support top performance.

The real problem may be the process or system. As Geary Rummler famously remarked, "Pit a good employee against a bad system, and the system will win every time."

From Pollock, Jefferson, & Wick, 2014, used with permission.

The problem is that doing something a new way, especially the first few times, requires more effort than persisting in the old way. It takes sustained effort to climb up the experience curve, which is why we have drawn the "new way" as a flight of stairs in Figure I.4. Moreover, performing the new way may initially take longer and even produce inferior results until the person achieves proficiency. In contrast, the "old way" is easy and predictable. It has the force of gravity behind it; no effort is needed to slide back into old habits. Indeed, habits are so powerful that "unless you deliberately *fight* a habit—unless you find new routines—the [old] pattern will unfold automatically" (Duhigg, 2012, p. 20).

Figure I.4.   THE "MOMENT OF TRUTH" IS WHEN AN EMPLOYEE DECIDES HOW TO PERFORM A TASK

Which path an employee chooses depends on the answers to two critical questions: "**Can I** do it the new way?" and "**Will I** make the effort?" (Figure I.5). It makes no difference how much an employee learned or how the knowledge was obtained; unless he or she answers "Yes, I can" and "Yes, I will" at the moment of truth, the learning adds no value to the organization (Pollock & Jefferson, 2012).

Corporate-sponsored learning needs to be conceived, designed, and delivered in the right way, at the right time, to the right audience, in a conducive work environment to ensure that both the "Can I?" and "Will I?" questions are answered in the affirmative (Figure I.6). Otherwise, the effort is a failure and the learning is just a pile of scrap.

Figure I.5.   WHICH PATH AN EMPLOYEE CHOOSES DEPENDS ON THE ANSWERS TO TWO QUESTIONS: "CAN I?" AND "WILL I?"

Figure I.6.   EMPLOYEES MUST ANSWER "YES" TO BOTH THE "CAN I?" AND "WILL I?" QUESTIONS FOR LEARNING TO ADD VALUE

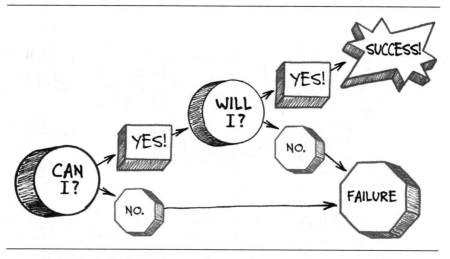

Learning Scrap

A product that fails to meet the customer's expectations and that therefore must be discarded or reworked is manufacturing scrap. Scrap is costly in terms of the raw materials and labor wasted, as well as the damage that defective products cause to the company and brand. In addition, there is the opportunity cost of tying up resources, producing waste instead of creating value (Table I.2).

As Deming (1986) famously pointed out: "Defects are not free. Somebody makes them, and gets paid for making them" (p. 11). No manufacturer nowadays can compete successfully against companies

TABLE I.2. COSTS OF MANUFACTURING SCRAP

Tangible (Out-of-Pocket Costs)	Intangible Costs
Materials	Customer dissatisfaction
Labor	Damage to brand reputation
Rework/recalls	Opportunity costs
Overhead	
Plant capital	

with more consistent quality and lower scrap costs. For these reasons, manufacturers have worked relentlessly to drive down the scrap rate by applying continuous-improvement methodologies. Many have achieved the goal of six sigma quality—less than one defect in 300,000 units.

What does manufacturing scrap have to do with training and development? In the first edition of *The Six Disciplines*, we coined the term "learning scrap" to refer to training that

Learning scrap is expensive.

employees attend, but never use in a way that improves their performance (Wick, Pollock, Jefferson, & Flanagan, 2006). Unused learning is the training equivalent of a defective product; it fails to meet the customers' expectations—in this case, the business leaders' expectations of improved performance.

Learning scrap—like manufacturing scrap—is expensive. It puts a company at a competitive disadvantage. The costs are similar (Table I.3). Learning scrap squanders the tangible costs of labor (of both trainers and trainees), travel, materials, technology, vendors, and so forth, as well as the opportunity costs of having people waste time in programs learning things they cannot or will not use.

As with manufacturing scrap, learning scrap also incurs the cost of customer dissatisfaction. When managers, having invested their people's time and departmental resources in some learning initiative, fail to see subsequent improvement, they are dissatisfied. They conclude that the training failed and are therefore reluctant to invest again in the future. Altogether, companies waste billions of dollars producing learning scrap and probably several times that in lost opportunities.

How much of training today is scrap? That indeed is the elephant in the room.

TABLE I.3. COSTS OF LEARNING SCRAP

Tangible (Out-of-Pocket Costs)	Intangible Costs
Materials	Customer dissatisfaction
Labor	Damage to brand reputation
Retraining	Opportunity costs
Overhead	
Training facility capital	

The Elephant in the Room

That training often fails to improve performance has been recognized for decades. As far back as the 1950s, Mosel pointed to "mounting evidence that shows that very often the training makes little or no difference in job behavior" (Mosel, 1957, p. 56). Thirty years later, Baldwin and Ford (1988) reviewed the literature and concluded: "There is growing recognition of a 'transfer problem' in organizational training today. It is estimated that while American industries spend up to $100 billion on training and development, not more than 10 percent of those expenditures actually result in transfer to the job.... Researchers have similarly concluded that much of the training conducted in organizations fails to transfer to the work setting."

Has anything changed? To find out, we have asked thousands of workplace learning professionals this question:

> After a typical corporate training program, what percent of
> participants apply what they have learned well enough and long
> enough to improve their performance?

The vast majority *of training providers themselves* estimate that less than 20 percent of corporate training actually leads to improved performance. Business leaders concur. In a survey conducted by McKinsey and Company, only 25 percent of business managers said that training and development contributed measurably to business performance (DeSmet, McGurk, & Swartz, 2010).

Of course, these are only estimates. Training professionals admit that their responses are simply a "best guess"; very few have actually measured how often training is transferred and produces improved performance. An ESI International study of learning transfer reported a similar observation: 60 percent of more than 3,000 respondents admitted that the primary method for evaluating transfer was either anecdotal feedback or "simply a guess" (Haddad, 2012). Even the most widely cited figure—10 percent—was also just an estimate (Georgenson, 1982).

Although precise measures are often lacking, the strong perception among both business leaders and learning professionals is that most training efforts fail to deliver improved performance. That explains

> The failure of training to improve performance is the elephant in the room.

why, as mentioned above, more than half of business managers were of the opinion that employee performance would not suffer if learning and development were eliminated completely! (Corporate Executive Board, 2009). The failure of training to improve performance is the elephant in the room: it is something that everyone knows about, but no one wants to discuss (Figure I.7).

The lack of attention to the issue is surprising, since no company could stay in business long if its other processes were as inefficient as most learning and development initiatives seem to be. To illustrate the point, we ask training professionals in our workshops what their reaction would be if they gave Federal Express one hundred packages to deliver but only 20 percent arrived as expected. They agree: FedEx would be out of business "overnight."

Figure I.7.   THE LEARNING TRANSFER PROBLEM

"I'm right there in the room, and no one even acknowledges me."

Successful companies, like FedEx, understand that meeting customer expectations is paramount. They relentlessly pursue the goal of zero failures by continuing to invest creativity, energy, technology, and money to improve the reliability and efficiency of their processes.

In stark contrast, companies have done relatively little to improve their training success rates in the sixty years since Mosel called attention to the problem, despite general agreement about the gross inefficiency of most initiatives. For our own survival, and for the good of the enterprises we serve, those of us in the learning and development business need a much greater sense of urgency about reducing the number of times our efforts fail to deliver improvement. We need to invest time, creativity, and technology to reduce the time and resources wasted producing scrap, just as our colleagues in manufacturing and service industries do.

A Multi-Faceted Challenge

As we began to look into the question of why some learning initiatives improve performance while others produce scrap, we discovered many and diverse reasons that training can fail to generate the desired results:

- Insufficient clarity of the business rationale and desired outcomes
- Trying to use training to solve problems it cannot and will not solve
- Training the wrong people, or the right people at the wrong time
- Trying to stuff too much content into too little time
- Insufficient opportunities for practice with feedback
- Treating training as a one-off event
- Lack of buy-in and support from the trainees' managers
- Failure to measure outcomes and act on the findings
- And many more …

Similar lists have been complied over the years by Spitzer (1984), Phillips and Phillips (2002), Latham (2013), and others. It became clear, given the many potential points of failure, that a rigorous and disciplined process would be required for an organization to consistently realize value from its investment in learning and development. The process would have to be different and more comprehensive than the instructional design systems already in use (ADDIE, SAM, and so forth), as they address only part of the problem. That is why, despite all the hype, learning technologies have had limited impact; the point of failure is not usually the learning itself, but rather, the lack of transfer.

The Six Disciplines are a business- and process-driven approach that complements and extends instructional design systems. The 6Ds provide a mnemonic for the discipline and thoroughness needed to extract maximum value from training and development. They have proven valuable in practice for reducing learning scrap and enhancing the business impact of learning interventions.

Introducing the 6Ds

The key themes of each of the Six Disciplines are briefly introduced below. In the remainder of the book, we devote a full chapter to each "D," exploring it in depth and providing examples, tools, and recommendations to maximize its impact. You can read straight through from D1 to D6, or you can use the 6Ds Application Scorecard (page 36) to identify which discipline offers the greatest opportunity for improvement in your organization and begin there.

Improving the practice of any one of the Six Disciplines will improve results; paying attention to all six will maximize the value that training delivers to your organization.

Define Business Outcomes

The First Discipline is to clearly and unambiguously define what the business expects to happen as a result of the learning intervention. The core concept is that learning is pursued in support of some organizational goal. The better the goal is understood, the easier it is to design an effective strategy (of which training may or may not be a part).

The fundamental logic of corporate-sponsored learning is that organizational value is created through people's actions—serving customers, developing new products, managing projects, making sales, leading people, or any of the thousands of other activities that take place in even a modest-sized firm. The better that people perform these actions, the better the organization is able to fulfill its mission, whether that is making a profit, saving lives, or serving constituents.

Training employees to perform better and more efficiently is thus one aspect of an organization's competitive strategy. An investment in learning is expected to pay returns in terms of improved performance, such as greater productivity, enhanced customer satisfaction, higher quality, better retention, lower cost, and so forth. Every company-funded learning initiative—whether classroom-based, e-learning, on the job, social learning, coaching, tuition reimbursement, or anything else—is ultimately intended to serve a business purpose.

Thus, corporate-sponsored learning is simply a means to an end—improved performance (Figure I.2). Business managers are willing to invest time and resources in learning initiatives *so long as* they deliver demonstrably improved performance. If they do,

> An investment in learning is expected to pay returns in terms of improved performance.

then learning and development is seen as a strategic asset; if they don't, then the training function is a drain on earnings and a target for reduction.

For that reason, the First Discipline (D1) of clearly **defining the business outcomes** for every learning initiative is the most critical and foundational. We do not mean *learning objectives;* we mean *objectives for on-the-job performance.* We do not question the value of learning objectives to guide instructional design. But we feel strongly that they are wholly inadequate to communicate the business rationale for the investment. Learning objectives define *what* people will *learn,* but not the *benefits* of doing so. They fail to answer the fundamental question that employees and business leaders are interested in:

- How will this initiative help me achieve my goals?

Learning objectives are written to explain what participants will *know* or be *able to do* at the *end of the program.* Business objectives for training, in contrast, specify what trainees *will do on the job* afterward and how that will *benefit the business.*

Getting clear about D1—the desired business outcomes—shifts the focus from learning to performance. It makes designing an effective intervention easier, assists in securing management buy-in, and is prerequisite to meaningfully documenting the results (D6). Perhaps most importantly, having clearly defined business outcomes allows training organizations to *win.* They can unambiguously demonstrate their value because they know what success means to the business.

Making the shift from learning to performance is not without its challenges. Surprisingly, some of the resistance comes from the business leaders themselves. That's because

> Clearly defined business outcomes give learning a chance to *win.*

many have become accustomed to thinking of training as a cure-all and something that you order the way you order a pizza. As a result, they may initially struggle to articulate the business rationale and may not welcome the realization that they have shared responsibility for the results.

Case in Point I.2
Extending Learning at Emerson

When Terrence Donahue accepted the leadership of the Charles F. Knight Learning Center at Emerson, he knew he had big shoes to fill. The former director had been highly respected and greatly admired. The learning organization he had built—which is responsible for leadership training for Emerson worldwide—enjoyed strong support from management and an excellent reputation throughout the company. They embraced the importance of learning transfer. How could Terrence and his team build on those strengths and take learning to an even higher level of excellence?

They decided to use the 6Ds to strengthen their ties to the business, drive learning transfer, and ensure that training delivered business impact. They started spreading the idea of a new finish line: that a leadership development experience isn't finished until leaders have transferred and applied their new skills and knowledge. The Learning Center staff kept repeating the message about business outcomes and began including transfer and achievement phases in program plans and descriptions.

And the message began to stick. "The concept of the new finish line for learning has struck a resonant chord here and across our enterprise," Terrence told us. "A global manufacturing company like Emerson really understands the concept of manufacturing scrap, so the concept of learning scrap has hit some people like a thunderbolt."

For example, one of the business unit presidents recorded a video for all supervisors in his company, outlining his expectations of them to drive learning transfer and provide performance support and how he intended to hold them accountable for outcomes. In India, front-line supervisors attending Leading at Emerson 2.0 are so excited about the implementation phase that they are calling their facilitators to share their successes.

In the company's 2015 Professional Development Learning Guide, the senior vice president for human resources, Michael Rohret, wrote: "We are making a significant investment in your future ... don't become a victim of 'learning scrap.' Attending a workshop and not applying what you learned is a wasted investment. To make sure your learning investments bring a return, we introduced a 'new finish line for learning.' "

The chief financial officer, Frank Delaquila, embraced the concept immediately, so much so that he agreed to record a video "call to action" for the company's flagship program, *Leading at Emerson*. The video is shown about 90 minutes before the end of the workshop phase of the program. In it, the CFO congratulates participants and explains how the workshop is an investment Emerson has made in a foundation for their careers. He goes on to emphasize that "there is more work to do" if that investment is to pay dividends. "The value of the training will be measured by what you do with that foundation; that is, *what you put to work when you are back to work.* The next twelve weeks are actually the most important part of the process." Coming from the CFO of a $25 billion global corporation, it's a clear and unambiguous message that learning needs to be converted into action.

"The new finish line and all the components around it continue to receive very strong positive support from senior executives and front-line managers alike," Terrence said. "It is a delightful situation for us to be in."

It will require patience and perseverance to re-educate the organization to think in terms of business outcomes for training (Keeton, 2014). The payoff is worth the effort (Gregory & Akram, 2014). Training providers—whether internal or external—who have shifted from a focus on learning to a focus on performance enjoy much greater buy-in from management as well as from program participants (see Case in Point I.2). When employees can clearly see the relevance of the training, they are more willing to engage and more likely to answer "Yes, I will" when they return to work.

In the chapter on D1, we underscore the concept that training is a business function that must deliver business value. We provide a process and tools to guide a dialogue between business leaders and learning professionals to achieve alignment. We underscore the importance of "starting with why" and agreeing on the criteria for success *in advance*, and we provide a checklist and suggestions for practical application.

Design the Complete Experience

The Second Discipline practiced by the most effective learning and development organizations is that they **design the *complete* experience**, rather than just an "event." The emphasis is on *complete*, which means actively planning and managing what happens before and after instruction with the same care historically afforded the instruction itself. The evidence is clear: the pre- and post-training environments profoundly impact the outcome (Salas, Tannenbaum, Kraiger, & Smith-Jentsch, 2012).

Generating business value from learning is a *process*, not a one-off event. As Linda Hudson, chief executive of BAE, remarked in an interview with the *Wall Street Journal,* "You don't go to class and next week, everything changes" (Lublin, 2014). To be effective, learning needs to be conceived and managed as a process, bringing to bear the tools of business process reengineering and continuous improvement. In today's results-oriented

Figure I.8.   TRAINING AND DEVELOPMENT NEEDS TO DESIGN THE COMPLETE EXPERIENCE, NOT JUST HOPE FOR A MIRACLE

"I think you should be more explicit here in step two."

© Sidney Harris/Condé Nast Publications/*www.cartoonbank.com.*

business climate, organizations need to be much more explicit and deliberate about the steps required to transform learning into results; it is no longer sufficient to just hope for a miracle (Figure I.8).

Managing something as a process requires taking into account *all* of the factors that affect the quality of the outcome. Process improvement involves identifying which elements are currently the weak links—the most common points of failure—and systematically addressing them. With respect to training and development, that means recognizing that learning itself is only one step in a chain of events leading to improved performance (Figure I.9).

Figure I.9. LEARNING IS ONLY ONE STEP IN THE PROCESS OF IMPROVING PERFORMANCE; NEW KNOWLEDGE AND SKILLS MUST BE TRANSFERRED TO THE WORKPLACE

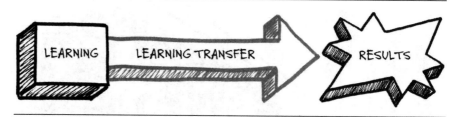

In any process, the quality of the end result is limited by the weakest link in the chain of value. Thus, a training program could produce outstanding learning, but still fail to create *value* if the process breaks down in the learning transfer step. In fact, that is frequently the case; learning transfer is far and away the most common point of failure in corporate learning initiatives, largely because it has usually been left to chance. Effective organizations recognize this and create structure, support, and accountability for this vital step.

Designing the *complete* experience (D2) recognizes that, from the participants' point of view, the learning experience is a continuum. It begins long before the planned instruction and continues long afterward. Participants learn what is actually expected of them from the actions of their managers and peers and from what the performance management system rewards. Unless these are in alignment with what is taught, training will have little impact on performance.

Traditional instructional design systems like ADDIE, and even proposed replacements like SAM (Allen & Sites, 2012), Agile (Islam, 2013), and LLAMA (Torrance, 2014) focus almost exclusively on "the course"—the period and method of planned instruction (Figure I.10). The learning, however, that happens before and after training, and therefore beyond the traditional scope of instruction design, is at least as important as the formal instruction in determining the eventual outcome. The "transfer climate" in particular, that is, the culture and environment in which participants work, has a profound impact (Gilley & Hoekstra, 2003); indeed, the work environment can make or break the value of any learning initiative.

That isn't to say that high-quality instructional design isn't still essential, but it is to say, as long-time learning researcher Frank Nguyen admitted, "Because of my ID roots, it pains me to admit that instructional design frankly is not enough" (Nguyen, 2011, p. 54). The 6Ds complement and

Figure I.10.   THE 6Ds EXTEND AND COMPLEMENT INSTRUCTION DESIGN SYSTEMS TO STRENGTHEN BUSINESS LINKAGE AND ON-THE-JOB RESULTS

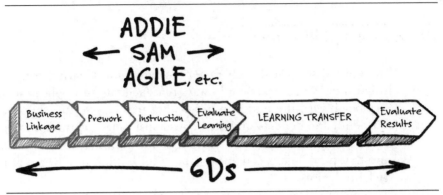

extend instructional design systems to ensure that learning creates business value (Figure I.10).

The Second Discipline seeks to optimize the learner's total experience, not just what happens during instruction (live, virtual, electronic, or on the job). The practice of D2 expands workplace learning professionals' roles and responsibilities in new, exciting, and challenging ways. Obviously, learning professionals do not *control* the learners' work environment, but they can, and should, learn to influence it for their own, their learners,' and their organizations' benefit.

In the chapter on D2, we examine what the "complete experience" includes and which elements have the greatest potential to influence the answers to "Can I?" and "Will I?" and thus whether training creates value or

> The real finish line for learning is improved performance.

scrap. We suggest methods and provide tools to optimize outcomes, some of which challenge conventional thinking. We show that improving the transfer climate is a particularly rich opportunity for a breakthrough. We argue that learning organizations need to redefine "the finish line" for training; participants should be recognized for completing a program only after they have demonstrated application and improvement on the job. The real finish line of learning is improved performance.

Because training and development programs take time and cost money, everyone benefits when they are planned and managed in a way that maximizes the likelihood of success. Designing for the complete experience enables learning professionals to realize their full potential to deliver business value.

Deliver for Application

The Third Discipline that characterizes high-impact learning organizations is that they deliver learning in ways that facilitate its application. That is, they begin with the end in mind—what participants are supposed to *do* differently and better—and then consciously select learning strategies that help participants bridge the learning-doing gap (Figure I.11). They make sure that participants can answer the "Can I?" question in the affirmative back on the job.

The practice of **delivering for application** (D3) involves selecting instructional methods, technologies, and supporting strategies that facilitate learning transfer and on-the-job application. Its success depends to a great extent on how well the business objectives and requisite skills and behaviors have been defined in D1. Delivering for application requires, in addition, a sound understanding of how people—especially adults—learn. It includes the application of instructional design principles such as spaced learning, scaffolding, active engagement, preparation, reflection, elaborative rehearsal, and practice with feedback. As Julie

Figure I.11.   THERE IS ALWAYS A GAP BETWEEN LEARNING AND DOING; THE PRACTICE OF D3 HELPS LEARNERS BRIDGE THAT GAP

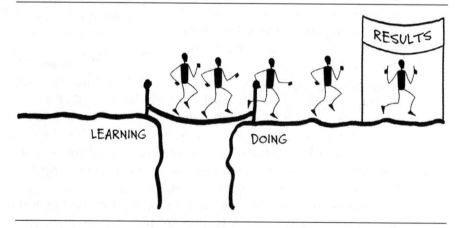

Dirksen wisely wrote: "a great learning experience is not about the content, but is about the way the content is taught" (Dirksen, 2012, p. x).

Professionals who practice the Third Discipline (Deliver) are open to new ideas and approaches, but eschew uncritical implementation of learning fads. They heed Karl Kapp's advice and select approaches best suited to achieve their goals, rather than what everyone else is doing at the moment.

> A great learning experience is not about the content.

> Organizations that match the learning needs to the right design achieve the most success ... focus on what these solutions can do for your organization. Don't jump on the bandwagon just to be on the bandwagon.
>
> Kapp, Blair, and Mesch, 2013, p. 17

The most effective learning providers appreciate that often "less is more"—that one of the most common problems in corporate learning is too much content in too little time. They are not wed to any one method or medium of instruction; they use a variety of techniques and approaches, depending on the nature of the topic, the audience, and the skills required. Because they are focused on delivering performance rather than training per se, they are willing to explore whether a good job aid or performance support system might suffice.

In Chapter 3, we review what makes learning memorable and actionable and leads to an affirmative response to the "Can I?" question. We also examine how the design and delivery of learning impacts the "Will I?" question, for example, by making the relevance of the material clear and showing how each element is connected to real business issues. We provide tools and recommendations to map the chain of value and monitor the perception of the program's utility.

Drive Learning Transfer

In any well-managed company, there are systems in place to set, measure, monitor, and reward the achievement of business objectives. Historically, however, there have been no similar mechanisms to ensure transfer of learning, even in those programs in which participants are supposed to develop action plans. Participants, managers, and instructors have thus been conditioned to treat learning initiatives as one-time events. The widespread practice of awarding credit and certificates at the end of instruction sends entirely the wrong message. It implies "You're done; no more is expected of you." In fact, the real work—that of transferring the learning and using it to improve performance—only begins when the class ends.

"Talk to any group of laymen or professionals about what's broken in the current learning and development process, and most will tell you it's the lack of serious post-training

> **The real work begins when the class ends.**

follow-through" (Zenger, Folkman, & Sherman, 2005, p. 30). It does not matter how much people enjoyed the training, how much they learned, or even how good their action plans are. Learning creates value only to the extent that it is transferred and applied to work, a relationship that can be expressed by the equation:

$$\text{Learning} \times \text{Transfer} = \text{Results}$$

Expressed this way, it is obvious that great learning is necessary to produce great results, but that, alone, it is insufficient. Even when the learning is a "ten out of ten," if the transfer is zero, then the results will be zero. From a business leader's perspective, "the training failed" if there is no change in performance. It doesn't matter that the real breakdown actually occurred in the transfer step; the investment was wasted (Figure I.12) and training is blamed. For that reason, high-impact learning organizations practice D4; they put in place systems and processes to drive learning transfer back to the work of the enterprise. They do not leave it to chance or individual initiative.

The extent to which training is or is not transferred is determined by the *transfer climate*—the constellation of factors in the workplace that communicate to employees whether or not transfer is expected and supported. The transfer climate determines the answer to the "Will I?" question. While no single factor defines the transfer climate, a learner's immediate supervisor has a very powerful influence. Thus, an important aspect of the practice of driving learning transfer (D4) is taking steps to ensure the active and effective engagement of managers in the transfer process.

Figure I.12.   WITHOUT TRANSFER, LEARNING IS SCRAP; IT CONSUMES RESOURCES BUT PRODUCES NO VALUE

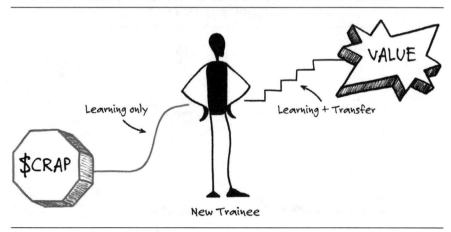

In the chapter on D4 we explain the elements that define the transfer climate and that determine the results that training ultimately delivers. We explain why great learning is not sufficient and why learning professionals need to take a leadership role in improving learning transfer. We provide case examples and practical advice on what you can do to improve transfer as well as a checklist and recommendations for action.

Deploy Performance Support

Trying something new always involves an element of risk. Whether employees make the effort to apply what they learned (do it the "new way") or cling to old habits (Figure I.4) depends, in part, on whether or not performance support is available. Job aids, apps, help lines, coaches, and other forms of performance support increase employees' confidence and the probability that they will attempt to apply newly learned skills on the job. Performance support also increases the probability of early success when they do—which encourages the continued effort needed to achieve proficiency (Figure I.13).

Companies that are serious about getting a return on their investment in learning and development practice the Fifth Discipline: they design performance support as an integral part of every learning initiative and they deploy support both during and after instruction. The most effective

**Figure I.13.   LEARNERS WHO EXPERIENCE EARLY SUCCESS ARE
MOTIVATED TO CONTINUE; THOSE WHO EXPERIENCE EARLY
FAILURE ARE LIKELY TO GIVE UP**

organizations work with senior leaders to develop a culture in which everyone understands that they have a responsibility to support learning. They "put their money where their mouths are" by reallocating some of their learning resources from pure instruction to performance support.

In the chapter on D5, we draw an analogy between product support and performance support. Consumer product companies understand that high-quality support is vital to customer satisfaction; we argue that this is also true for learning. We explore the characteristics of great performance support and the times at which it is most valuable. We stress the importance of providing support to the participant's manager as well, since he or she has a profound impact on outcomes. We include practical advice for designing and deploying effective performance support, a checklist for D5, and recommendations for action.

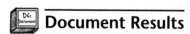

Document Results

In today's hypercompetitive global business climate, no company can afford to waste resources, especially its human capital. Every investment must ultimately be judged in terms of its contribution to the organization's mission and success. Leaders have a fiduciary responsibility to invest their company's resources—time, people, and money—in ways that are most likely to secure its long-term success. To do so, they need reliable data with which to weigh the merit of various initiatives so that they can revise or replace those that fall short of expectations.

The investment in learning is no exception. The bottom-line questions that must be answered about any learning and development initiative are:

- Did it achieve the results for which it was designed?
- Was it worth it?

Workplace learning professionals must be prepared to answer those questions. To justify the investment, leaders need to see the impact on performance, not just the level of learning activity (Figure I.14).

Therefore, the Sixth Discipline practiced by the most-effective learning organizations is to document results in a manner that informs decisions about future investment and that facilitates continuous improvement. Documented results must be:

- *Relevant.* That is, they must directly assess the behaviors or results for which the program was created in the first place. It is not enough to measure activity, satisfaction, or even learning. You must measure the outcomes the program was designed to deliver.

Figure I.14. WHAT THE BUSINESS REALLY WANTS TO KNOW IS WHETHER THE LEARNING HELPED IMPROVE PERFORMANCE

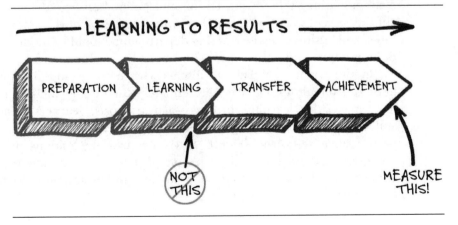

- *Credible.* The data you present and the way in which they were generated must be credible—that is, believed and trusted by the stakeholders. If they do not believe your data, they will not believe your conclusions and will not implement your recommendations.
- *Compelling.* The results must be significant enough and presented in an interesting enough way to persuade stakeholders to take action to continue the program, expand it, revamp it, or abandon it.
- *Efficient.* The evaluation should not cost more than the value of the decision it is meant to inform. Efficiency only matters, however, if the first three criteria have been satisfied. Obtaining the wrong information quickly and inexpensively is *not* efficient.

Finally, measurement is prerequisite to improvement. Companies must continuously improve the effectiveness and efficiency of their business processes—including learning and development—to stay competitive. But continuous improvement is impossible without relevant data about which activities are adding value and where processes are breaking down. The rigorous practice of documenting results (D6) is essential to support a cycle of continuous learning, innovation, adaptation, and improvement. The results of one program should become the raw material for the next cycle of defining outcomes, designing experiences, delivering, driving, deploying, and documenting (Figure I.15). A never-ending cycle of reinvention and renewal ensures that corporate education keeps pace with the changing competitive environment, workforce, and business needs. Training departments should be models of continuous improvement.

> Training departments should be models of continuous improvement.

In the chapter on D6, we discuss why learning and development must document results. We differentiate between the metrics needed to manage the learning process—activity, costs, learners' reactions, and amount learned—and what the business really wants to know: Did performance improve? (Figure I.14). We provide guiding principles for program evaluation and advice on what to measure, how to collect and analyze the information, and, no less important, how to market the results.

Figure I.15.   THE RESULTS OF ONE ITERATION SHOULD BE USED TO INFORM THE DESIGN, DELIVERY, SUPPORT, AND ASSESSMENT OF THE NEXT

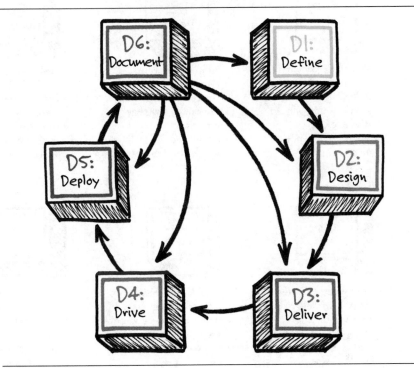

Summary

Companies invest in learning in order to enhance the value and effectiveness of their human capital and, therefore, their ability to achieve their objectives. Management has a fiduciary and ethical responsibility to ensure that such investments produce a return in terms of improved performance and competitiveness.

We have identified Six Disciplines—the 6Ds®—that characterize high-value, breakthrough learning and development initiatives. Organizations that have adopted and practiced the 6Ds have increased the contribution that learning makes to their companies' success. As a result,

Figure I.16.   THE SIX DISCIPLINES

D1: Define

- Always start with business objectives
- Describe what the participants will do differently
- Agree on definition of success

D2: Design

- Include all four phases of learning
- Plan and manage learning transfer process
- Redefine finish line as on-the-job results

D3: Deliver

- Make relevance and utility clear
- Provide enough time for practice
- Use methods that make learning memorable

D4: Drive

- Recognize transfer as a critical part of the process
- Engage participants' managers
- Put in place systems of accountability

D5: Deploy

- Provide job aids and performance support
- Make them an integral part of the plan
- Ensure availability of feedback and coaching

D6: Document

- Measure what matters to sponsors
- Use insights to drive continuous improvement
- Market the results to stakeholders

they enjoy greater recognition and support from the business (Pollock, Jefferson, & Wick, 2014).

In preparing this edition and *The Field Guide to the 6Ds*, we solicited examples from readers and professionals who had attended our 6Ds workshops. Learning leaders around the globe generously shared their ideas, successes, and advice. Our experience has renewed our optimism about people, learning, and organizations. We are convinced that we are at the beginning of a true renaissance in corporate education. We are confident that you will extend these principles and will achieve even greater successes.

We look forward to hearing your story.

Recommendations

For Learning Leaders

- Share this book with other members of the learning team. Read and discuss it. How should it influence your approach to learning?
- Build 6Ds principles into your processes and standard operating procedures; they are most effective when they become habit and "the way we do things around here."
- Consider training your whole team on the 6Ds to establish a common understanding and language.
- Check with a sample of participants from a recent, high-profile program. How did they answer the "Can I?" and "Will I?" questions?
- Select an important learning initiative for which you are responsible.
  - First, assure yourself that training is an appropriate part of the solution. Use Exhibit I.1 to help you.
  - If training is not the right solution, help educate management about the kinds of performance gaps that learning will, and will not, help close.
  - If training is part of the solution, score it using the 6Ds Scorecard (Exhibit I.2) to identify which discipline, if strengthened, will produce the greatest performance improvement.
- Use the relevant chapters of this book and *The Field Guide to the 6Ds* to develop a plan.
- Present your findings, the target, your plan, and the business rationale to the relevant management team.
- Ask for the resources and cooperation needed to implement your recommendations.
- Evaluate the results and repeat the process to drive continuous improvement.

For Business Leaders

- Commit to investing more of your time and attention to learning and development; it is a strategic investment that can and should deliver greater value than it does today.
- Write down what you really want from learning and development—how you define value.
  - Now rate your current level of satisfaction with the results.
  - Share these with your head of learning.

- Give your head of learning a copy of this book and ask him or her to read it and explain how it should influence your organization's learning strategy.
- Use the 6Ds Scorecard (Exhibit I.2) to rate a strategically important program. Ask your learning leader to do the same and compare results.
- Jointly develop a plan for improvement.
- Keep in mind that creating value from training is a shared responsibility between the business and the learning provider.

Exhibit I.2
6Ds Application Scorecard

Use this tool to evaluate a learning initiative and identify opportunities for improvement. For each item, check the box that best describes the initiative using the following key:

0 = Not at all 1 = To a small extent 2 = Somewhat 3 = To a large extent 4 = To a very great extent

			0	1	2	3	4
Define	1.	The business needs are well understood. Anticipated on-the-job results of the training are clearly defined and measurable.	❏	❏	❏	❏	❏
	2.	Course objectives are communicated to participants and managers in terms of expected business impact.	❏	❏	❏	❏	❏
Design	3.	The pre-instruction preparation phase is an integral part of the design. Meetings with managers are facilitated. Pre-work is fully utilized during exercises and instruction.	❏	❏	❏	❏	❏
	4.	The training is considered complete only when there is evidence of successful transfer and application on the job.	❏	❏	❏	❏	❏

			0	1	2	3	4
Deliver	5.	The cognitive load of the program is manageable; there is sufficient time for practice with feedback for participants to develop basic proficiency.	❑	❑	❑	❑	❑
	6.	Each topic and exercise has a clear "line of sight" to required behaviors and business results. Participants' perception of the program's utility and relevance are monitored and acted upon.	❑	❑	❑	❑	❑
Drive	7.	After the program, participants are periodically reminded of their learning in ways that encourage reflection, retention, and application.	❑	❑	❑	❑	❑
	8.	Participants' managers are actively engaged during the post-training period. They monitor and actively support application on the job.	❑	❑	❑	❑	❑
Deploy	9.	Post-training performance support is an integral part of the design. Participants are provided job aids, expert help, coaching, and other support as needed to facilitate transfer.	❑	❑	❑	❑	❑
	10.	Participants continue to learn from each other after the program. Peer coaching and sharing of best practices are facilitated.	❑	❑	❑	❑	❑

			0	1	2	3	4
Document	11.	On-the-job actions and results are evaluated based on the business outcomes agreed to by the sponsor prior to the program.	❑	❑	❑	❑	❑
	12.	Information to support continuous improvement of the preparation, program, and learning transfer is actively solicited, analyzed, and acted upon.	❑	❑	❑	❑	❑

DI:
Define

DEFINE BUSINESS OUTCOMES

"The only reason that learning functions exist is to drive business outcomes."

—Rita Smith, *Strategic Learning Alignment*

IN THE PALACE OF TRUTH, business managers don't care about training. They care about performance. That's because, in a competitive market, those companies and individuals who perform well prosper and grow; those who perform less well than their competitors fall behind and are ultimately replaced.

Actually, managers *do* care about training, but only to the extent that it helps improve performance. They consider training as simply a means to an end, one strategy among many in the organization's armamentarium. In a corporate setting, learning matters only if it meaningfully contributes to achieving the organization's mission and goals.

That is why effective organizations practice the First Discipline: they **Define the Business Outcomes** *before* they embark on *any* learning initiative. In this chapter we will examine why that is so important and what is required to execute this discipline well. Topics include:

- Performance is the goal, not learning
- Why you need to start with "why"
- A process for defining business outcomes
- How to map the journey
- Managing the learning portfolio
- A checklist for D1
- Recommendations for learning and business leaders

D1: Define It Is All About Performance

Anyone at all familiar with the stock market knows that current and future *performance* are investors' overriding concerns. Companies that outperform expectations are rewarded with rising share prices—reflecting increased investor confidence and willingness to invest; those that under-perform are punished by falling share prices as investors abandon them to pursue more attractive alternatives.

While many factors contribute to a company's success, an organization's performance is increasingly a reflection of the strength of its human capital. "People, not cash, buildings, or equipment, are the critical differentiators of a business" (Fitz-enz, 2000, p. 1). The algebraic sum of peoples' performance over time determines how well the organization performs.

Gilbert introduced the concept of *worthy performance*, which he defined as performance in which the value of the accomplishment exceeds the cost of the behaviors required to achieve it (Gilbert, 1978, p. 17). Gilbert carefully distinguished between mere activity (behavior) and performance. Performance is the more comprehensive concept; it includes not only the activity, but also its consequences (outcomes) and their worth. So "good performance," in the business sense, is activity that produces high-value outcomes at relatively low input cost.

Factors at the worker, work, and workplace levels influence whether performance is ultimately "worthy" or not (Rummler & Brache, 2012; Van Tiem, Moseley, & Dessinger, 2012). Learning initiatives are intended to enhance performance by increasing capabilities and proficiency at the worker level (Figure D1.1). Whether they ultimately succeed in doing so depends on whether training was an appropriate intervention, how well it was conceived and delivered, and, as we will discuss in greater depth in subsequent chapters, the work processes and workplace climate.

The key point here is that corporate-sponsored learning is a business activity pursued for the purpose of improving performance. In a study by *The Economist* Intelligence Unit, 295 executives from around the world chose "increased productivity" as the main justification for investing in workforce development (CrossKnowledge, 2014). Business leaders expect their workplace learning professionals to help them achieve business objectives, not just to provide classes, tools, and learning. An investment in learning is worthy to the extent that it pays a return as a result of improved performance (Figure D1.2).

FIGURE D1.1.   PERFORMANCE IS THE RESULT OF THE INTERACTION OF THE WORKER, WORK, AND WORKPLACE. TRAINING IMPACTS ONLY THE WORKER

FIGURE D1.2.   TRAINING IS AN INVESTMENT THAT IS EXPECTED TO PAY A RETURN IN TERMS OF IMPROVED PERFORMANCE

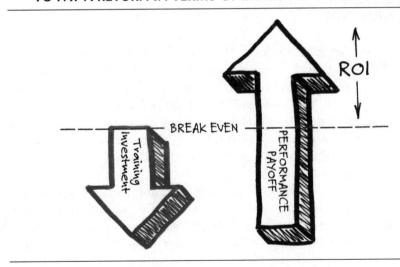

As with any business activity, the performance of the training department itself must be "worthy"—that is, generate outcomes that are aligned with the business goals and have greater value than the cost of the activities required to achieve them. "It's not about the training; it's about the results" (Trolley, 2006, p. 101). "To enjoy strategic influence, [learning] leaders must understand their company's goals and execute their plans to deliver results for the company and its customers" (Wik, 2014).

> It's not about the training; it's about the performance.

Practical Application

- Shift your focus from delivering training to delivering improved performance.
- Keep in mind that performance depends on more than just the worker; do not lose sight of the impact of work processes and workplace policies.

 D1:
Define

Start with Why

Simon Sinek's TED talk, "How Great Leaders Inspire Action" (Sinek, 2009b) is one of the most-viewed TED talks. His message is simple: to inspire people to action, you have to start with *why*. *Why* is at the center of what he calls the "Golden Circle" (Figure D1.3). *Why* should inform what a company does and how it does it. Sinek argues that great leaders and great companies always start with *why* (Sinek, 2009a). They give people a reason to take action. Less effective organizations start with *what* they do or *how* they do it.

The same applies to training. If we want to inspire people to learn and to take action to apply what they learn, if we want to inspire managers to send their employees to training, if we want to inspire supervisors to invest the time and effort to pull the learning through on the job, then we need to start by answering "why?" In corporations, that means beginning the process by defining the business outcomes that learning will help achieve (Figure D1.4).

FIGURE D1.3.   "WHY?" IS AT THE CENTER OF SINEK'S "GOLDEN CIRCLE"

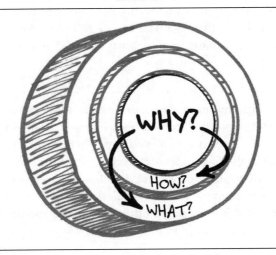

 ## The End in Mind

The first and vital step in generating value is to understand what value means, or to use Stephen Covey's famous phrase, "begin with the end in mind" (Covey, 2004, p. 96). But what defines value? For corporate learning, value is defined in terms of the organization's vision and mission.

FIGURE D1.4.   STARTING WITH "WHY?" (BUSINESS OUTCOMES) INFORMS THE ANSWERS TO WHAT AND HOW

Learning that helps the organization achieve its goals has value and is worthy of investment. Learning that is irrelevant to the purpose of the organization may still be of great value to the individual or to society, but if it does not create value for the organization, then it does not warrant investment.

The great management guru Peter Drucker summarized the point this way:

Management must always, in every decision and action, put economic performance first. It can only justify its existence and its authority by the economic results it produces. There may be great non-economic results: the happiness of the members of the enterprise, the contribution to the welfare or culture of the community, etc. Yet management has failed if it fails to produce economic results.... It has failed if it does not improve, or at least maintain, the wealth-producing capacity of the economic resources entrusted to it.

Drucker, 1974, p. 37

Drucker's point was that management has a fiduciary responsibility to "improve, or at least maintain, the wealth-producing capacity of the economic resources entrusted to it." That is true whether or not the organization is expected to produce a profit. Sometimes the expected value of learning is immediate and apparent—such as teaching sales people how to explain the benefits of a new product; sometimes the business benefit is less direct and longer term—such as teaching managers how to give more effective feedback to improve retention and reduce the cost of replacing workers. Regardless, learning that is sponsored and paid for by the organization must have a line of sight to some expected organizational benefit.

 ## Practical Application

- Start with the end in mind—the business need.
- Always ask "Why? What is the expected benefit to the organization?"

Benefits of Defining Business Outcomes

The benefits of defining the business outcomes expected from learning initiatives are numerous.

1. A clear understanding of how the business hopes to create value through learning enables you to design more effective interventions. Knowing what learners are expected to do on the job informs the selection of methods, media, timing, sequence, and support. It also helps avoid creating just another "feel-good" training program (Banerjee, Wahdat, & Cherian, 2014).

2. A clear and compelling link between the training and the organization's mission secures greater support and engagement by participants' managers, who, as we will discuss in greater depth in D4, have a profound impact on the initiative's success. Managers who understand the business case for learning are more willing to send their direct reports to training and are more likely to support their efforts to apply what they learn.

3. Being able to state the overarching business objectives helps answer the "What's in it for me?" (WIIFM) question for participants. As we will discuss in D3, participants' willingness to learn the material in the first place—as well as to answer "yes" to "Will I?" afterward—is enhanced when the business rationale is clear.

4. Expected benefits provide a sound rationale for prioritizing learning initiatives. Inevitably, there are more requests than there are staff and funds. The decision of which to take forward and which to forego should be based on the magnitude and strategic importance of the benefits, not merely a program's popularity or the training department's enthusiasm for a particular approach.

5. The outcomes that management expects from training are the criteria for its success. They are what need to be measured to ensure that the effort is, in fact, meeting its objectives (see D6).

6. A shared focus on business outcomes is the basis for partnership between the learning organization and the business (see Case in Point D1.1). It transitions learning professionals from "order-takers" to strategic business partners and gives them a "seat at the table."

Case in Point D1.1
Renewed Partnership at Marathon Pipe Line

When Steve Rodzos accepted the role as manager of human resources and learning & development for Marathon Pipe Line LLC (MPL), his manager, MPL President Craig Pierson, charged him with reviewing hourly training as his first priority.

Marathon Pipe Line moves millions of gallons of petroleum feedstocks and finished products through thousands of miles of pipeline every day. Doing so safely and in accordance with federal and state regulations requires well-trained and highly knowledge-able employees. Pierson wanted to transform MPL into a "premier learning organization" to ensure that the company maintained its commitment to safely and reliably operating its pipelines and growing the business in the best interest of shareholders.

Pierson visits the field regularly to get first-hand feedback on the connection between MPL's strategic business plan and the work being performed at all levels. When discussing training with field personnel and managers, he learned that some felt the training programs needed improvement. They noted that training was outdated, not responsive to their needs, or too dependent on lectures and PowerPoint presentations. Pierson determined that these concerns needed to be addressed, and quickly.

Steve held one-on-one meetings with the trainers to gather their perceptions, which, naturally, differed from those of the trainees. While most of the trainers acknowledged that they could use more time to revamp their content, by and large, from their perspective, there were no insurmountable problems, just a disconnect between the trainers' goals and techniques and the field employees' expectations of training.

Knowing the trainers were well-intentioned and skilled, Steve diagnosed the most press-ing problem as a "fractured partnership." He took the bold move of shutting down training for a full month to bring in hourly technicians, supervisors, and managers from the field to two "Check and Adjust Forums" to help repair this fracture.

"By shutting down the Training Center for a month, we sent a strong message to the business that training wasn't going to just be 'business as usual' anymore. We wanted all to know that we were serious about making significant and sustainable change by developing a strong partnership with the field.

"During the forum, we planned to ask the trainers and field representatives to review the current training materials together using the ADDIE model. After reading *The Six Disciplines*, however, I decided the 6Ds model was a better fit for the MPL organization. It requires fewer occasions in which field needs are shoe-horned into a learning model. Instead we start with the business objectives and co-create a training plan to meet those objectives."

The first Forum focused primarily on evaluating the current state of content and delivery against the principles of D2 and D3. Steve knew that the most important step in repairing the partnership was honing in on the business outcomes and building consensus among the business leaders and L&D. The second Check and Adjust Forum included the president and VP of operations and their respective staffs and the L&D staff. It focused on D1: Define Business Outcomes and the vision for MPL as a premier learning organization. The results were exceptional, with the following stretch goals identified and agreed on:

1. Within eighteen months, shorten the time to proficiency for hourly technicians by 25 percent or more.
2. Transform the reputation of the Learning Center so that technicians look forward to attending training there because they know it will be consistently valuable, positive, and practical.

3. Immediately incorporate lessons learned in safety incident investigations into training so incidents are not repeated.
4. Reduce computer-based training time by 50 percent within twenty-four months.

According to Steve, "The feedback regarding L&D is beginning to make a 180-degree turn since the renewed partnership, and continues to improve. By strengthening partnerships between the business and learning professionals and diligently connecting training to business outcomes, Marathon Pipe Line, LLC, will continue to make progress toward becoming a premier learning organization."

Everything Depends on Getting D1 Right The definition of expected business outcomes is the bedrock on which the design and delivery plans for learning must rest. If that foundation is weak, then the entire edifice is likely to fall. Thus, D1 is arguably the most important of the six disciplines. If you do not get D1 right, you cannot salvage the effort by clever design, brilliant facilitation, or nifty technology. "We will never succeed if we think about solutions first" (Israelite, 2006, p. 210).

> We will never succeed if we think about solutions first.

Kevin Wilde, chief learning officer of General Mills, underscored this point in his preface to the first edition of *The Six Disciplines*: "I've been there—so caught up in crafting the excellence of the learning event that we failed to ground everything in the real business case. When that happens, the results leave you heartbroken, far short of the learning breakthrough you intended" (Wilde, 2006, p. xv).

The learning leadership at KLA-Tencor feels so strongly about the importance of defining business outcomes that they have established the policy that no learning project will be released without a sponsor and a clear outcome, typically one tied to at least one of the company's four strategic goals: Growth, Operational Excellence, Customer Focus, and Talent. At Qualcomm, the learning and development staff conduct annual business needs assessments with each division's executive leaders and their staffs (Elkeles & Phillips, 2007). At Ingersoll Rand, learning is prioritized based on the expected business value, just like any other investment option (see Case in Point D1.2).

"The first best practice for creating a world-class training organization is to establish a formal link to the business at all levels, with the intent of becoming a strategic partner" (Schmidt, 2013).

Case in Point D1.2
Learning As a Business Strategy

One company that really understands the strategic nature of learning is Ingersoll Rand. As Rita Smith, vice president of enterprise learning, puts it: "We're here for only one reason: to help drive business outcomes. We need to understand the business strategy, key strategic drivers, external threats, and financial metrics. We literally need to be bilingual, speaking the languages of both learning and business" (Smith, 2008).

Ingersoll Rand utilizes a governance board to ensure that investments in learning are business-relevant and tied to business-strategy priorities. Every program must have an executive-level sponsor; no sponsor, no program.

Ingersoll Rand's CEO, Herb Henkel, considers learning a key strategic lever, so much so that he made it an integral part of the strategic planning process: "When we go through the strategic planning process, we come up with ideas, strategies, and visions of where we're going to be. Then we decide what to invest in to get the things we want. So I look at how many dollars we spend on bricks and mortar; how many on developing new products; and how much training we need to be able to meet our goals. Built into the planning process is the assumption that there will have to be some kind of training. So we consider it no different than we would anything else in terms of investment decisions" (quoted in Bingham & Galagan, 2008).

Unfortunately, too many learning interventions today are still initiated for the wrong reasons. Sometimes it's because training is the only solution a harried manager can think of (Pollock, 2013) or sometimes it is simply to be seen to be doing *something* (Figure D1.5). Such efforts are doomed to failure. They contribute to learning scrap and undermine support for legitimate learning initiatives. Learning professionals need to constructively challenge proposals whose sole purpose is to "have a program."

 Practical Application

- Establish a policy that no learning initiative will be designed or delivered without a sound and explicit business rationale.
- Be sure you use the language of business, rather than the language of learning.

FIGURE D1.5.   "WE NEED A PROGRAM" IS NOT A SUFFICIENT REASON TO CREATE ONE

"Quick, we need a leadership development program that I can announce to the Board of Directors' meeting on Friday."

Copyright 2006 by Randy Glasbergen. *www.glasbergen.com.* Used with permission.

Learning Objectives Are Not Business Objectives

We want to emphasize that when we speak of business or performance objectives for training, we do not mean learning objectives. We know that learning objectives are prerequisite to effective instructional design; "they guide the remaining steps in the instructional design process by describing precisely what the targeted learners should know, do, or feel on completion of a planned learning experience" (Rothwell & Kazanas, 2008). But therein lies the problem. Although learning objectives are sometimes called "performance objectives" or "behavioral objectives," their focus is always "on completion of a planned learning experience." They describe what

> Learning objectives are necessary, but not sufficient.

learners will be able to do at the end of instruction, but they do not explain how that relates to on-the-job performance or the business value that will be created.

In our view, instructional objectives should be used for communication *only among training professionals.* They should not be used to communicate with management or to learners; they are too internally focused. As a result, they fail to communicate the business benefit or rationale and "it also means that learners are subjected to horrible instructional design jargon" (Dirksen, 2012, p. 72).

We need a better way to communicate with business leaders, learners, and their managers, something that explains the business rationale for the investment of time and resources. We need to explain the *expected business benefit (outcome)* in terms that are familiar to the business leaders and are of interest to them such as:

- Increased sales
- Improved customer service
- Reduced time to proficiency
- Less scrap
- Greater employee engagement
- More efficient use of time
- Fewer accidents

All of these ultimately contribute to either increased income or decreased costs; all of them are the kinds of concerns that keep business leaders up at night.

Every discussion of a training initiative—whether in a budget review or in the course catalog—should include reference to its overall business purpose because that ultimately is its reason for being and provides the answer to "why?" Terrence Donahue, director of global learning at Emerson Electric, and his team took this message to heart and included a section in every course description entitled "Business Outcomes: (How You Will Benefit)" (Exhibit D1.1). The response—from both managers and participants—has been overwhelmingly positive.

Start with the Business Objectives For corporate-sponsored learning, the business objectives always come first. Expected outcomes must be defined *before* the learning objectives; learning objectives only exist to support achievement of business goals.

How Much Detail? How detailed do the expected business outcomes need to be? It depends on the purpose of the communication and to whom. In a high-level overview to management or as the introduction to a program, the bullet points above—for example, "the purpose of this program is to help increase sales of product X"—will suffice. In developing a new program and in evaluating its success, a more precise definition is needed that

Exhibit D1.1.   AN EXCERPT FROM THE CAREER DEVELOPMENT GUIDE AT EMERSON SHOWING HOW BENEFITS ARE MADE EXPLICIT.

Who Should Attend. Any supervisor or manager responsible for leading a function or department who has direct reports and is responsible for the performance and development of employees. Those with supervisor or manager titles who do not have direct reports may benefit from many of the skills taught in the workshop.

The workshop is well-suited for those who are new to their role; however, it is also valuable for experienced leaders who want to improve their skills and learn Emerson's best management and leadership practices.

Duration. 3 days

Facilitated By. Learning Center-certified facilitator.

Strategic Purpose. This required workshop equips front-line leaders with Emerson's best leadership practices and standards to effectively and efficiently lead people and drive business results.

Business Outcomes (How You Will Benefit)
The ultimate success of any training investment is measured by the results it delivers to your business. The business and personal benefits that you can expect to receive by applying the skills include:

- Leading your team with confidence and credibility by *applying proven leadership skills*.

- Improving the productivity and effectiveness of your team *by having clearly defined job roles and expectations*.

- Increasing employee engagement through an effective *performance-management process*.

- Building healthy and productive work relationships *through open, two-way communication*.

Learning Objectives (What You Will Learn)
This workshop will equip you with Emerson's best leadership practices and proven performance tools in order to be effective in the critical competencies required of a leader. You will:

- Communicate to your team how it contributes to the *Emerson mission*.

- Develop performance objectives for yourself and your *direct reports*.

- Determine the motivational drivers for each of *your employees*.

- *Influence others without using formal authority*.

- *Apply active listening skills*.

- *Coach employees to become self-directed in their work*.

- *Delegate work effectively*.

- *Give supportive and constructive feedback*.

- *Resolve employee performance issues and problems*.

- *Lead with integrity*.

Lominger Competencies Addressed in This Workshop

7 – Caring About Direct Reports
18 – Delegation
19 – Developing Direct Reports and Others
20 – Directing Others
23 – Fairness to Direct Reports
27 – Informing
29 – Integrity and Trust
33 – Listening
35 – Managing and Measuring Work
36 – Motivating Others
54 – Self-Development

indicates how much by when: for example, "increase employee engagement scores by 5 points on the next annual survey." Making the business case for an expensive or strategically vital program may also require an estimate of the projected financial value (Basarab, 2011; Smith, 2010; Vance, 2010).

Since individual initiatives target only specific aspects of sales, marketing, management, safety, and so forth, the statements of business outcomes usually need to be qualified by the specific focus of the training: "The purpose of this program is to improve employee retention by teaching shift supervisors to have more effective conversations." See, for example, the Plastipak case study in the *Field Guide to the 6Ds* (Hinton, Singos, & Grigsby, 2014).

Some authors have suggested defining objectives at multiple levels, for example, reaction objectives, learning objectives, application objectives, impact objectives, and ROI objectives (Phillips & Phillips, 2008) or intention, adoption, and impact goals (Basarab, 2011). While the intent is laudable, we are concerned that that level of detail may seem overwhelming and inhibit efforts to link learning more tightly to the business. Start with something short, simple, and easily communicated.

 Practical Application

- Require that every learning initiative has both (a) a clear statement of expected business outcomes and (b) a well-crafted set of the learning objectives necessary to achieve them.
- Always create the business objectives first.
- Communicate the business benefits to participants and managers.
- Use the learning objectives only for communicating requirements to instructional designers and facilitators.

The Downside   Oscar Wilde famously wrote that "Nowadays, to be intelligible is to be found out" (Wilde, 1893). The most common objection we hear to being explicit about the expected business outcomes is: "How can we promise those results when we only control the training environment?" We have no sympathy with that argument. Every other unit in a business has to promise—and then deliver—results from processes that it does not entirely control. For example, a product manager is expected to project sales a year or more in advance and then achieve them, even though he or she has no direct control of the sales force. A plant manager must commit to production volumes and cost per unit, even though he or she has no direct control of suppliers and many of the other variables in production.

To achieve their targets, managers must learn to influence those elements of the process they do not control directly. They put in place reliable processes and monitoring systems so that they have "early warning" and can take corrective action if they are not on target to achieve their goals. Learning and development organizations need to also commit to targets and achieve them if they are to command respect as legitimate business partners.

> Learning and development departments need to commit to targets.

How to Define Business Outcomes

How do you discover what the business really wants from learning? The obvious answer is to ask the business leaders. But it is not quite that simple, for several reasons. The first is that many business leaders have become accustomed to ordering training like they would order a burger. They may not have given much thought to what they really want beyond "training," or they may have difficulty articulating what they are really looking for.

You will need to develop your active-listening and consultative skills to help business leaders define what they are ultimately trying to accomplish. We have provided some suggestions in the discussion of the Outcomes Planning Wheel (page 55). Dana and Jim Robinson's book, *Performance Consulting* (1996), also contains helpful advice on the art of performance consulting.

Second, you need to have a working knowledge of business terms and concepts as well as a deep understanding of the specific business of your organization or client so that you can ask intelligent follow-up questions. Use the self-test in Exhibit D1.2 to gauge your current level of understanding.

Exhibit D1.2
Self-Test of Business Knowledge

Answer the following questions about your business:

1. The most important source of our revenue is:

2. The most important driver of our growth is:

3. The core elements of our strategy are (list):

4. Our main competitor is:

5. The greatest threat we face is:

6. The greatest human capital challenge we face is:

As a workplace learning professional, you are expected to have special expertise in instructional design, adult learning principles, learning technologies, and so forth. But those are not sufficient. Since training is ultimately a business endeavor, you must be able to speak the language of your business if you want to be considered a true contributor. As Jeff Thull wrote in *Mastering the Complex Sale:* "Expected credibility is what you know about your solution. Exceptional credibility is what you know about your customer and his or her business" (Thull, 2010, p. 102).

> You must be able to speak the language of the business.

You don't need an MBA to be able to speak knowledgeably and credibly about business matters. You just need a healthy curiosity, a genuine interest in learning about how your enterprise creates value, and the willingness to invest some of your time—an investment that will pay dividends in greater effectiveness, contribution, and appreciation by your business partners.

Start by reading the business or strategic plans for the units you support. Pay particular attention to sections that discuss key opportunities and threats the organization is facing, as these may be situations in which targeted learning can make a significant contribution. Use the Internet or other references to help you with unfamiliar terms and find a mentor or colleague who can help explain parts you do not understand. Ask to sit in on budget reviews and marketing discussions; you will pick up a lot of the business lingo and concepts by osmosis.

Practical Application

- To gain a "seat at the table," learn your business—its challenges and language—in depth.
- Speak to business leaders in their language, not learning or HR jargon.

Outcomes Planning Wheel

A simple device that has proven to be surprisingly valuable is the 6Ds Outcomes Planning Wheel (Figure D1.6). The Planning Wheel is a way of structuring a conversation with business leaders to help you arrive at a common understanding of the results they are trying to achieve through learning and how success will be defined. On follow-up calls after our 6Ds workshops, participants tell us that using the Planning Wheel and focusing on business outcomes are two of the most valuable things they have done. Numerous case examples describing the use of the Planning Wheel can be found in the *Field Guide to the 6Ds* (Pollock, Jefferson, & Wick, 2014).

Using the Planning Wheel

Ask the four questions of the Planning Wheel whenever you receive a request for training, whether you are part of an internal learning and development team, a consultant, or a training provider. The exchange sounds something like this:

> *Business leader:* "I need a training program on X."
> *Learning professional:* "I can help you."

**Figure D1.6.   THE FOUR QUESTIONS OF THE OUTCOMES
PLANNING WHEEL**

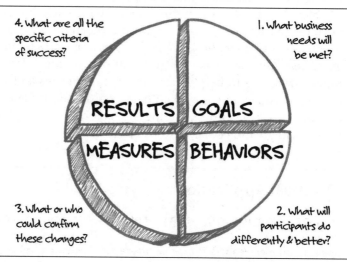

It is important to be positive about your ability to provide assistance, even if you already suspect training will not ultimately be part of the solution. Avoiding unnecessary or inappropriate training is just as valuable as delivering effective training. Stolovitch and Keeps (2004) recommend using the phrase "I can help you solve your problem" in response to any request for training, because it is "friendly, encouraging, and supportive. It shows interest but does not promise training—a professional response" (p. 16).

We then usually say something like this: "Training takes time and costs money. We want to be sure that you gain value from the investment. The better we understand your performance challenge and what you are trying to accomplish, the better an intervention we can deliver. Would you be willing to spend a few minutes to answer some questions and provide additional insight?" When you frame it that way, it is hard for managers to say no, since you have positioned the discussion as being in their best interests.

If the business leader has the time to discuss the issues right then, seize the moment. If not, set up a time to meet for about 30 minutes. Prior to the meeting, do your homework: review business plans or other relevant documents, including guidelines for the interview (Exhibit D1.3).

Exhibit D1.3
Interview Guidelines for Discovering Business Needs

Preparation

- Do your homework; read the relevant business plans, reports, and related materials.
- Schedule your interview with the business leader in advance; state the objective, the questions to which you need answers, and time required.
- Know what you want to get out of the interview before you begin.

The Interview

- Follow the classic sales opening: meet and greet, state the value, propose an agenda, check for agreement.
- Start on time.
- Summarize what you already know and check your understanding: "From what I was able to read, it seems like the most important things you are trying to accomplish are X, Y, Z. Did I summarize that correctly? What have I missed?"
- Use the Outcomes Planning Wheel (Figure D1.6) to help structure the discussion.
- Use open questions; check for understanding by restating; probe for the deeper issues.
- End on time. If there are still some issues that need to be clarified, schedule a follow-up meeting or resolve them by email.

Follow-Up

- Immediately following the interview, summarize the discussion in writing. A sample memorandum is included below as Exhibit D1.4.
- Send a note thanking the manager for his or her time and include a copy of your summary.
- The purpose is four-fold:
  - Summarizing your notes will encourage you to reflect on what you have learned and better cement it in your memory.
  - The document will be a useful reference as the planning process proceeds.
  - Your summary acknowledges that you valued the leader's time and input.
  - Finally, sharing your summary affords the person you interviewed an opportunity to correct any oversights or misunderstandings, which will lead to a superior solution.

There is both a science and an art to using the Planning Wheel. The science is using the questions to structure the interview to help clients stop focusing on the solution (training) and shift their focus to the required performance and results. "The key to a successful reframing discussion is to ask powerful, thought-provoking questions with a compelling logic" (Robinson & Robinson, 2008, p. 172).

**Exhibit D1.4
Sample Follow-Up Memorandum.**

Date: _____

Subject: Summary of Our Discussion

Dear _____:

   Thank you for taking the time yesterday to meet with me to discuss your training needs. I am writing to confirm my understanding of the business drivers and the criteria for success.

   The underlying business need that this program is designed to address is _____.

   If the training is a success, then the trainees will do (more/less) of _____ and _____ in their work.

   These changes will be evident to _____ and will be measured by _____.

   To ensure these actions and behaviors occur on the job, the following steps need to be taken by their managers: _____; and the following changes need to be made in the work environment: _____ _____.

   The program will be considered a success if _____ _____.

   Please let me know if I have correctly summarized our discussion so that we can work together to maximize the return on this investment in learning.

   Sincerely,

   _____

The art is how to ask follow-on questions that help business leaders clarify their thinking about what they really want. Throughout the interview, use open-ended questions (as opposed to those that can be answered yes or no). Stop and restate frequently, both to illustrate that you are listening and also as a check to be sure that what you think you heard is what they think they said.

"*Help me understand …* " is a very useful phrase that can be used to genuinely seek understanding, and also as a graceful way to point out inconsistency or confusion, as in: "*Help me understand how the training course you have requested will help address your business needs.*"

Specific suggestions about using each of the four questions follow.

1. What Business Needs Will Be Met? The goal of the first question is to shift the focus from the discussion of a particular solution (training) to an exploration of the underlying business drivers—the real business issue or opportunity behind the request. Such understanding is critical to make sure that training is even appropriate.

The better you are able to link a learning initiative to specific business needs, the greater the buy-in you will enjoy from participants and their managers. Learning organizations that have shifted their focus to business outcomes instead of learning objectives also enjoy much greater support from management. According to Patricia Gregory and Steve Akram at Oracle:

The statistic that most tellingly demonstrates the value of this approach is this: when we began the initiative to shift our focus from courses to business needs, 70 percent of the sales training programs were open enrollment and only 30 percent were VP-sponsored. Now, several years into the process, the ratio has completely reversed: 70 percent of the courses are VP-sponsored and only 30 percent are open enrollment.

Another telling metric is that requests for training have actually *increased* as a result of doing a better job of addressing business needs up front, as well as reporting the impact of training on the job.

Finally, as training directors, we are now viewed much more as business partners than simply training providers. We are brought into discussions earlier, we receive greater management support for training, and our opinions are more highly valued.

Gregory and Akram, 2014, p. 283

Surprisingly, many business leaders struggle to answer the business-needs question because they have not thought about training in those terms. You will probably need to ask a series of clarifying questions to reach a specific enough definition of the business need. For example, when asked about the business need, some managers simply re-assert the need for training: "We need a training program on the order-entry system." The challenge in such cases is to help the client *reframe* their focus. Training is not a business need; training is one of many potential solutions. Continue to probe for the ultimate goal—the business-relevant outcome behind the request for training: "*Can you help me understand the business driver behind your request for training?*" or "*Assuming that the training is successful, what will the benefit be to the organization?*"

The perceived need for training usually originates because management believes that something is not happening that should be ("the sales clerks are not asking customers about related supplies") or because something is happening that should not be ("too many mistakes," "inappropriate behavior," and so forth). Your goal is to clarify the perception of the problem and why it has to be addressed. You could ask, for example, *"What is the gap between our current performance and what it needs to be?"* or *"What is the cost of the current level of performance?"*

Books on performance improvement often use the idea of "filling a performance gap"—for example, Robinson and Robinson (2008) or Gupta (1999)—but that does not mean that training is only useful for solving a performance problem. Learning initiatives can help an organization seize new opportunities, such as entering a new market or launching a new product. Indeed, when Herb Henkel was CEO of Ingersoll Rand, he required that every business plan include a section on training and development because he felt that any plan worth its salt included new initiatives, and that the success of any new initiative depended on ensuring that employees had the knowledge and skills needed to execute it (see Case in Point D1.2).

Alternatively, the business leader may state the business need in terms too broad and general to be operationalized, for example, "We need to increase sales." In such cases, you need to probe for details, for the intermediate steps or aspects of the process that require attention: *"You have been very clear about the urgent need to increase sales. Can you say more about the specific areas that you feel we most need to address or improve? Where is the process breaking down?"*

If the business manager still struggles to clearly define the business need, you can do what one of our global partners—Conrado Schlochauer of AfferoLab in Brazil—does and ask about the desired behaviors (Question 2). Business leaders often have a very clear idea of what they want employees to do better and differently. Conrado approaches the discussion this way: *"Imagine you had a magic pill that would cause all employees to perform optimally. What would that look like?"* He then follows up by asking *"and what would be the benefit to the business?"* He has discovered that asking about the benefits of optimal behavior is a good way to help leaders clarify the business objectives for the training.

2. What Will Participants Do Better and Differently? The second question of the Planning Wheel is designed to identify the vital behaviors or actions needed to achieve the desired results. This reflects what Brinkerhoff (1987) called the "fundamental logic of training." That is, the purpose of learning initiatives is to help employees *perform* better—to do their jobs in new and more effective ways. Behavior change is key because, as Einstein supposedly quipped, "One definition of insanity is to continue doing the same thing and expect a different result." To use learning to improve results, you have to know what behaviors are required and then design learning and transfer environments that support them.

Ask the client to describe the desired changes in behavior: "*If the training is a success, and we were to watch how people perform their jobs afterward, what would we see them doing that is different and better?*" Another useful approach is to ask about the behaviors of better performers: "*What do the better performers do that lesser performers don't? If the goal is to have more people do what the top performers do, what would that look like?*"

Of course, one conversation is not a complete performance analysis. But we think it is essential to start with the perspective of the business sponsor, as he or she will ultimately judge the success of the initiative. You will need to follow up with additional interviews and observations to truly understand the performance required and the requisite skills and knowledge (see Case in Point C.1, page 282). For detailed descriptions of performance analysis, see Van Tiem, Moseley, and Dessinger (2012), Addison, Haig, and Kearney (2009), Kaufman and Guerra-López (2013), and Robinson and Robinson (2008).

3. Who or What Could Confirm These Changes? The goal of the third question of the Planning Wheel is to start the dialogue about how to validate whether or not the initiative is producing the desired outcomes. The principle is that success is defined *by the customer, not by the training department.* The latter phrase is in italics because, as we will explain in greater detail in D6, it is the sponsor who ultimately decides whether the initiative was a success or failure. That assessment depends on whether the change in performance met their expectations or fell short. Engaging the customer (which, in business, usually means the department that is paying the bills) in a discussion of what *could* be measured (Question 3) facilitates the discussion of what *should* be measured and their criteria for success (Question 4, below). The right time to discuss the criteria for success is *as the project is being defined*, since the definition of success affects everything else—from program design to evaluation strategies.

The initial discussion of Question 3 should be a shared brainstorming session: "*How can we be sure the initiative is producing the desired results? Who will notice the changes first? What will change or be observable?*"

Try to focus the discussion on what changes will be detectable first (leading indicators, see page 259), because you want to know as soon as possible whether the intervention is working or not. In the discussion of

Question 3, you may need to "prime the pump" by offering some suggestions to help your client think about potential outcomes and how they could be confirmed. Examples include:

- *If we were to actually observe participants doing their jobs following the program, would we be able to see the change? What would we look for?*
- *Who would notice a change as part of his or her normal interactions with the participants—for example, customers, managers, or direct reports?*
- *Would any of the business metrics that we track routinely (sales, quality, customer satisfaction, and so forth) change? Which?*

It turns out that, while there are as many different potential outcomes as there are kinds of training, there are a relatively small number of *types* of outcomes and ways to assess them. Use Table D1.1 to help guide your brainstorming.

The goals of Question 3 are to (a) explore a variety of potential ways in which the outcome could be assessed, (b) generate buy-in, and (c) gain a sense of what matters most to the client.

It's important to explore a variety of options since some will be much easier or quicker to assess than others. For example, the ultimate goal of the program might be to enhance employee retention. However, that would not be the best measure of whether the training is having an effect because it would take months to become evident. At that point, it would be nearly impossible to ascribe the change to the training and not to other factors, such as changes to the economy or the benefits package, and it would be too late to make adjustment to the initiative if it is not producing the expected results.

Finding ways to get an "early read" on the output is important to be sure things are working as planned and to identify potential improvements. Also, early changes can be more credibly ascribed to the training. The discussion might sound like this:

"We agreed at the beginning of our discussion that improving retention is a long-term business need and goal. The problem with relying solely on that to measure the impact of the program is that we won't see a significant change in retention rates for months. By then it will be hard to figure out whether it was the training or something else. What could we measure sooner that would give us an indication that the initiative is having the desired effect? A survey? Employee commitment scores? 360-degree feedback?"

TABLE D1.1. MAJOR CATEGORIES OF POST-LEARNING OUTCOMES AND WAYS TO DOCUMENT THEM.

Type of Outcome	Potential Data Sources	Potential Data Collection
Change in behavior	Customers Co-workers or direct reports Participants themselves Participants' managers Trained observers	Surveys Interviews Observation
Improved opinion by key stakeholders	Customers Direct reports Managers Others	Satisfaction surveys Interviews Focus groups
Improved business metrics	Company IT system/reports Independent tracking agency	Data extraction Data purchase
Improved work product (writing, strategic plan, computer code, presentation, etc.)	Samples of work	Expert review Comparison to standards/rubrics Observation

RESULTS

4. What Are the Specific Criteria of Success? Once you have explored the possible outcomes that *might* be measured, it is time to agree on what *will* be measured and when, as well as how much of a change is required to consider the program a success. It is vital to reach agreement on the "conditions of satisfaction" *in advance,* since these are the deliverables section of the contract between the learning organization and line management (see Case in Point D1.3). If you don't know how the business leaders define success, you are likely to miss the mark. Nothing is more discouraging than to present the results of an initiative that you feel was a runaway success, only to find out that the results you tracked were not what the customer was looking for.

For example, we know of one company that spent over $100,000 on an ROI study only to have the chief financial officer say: "These data are worthless; that is not how I define ROI at all" (see Case in Point D6.6).

The point is not whether ROI is a valuable measure. The point is that it was the wrong measure for *their* stakeholder. They should have asked the management team *during the planning stage* how they would define success.

The discussion of Question 4 should be primarily a selection process, winnowing down the possible choices identified in Question 3 (who or what?) to the critical few. It should include a high-level discussion of what the sponsor considers credible (believable, trustworthy) evidence. For example, will self-reports suffice? Do the raters need to be completely independent? The goal at this point is to understand what the business leaders consider relevant and credible outcome measures, not to create a detailed evaluation plan—that is the work of D6. Nevertheless, you have not completed D1 until you have a clear idea of how the sponsor defines success. There is no one right answer; the conditions of satisfaction are defined *by the customer*. That is not to say that learning professionals should have no say in setting the criteria. Defining the measures of success should be a "give and take" discussion. Blindly accepting impossible targets guarantees failure.

Committing to specific levels of achievement may be uncomfortable for many learning professionals, but it is, as Basarab (2011) points out, the norm in business. Having a specific target allows the learning organization to optimize the learning experience, to influence the transfer climate, and to implement continuous improvement. Perhaps most important, an agreed-on target for expected business results enhances the credibility of the learning organization, earns it a seat at the table, and achieves its long-sought goal of being embraced as a true business partner.

 Practical Application

- Use the Outcomes Planning Wheel to structure the discussion about the business purpose of any proposed learning initiative.
- Supplement the insights from the Planning Wheel with a more detailed performance analysis.

Case in Point D1.3
Conditions of Satisfaction

When we asked Richard Leider, award-winning co-author of *Whistle While You Work* and *Claiming Your Place at the Fire*, about the importance of defining objectives, he told us it was vital:

"We teach leaders how to create what we call COS—conditions of satisfaction. What are your conditions of satisfaction? What is it that we are supposed to do differently after this and by when? What is it that you want delivered by when?

"You could call it accountability, but when leaders lead, they are customers. For leadership development, the line leader is a customer. She makes a request; she puts out certain conditions of satisfaction. And so this whole notion of leader as customer translates into the training, and therefore the follow-up practice; leaders have certain conditions of satisfaction for training.

"So often leaders are not clear about their conditions of satisfaction. There is a certain language and a certain rigor that leaders need to learn in order for meetings and training and transactions to be effective. It really clears up all that murkiness. You could say it is common sense; well, the fact is—look where the breakdowns are."

Create Co-Ownership

There is actually a fifth question to the Planning Wheel, but you should wait to broach it until you have explored the first four. It is this: "What else needs to be in place to ensure these behaviors and results?" (Figure D1.7)

The conversation sounds something like this: *I genuinely appreciate the time you have taken to clarify the business outcomes you are looking for and the*

Figure D1.7. THE FIFTH AND CRITICAL QUESTION FOR THE PLANNING DISCUSSION

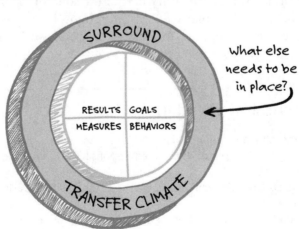

behaviors needed to achieve those results. I have just one last question: 'What else will be required to ensure those behaviors and results?' I am thinking of things like reinforcement by supervisors, recognition for application, consequences for not adopting the new behaviors, and so forth. We will make sure that when people leave the class, they can answer 'Yes, I can.' But whether they will use what they learn or not depends on their work environment. What do we need to do together to be sure the new skills and behaviors are reinforced back on the job?"

Having just given the manager the opportunity to say what he or she considers to be the necessary and important business results from learning (the first four questions), now is a perfect time to point out that whether or not learning improves performance depends as much on the post-training environment as on the learning itself. Unless the desired behaviors are supported and reinforced on the job—which is management's immediate sphere of influence—then the initiative is likely to have little effect. Recall that worthy performance depends on the quality of the work processes and workplace policies as much as on the skills and efforts of the workers (Figure D1.1, page 41).

Once you shift your focus from delivering learning experiences to delivering improved performance, then you appreciate the importance of what has been called the "learning ecosystem" (Frielick, 2004)—the environment in which the learner is embedded (see Table D1.2). Unless the approaches that people learn are supported by the performance management system, the incentive structure, and especially managerial practice and style, they will wither and die, like a plant transplanted into unsuitable soil. Since management owns the post-training work environment, they are either part of the solution or part of the problem. You need to plant that seed with the sponsor now because you will need management's support for changes in the work processes and work environment to optimize learning's impact.

 ## Practical Application

- Use the fifth question—"What else needs to be in place?"—to educate managers about their part in the shared responsibility of ensuring that learning pays dividends.
- Always consider the work environment of the learner; it will make or break any initiative.
- Call out the key points of "what else needs to be in place" in your written summary of the discussion (see Exhibit D1.4)

TABLE D1.2. EXAMPLES OF "WHAT ELSE NEEDS TO BE IN PLACE?"

Category	Notes
Feedback	People want and need feedback to improve their performance. Feedback can come from many sources, including their manager, peers, and even self-assessments.
Recognition	Recognition for effort is a powerful motivator; it is one reason gamification works. Simple acknowledgement by managers is, in general, more motivating than material rewards.
Incentives	The motivation provided by material rewards is not so great as often supposed, but incentives can facilitate change, provided they reward the behaviors taught in training. Surprisingly often, what is taught and what is rewarded are in conflict, or only the result is rewarded without regard for how it was obtained, which can lead to all sorts of undesirable behaviors.
Performance Management System	The performance management system, annual reviews, and any employee rating forms must all be in synchrony with what is being taught, or the training will end up as learning scrap.
Managerial Practices	"I hear what you say, but I see what you do. And seeing is believing." Unless the supervisors of those being trained actively practice and model what was taught, the training is likely to have limited impact. As Mosel pointed out more than fifty years ago: "It is top management, through the organizational climate or reward structure it creates, that is *really* doing the training, regardless of what the training staff does. The training administered by the training staff 'sticks ' only if it coincides with what top management is teaching every day" (Mosel, 1957, emphasis in original).
Consequences for Non-Use	Just as there need to be incentives and recognition for applying the training (carrots), there need to be consequences for not making the effort to perform as taught (sticks). As the saying goes: "People respect what you inspect." If no one cares whether the learning is applied or not, it won't be.

Map the Journey

Going from learning to improved performance is a journey. Creating a map of the journey helps designers, participants, and stakeholders visualize the process and its rationale. It's what Dan Roam, in *The Back of the Napkin* (2013), calls "visual thinking."

Visual thinking means taking advantage of our innate ability to see—both with our eyes and with our mind's eyes—in order to discover ideas that are otherwise invisible, develop those ideas quickly and intuitively, and then share those ideas with other people in a way that they simply "get" (p. 3).

A logic model is a way of mapping the critical elements of an initiative to illustrate their interrelationships, and how they are expected to contribute to the desired outcomes. A logic model makes explicit the "theory of change"—the assumptions behind the initiative—as well as what needs to be evaluated. The approach is widely used in illustrating and evaluating pro-

> A logic map makes explicit the theory of change.

grams in general (Frechtling, 2007) and has proven to be valuable for designing and evaluating corporate learning initiatives in particular (Parskey, 2014).

The generic form of a logic map is shown in Figure D1.8 and illustrates the rationale for company-facilitated learning: **resources** (time and money) are invested in **activities** (training, action learning projects, performance support, etc.); these generate **outputs** (number of people trained, number of coaching sessions, number of participants in social networks, and so forth), which contribute to the **outcomes** of interest (such as increased customer satisfaction, higher sales, faster cycle time). It is important to note that, although the map is usually drawn in time sequence from left to right (resources to outcomes), developing an effective intervention proceeds in the opposite direction, beginning with defining the desired outcomes (Frechtling, 2007).

Figure D1.8.   A HIGH-LEVEL, GENERIC LOGIC MAP

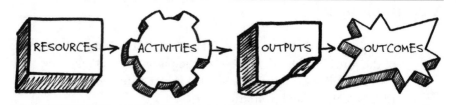

We will return to the concept of a logic map throughout *The Six Disciplines*, enriching it and illustrating how all of the components need to work together to achieve the desired outcomes. At this point in the process—when you have completed the Planning Wheel discussion with the sponsor(s)—your map will be very incomplete. Only the outcomes will have been defined. But the destination will be clear, which is prerequisite to selecting the right route and investing the right level of resources.

Practical Application

- Construct a logic map to illustrate the relationships among activities, outputs, and outcomes.
- Use it to guide both planning and evaluation.
- Develop the map in concert with key constituencies so that everyone is clear about the destination and the journey required to get there.

Manage the Portfolio

According to the great military strategist Clauswitz, the essence of strategy is to concentrate resources on the "decisive point." One of the principal tasks of a business manager is to manage the company's portfolio of products and services, matching investment to potential. Not all products are created equal; some have more potential to contribute to growth and profitability than others, for a variety of reasons, including market size, competition, and where they are in their life cycles. Products with greater potential deserve greater investment and nurturing; those with little potential should be ignored or dropped.

One of the best-known classification schemes for classifying business portfolios is the Boston Consulting Group (BCG) grid, which classifies lines of business along two dimensions—market growth and market share. It is divided into four quadrants or types of business/product (Figure D1.9).

- **Stars.** Entries with a high market share in a fast-growing industry or segment. Stars need high rates of funding to maintain their growth and maximize their potential.
- **Cash cows.** Have high market share in a slow-growing segment. They are called cash cows because they can be milked for cash to support investment in stars and new ventures. They require a limited amount of

Figure D1.9. THE BOSTON CONSULTING GROUP GROWTH-SHARE MATRIX

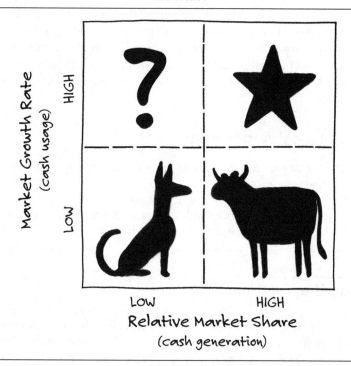

investment, since their potential for growth is low, but they mustn't be starved to death. Cash cows are critical to any company and should be valued appropriately.

- **Dogs.** Have low market share in a mature, slow-growing industry. They have no real strategic value since they typically contribute little cash, have limited potential for growth, and consume time and resources that could be more profitably deployed elsewhere. In his essay, "What Is Strategy?" Michael Porter pointed out that choosing what *not* to do is just as important as choosing what to do; there are always tradeoffs (Porter, 1996). Dogs should be sold or otherwise disposed of and the resources redeployed.

- **Question Marks** (also called **Problem Children**). Products or businesses positioned in high-growth markets, but which have failed to live up to their potential to achieve significant market share. They need attention. If they can be turned around, they might become stars and eventually cash cows; otherwise, they will turn into dogs and be a continuing drag on the organization.

The business manager's task is to continually assess the portfolio and adjust the level of investment to ensure that time, energy, money, and creativity are expended on those lines of business with the greatest potential.

> The essence of strategy is to concentrate resources on the decisive point.

These concepts should be applied to the learning portfolio. Not all learning initiatives have equal potential to contribute to organizational success. The most effective learning organizations practice portfolio management, maximizing their investments in those programs that are stars and killing off low-value or ineffective programs. The BCG grid can be adapted to the management of learning initiatives by modifying the axes to "potential business contribution" and "current level of effectiveness"—to create the Training Potential/Actual or TP/A Grid (Figure D1.10). Programs would then fall into the same four categories with the following definitions.

- **Stars.** Highly effective programs in areas of key strategic importance to the business, such as leadership effectiveness, new product introductions, new market penetration strategies, and so forth. They deserve the best talent, creativity, and highest levels of investment.
- **Cash cows.** Very effective programs that are not necessarily sexy or glamorous, but are nevertheless essential to organizational effectiveness, such as safety training, on-boarding, and compliance training. Like cash cow products or businesses, they must not be starved, but they should not be overfed either.
- **Dogs.** Programs that either are simply not working or that make a minimal contribution. It may be that they were created some time ago to address an issue that is no longer relevant, or it may be that training was not the right solution to begin with. Regardless, programs that are dogs should be discontinued; they sap the organization's resources, energy, and morale.
- **Question Marks.** Training initiatives that should be making a much greater contribution than they are currently. They need to be studied to determine whether the issue is an overstatement of their potential, a misdiagnosis of the problem, ineffective training, or lack of transfer

Figure D1.10.   THE TP/A GRID FOR ASSESSING LEARNING PORTFOLIOS

support. If they have the potential to become stars or cash cows, they should be fixed. Otherwise, they should be discontinued and their resources redeployed in more productive areas.

Effective management of the learning portfolio requires a periodic (quarterly or annual) prioritization process that includes business leaders as well as learning professionals, since learning is a business-support function. Many organizations maintain learning advisory boards or committees for this purpose. Learning professionals should be active contributors to the process. They should come forward with a point of view and recommend specific programs to eliminate in order to free up resources to invest in new or more promising initiatives.

It is important to note here that responsible prioritization of training investments is based on their potential and actual contribution to business outcomes—not their learning objectives, reaction ratings, or whether they're the latest fad in instruction. Training is a business function that needs to be managed as such. The first step in managing learning like a business is clearly defining the expected outcomes (D1).

Practical Application

- Remember that not all learning is equally valuable.
- Maximize your contribution by investing in initiatives with the highest potential for payback.
- Use the TP/A grid to identify your stars as well as your dogs; make strategic decisions about what to keep and what to eliminate.

Summary

The first, crucial, and frequently underdeveloped discipline in successful learning and development is to define the desired outcomes in business terms (D1). Successful learning organizations focus on performance and always start with why. In collaboration with the key stakeholders, they define the rationale for the program in terms of the business benefits to be delivered, rather than just the learning objectives to be achieved. They prioritize their efforts and resources, concentrating on initiatives that will have the greatest impact and probability of success. Together with the sponsors, they agree, *in advance*, on the criteria for success before they embark on design.

Defining business outcomes is the keystone for the success of any learning initiative. When learning professionals don't make the effort to articulate the expected business outcomes, they put the success of the initiative, and perhaps the company itself, at risk.

**Exhibit D1.5
Checklist for D1**

Use the checklist below to ensure that training is the right solution and that the objectives for the learning initiative are stated as business outcomes.

Overall

❑ The proposed initiative addresses a performance issue related to lack of knowledge or skill.
❑ Non-training solutions have been explored or tried and rejected.
❑ A needs analysis has identified the specific knowledge and skills that must be mastered to improve performance.
❑ Environmental factors that will affect successful implementation (such as accountability, consequences, coaching, and so forth) have been identified and discussed.
❑ A high-level logic map has been drafted to illustrate the proposed relationship between learning activities and expected outcomes.
❑ Management understands the impact of the transfer climate on the success or failure of learning initiatives.
❑ Management accepts its responsibility and role in creating a positive environment for learning transfer.
❑ The "conditions of satisfaction" of the sponsor(s) have been spelled out.

Each Program Objective

❑ Is clearly linked to a high-priority, high-value business need or opportunity.
❑ States the actual performance that will be achieved (as opposed to knowledge, ability, or capability).
❑ Specifies the performance standard that will be met and by when.
❑ Uses business terms, concepts, and language.
❑ Clearly indicates how success could be measured.

Recommendations

For Learning Leaders

- Read and understand the business plan. Be proactive in identifying areas in which learning and development can contribute.
- Never offer a program simply because you were asked to offer a program.
  - Always ask: "Why? What is the expected benefit to the company?"
- Use the Outcomes Planning Wheel to help negotiate a clear "contract" with management that specifies, in advance, the business objectives and how success will be assessed.

- Use the "What else needs to be in place?" question to help business leaders understand that training will fail unless supported by managers, incentives, and so forth.
- Review all the programs for which you are responsible to be sure each has objectives that are credibly linked to business imperatives.
- Be proactive in managing the learning portfolio.
  - Use the TP/A Grid to categorize initiatives by their strategic importance and effectiveness.
  - Propose redistribution of resources as appropriate to maximize value.

For Line Leaders

- Tell your learning professionals the results you want—not the solutions (e.g., a one-day workshop); it's their job to propose the best solution.
- Review the portfolio of learning and development initiatives in the business unit for which you are responsible.
  - Are they clearly aligned with the most pressing needs of the business?
  - Are there critical needs that are not being addressed?
  - Are resources being squandered on low-value programs that could be profitably redirected to higher-value initiatives?
- If the current learning initiatives are not aligned with the business needs, work with your learning leader to ensure that they are.
- Rebalance your learning and development portfolio to redirect resources to the initiatives with the greatest potential payoff for the business.
- Identify a business need that you believe requires training to achieve.
  - Confirm that training is an appropriate part of the solution.
  - Work through the Outcomes Planning Wheel with your learning and development partners.
  - Agree on the behavioral changes that are needed to achieve your objectives and how they can be confirmed.
  - Be clear about your "conditions of satisfaction"—the results necessary for you to consider the initiative a success.
- Ask learning and development to propose a plan for achieving these results.
  - Review it critically, using the 6Ds Scorecard (Exhibit I.2, page 36).

D2:
Design

DESIGN THE COMPLETE EXPERIENCE

"If you can't describe what you are doing as a process, you don't know what you're doing."

—W. EDWARDS DEMING

A PROCESS IS "a series of planned activities that convert a given input into a desired output" (Rummler, 2007, p. 197). Since its introduction after World War II by Deming, Juran, and others, process thinking has transformed businesses and generated consistently higher-quality goods and services at lower cost. Process thinking has also reshaped the nature of competition, so that today "competition is not between people, products, or companies: it is between processes" (Tenner & DeToro, 1997, p. 15). The organization with the process that produces the greatest value, most reliably, at the lowest cost, wins.

Corporate-sponsored learning fits the definition of a process: a series of steps is required to transform inputs of people, time, and materials into the value-added outcome of improved performance (Figure D2.1). As with any other business process, the quality of the outcome is only as good as the weakest link in the causal chain. Thus, even if the learning itself is superb, the value it creates for the organization will be minimal if the application step is weak. That is why the most effective learning organizations practice the Second Discipline: they **Design the *Complete* Experience**, not just what happens during the "event" (classroom, simulation, e-learning, and so forth).

Designing the complete experience is vital because people are learning all the time—including lessons the enterprise did not intentionally set

77

FIGURE D2.1.   TRAINING IS A PROCESS

out to teach. They learn from the way the training is designed and exe-cuted, from the way their managers react, from what other participants say about it, and so forth. Employees have learned, for example, that they can safely ignore pre-work assignments since the facilitator will present the same material in class anyway. They have learned that there is rarely any follow-up to training, accountability for its use, or consequences for non-use. If we are to improve the effectiveness of corporate learning, we need to pay attention to *everything* a program teaches, implicitly as well as explicitly; we need to design and manage the *compete* experience.

In this chapter we examine what it means to design and manage the learning process holistically and systematically—to actively plan and influ-ence what happens before as well as after the traditional boundaries of corporate education—and the benefits that accrue from doing so.

Topics include:

- Learning is not an event
- Many factors affect the outcome
- The four phases of transforming learning into results
- Redefining the finish line for corporate learning
- A checklist for D2
- Recommendations for learning and business leaders

Learning Is Not an Event

Everyone has heard the expression "learning is a process, not an event" and most workplace learning professionals agree. And yet the event men-tality is so firmly embedded in our thinking that we unconsciously use the language of "events" when we discuss learning. As a result, we continue to reinforce the "one and done" paradigm. Even the recent *Leaving ADDIE for SAM* (Allen & Sites, 2012), for example, talks about the "anatomy of effec-tive learning events" and the need for "concise, effective learning events" (pp. 21–22).

Concise, effective learning experiences are an essential *part* of the learning-to-performance process. The message of D2, however, is that when learning organizations focus all their attention, resources, and energy on the "event," they sub-optimize learning's potential and add to the learning scrap heap. As professionals, we need to move beyond the learning-as-event paradigm.

The concept of paradigms (accepted "truths") and their power to shape thinking was popularized by Thomas Kuhn in his classic *The Structure of Scientific Revolutions* (Kuhn, 2012). While paradigms are essential for what Kuhn called "normal science" and day-to-day problem solving, there comes a point at which prevailing paradigms are counter-productive to progress and need to be discarded. That time has come in learning and development; real progress in learning effectiveness cannot occur until learning professionals abandon the "learning as event" paradigm.

> When we treat training as an event, we sub-optimize the results.

Writing in the *Journal of Organizational Excellence*, Teresa Roche, CLO of Agilent Technologies, explained: "At Agilent, every department is expected to innovate, learn continuously, and deliver bottom-line results. Global Learning and Leadership Development knew it could not fulfill these expectations simply by delivering traditional programs in traditional ways—no matter how high the end-of-course ratings. To reap the full benefits of corporate training investments, it needed to broaden its perspectives about when, where, and how learning occurs" (Roche, Wick, & Stewart, 2005, p. 46).

Isolated initiatives rarely solve business issues because business issues are inherently systemic in nature (Senge, 2006). "At its fundamental level, every organization is a human performance system. It was founded by people, run by people, for the sole purpose of delivering value to the people who are its stakeholders ... a comprehensive approach to organizational improvement must begin with such a premise" (Tosti, 2009).

Since its inception, the International Society for Performance Improvement (ISPI) has emphasized the need to think holistically and systemically about human resources interventions. Its performance standards state: "Taking a systems view is vital because organizations are very complex open systems.... A systemic approach considers the larger environment that affects processes and other work. The environment includes inputs, but, more importantly, it includes pressures, expectations, constraints, and consequences" (Van Tiem, Moseley, & Dessinger, 2012, p. 591).

The problems with the event paradigm are manifold, not the least of which is that it teaches employees to think of learning initiatives the way they think about a football game or a theatre production—as simply spectators. An event paradigm implies that employees have done their part by showing up. When an event is over, it's over; no more is expected of you. Corporate learning initiatives should be very different. Attendees should expect to play an active role in their own learning and to carry on the process long after the period of instruction ends. That is what actually creates value—a topic we will return to below and in the discussion of D4: Drive Learning Transfer.

Practical Application

- Pay attention to how deeply embedded the "learning-as-event" paradigm is in the way that learning and business professionals talk about training.
- Avoid portraying learning initiatives as "events."

Many Factors Influence Outcomes

Moving from an event paradigm to a systemic approach acknowledges the reality that learning doesn't happen in a vacuum. What each person takes away from a learning experience is shaped by many things, including expectations, attitude, prior experience, aptitude, and emotional state. Similarly, numerous factors influence the extent to which people subsequently transfer and apply their knowledge. These include opportunity, encouragement, reinforcement, and early successes or failures (Figure D2.2).

Indeed, research has shown that what happens before and after the formal period of instruction is as important, if not more important, than what happens in the course itself (Broad, 2005; Broad & Newstrom, 1992; Saks & Belcourt, 2006; Salas,

> What happens before and after instruction is as important as the learning itself.

Tannenbaum, Kraiger, & Smith-Jentsch, 2012). Workplace learning organizations, therefore, need a new paradigm about the scope of their responsibility: one that goes beyond "delivery of events" to "delivery of performance." Delivering improved performance requires attention to

FIGURE D2.2. MANY FACTORS INFLUENCE THE LEARNER'S EXPERIENCE, IMPACT LEARNING TRANSFER, AND AFFECT RESULTS

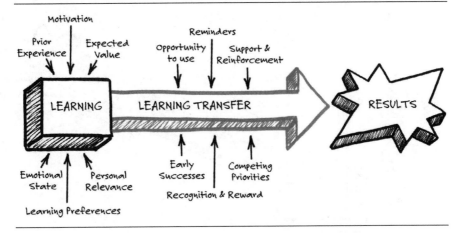

all of the factors that influence outcomes and to all four phases of the learning-to-results process (see below).

Crozier, in the *Engagement Manifesto* (2011), put it well:

> For an intervention to be successful, it has to be supported elsewhere in the system. There must be communication about the aims and objectives of the process, the desired outcomes, and how everyone will benefit. Leaders must focus on the new behaviors in the performance management system and how they will be assessed, rewarding people who successfully demonstrate the desired behaviors. Doing these things will ensure that the change is embedded and sustainable. (p. 58)

A Four-Phase Process

The process of turning learning into business results has four phases (Figure D2.3):

I. **Preparing** the learner, plan, and environment
II. Guided **learning**
III. **Transferring** and applying
IV. **Achieving** improvements

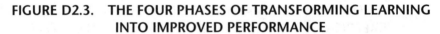

FIGURE D2.3.   THE FOUR PHASES OF TRANSFORMING LEARNING
INTO IMPROVED PERFORMANCE

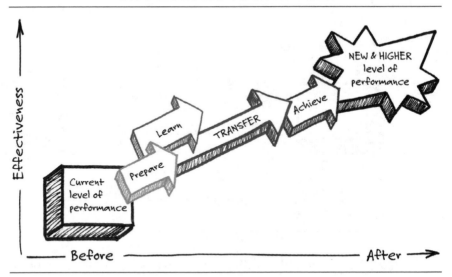

Each contributes to how participants answer the "Can I?" and "Will I?" questions and, hence, to the effectiveness of the initiative. All four are essential to improve performance, leverage corporate learning assets, and execute the organizational strategy (see Case in Point D2.1).

Case in Point D2.1
The Complete Learning Experience at the UBC

The United Brotherhood of Carpenters and Joiners of America (UBC) represents more than a half-million men and women who provide the construction industry with productive, competitive, and expert work. Learning is at the heart of General President Douglas McCarron's strategy to ensure the competitiveness of UBC's members and increase market share.

Dr. Randy Eppard, UBC's chief learning officer, was tasked with making sure that learning fulfilled its promise and became a strategic asset of the Brotherhood. To maximize the value of UBC's 1.2 million-square-foot training center in Las Vegas, Randy focused his team on moving away from an event-driven approach, re-conceptualizing learning as a business process. He challenged them to deliver complete learning experiences that included all of the elements necessary to support UBC's market strategy.

Randy began by immersing his team in the 6Ds. They selected their new flagship Journeymen Leadership Program as their top priority for implementation because it touched the people who had the greatest potential to make the biggest difference to the future of the UBC: the journeymen. The goal of the program was to ensure that journeymen put into practice the principles of transformational leadership.

Randy and his team designed the program to include all four phases of learning. Participants were told explicitly that they would be attending a six-month learning initiative and that the instruction was merely the catalyst to the real work back on the job. The UBC learning team deployed support back into the workplace using a new, purpose-built LMS, coaching, and tools to help drive learning transfer and ensure success.

Before the application of the 6Ds and process thinking, evaluations revealed a transfer rate of 35 percent. Since revising the program with an emphasis on all four phases of learning, the transfer rate is now 80 percent. More than twice as many participants in the Journeymen Leadership Program are now putting their learning to work in a way that aligns to the overall strategy of the UBC.

According to Randy, "Learning at the UBC Training Center is now governed by process thinking and a focus on business results. All new programming is designed with a view to creating a complete learning experience that optimizes for application and produces impact."

Phase I: Preparation

The first phase is preparation. By that we mean much more than traditional pre-work. Preparation in the context of D2 includes:

- Preparing the learning plan
- Preparing the learner
- Preparing the environment

Prepare the Learning Plan

When you conceptualize learning as a process rather than an event, preparing the learning plan involves more than traditional instructional design. Plans need to be made for all four phases: what needs to be done *before* the guided learning activities and what needs to be done to support continued learning and transfer *afterward*.

The logic map for a learning initiative needs to be expanded to include the activities in each of the four phases of the learning-to-

> Plans need to be made for all four phases of learning.

**FIGURE D2.4.   THE LOGIC MAP OF A LEARNING INITIATIVE
SHOULD INCLUDE THE ACTIVITIES REQUIRED IN EACH OF THE
FOUR PHASES OF THE LEARNING-TO-PERFORMANCE PROCESS**

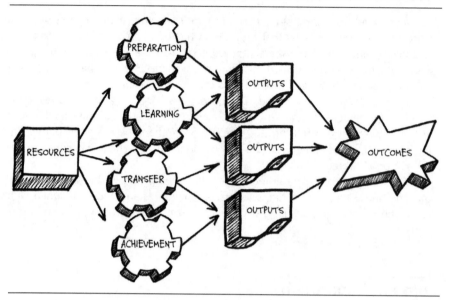

performance process (Figure D2.4). Review learning designs prior to implementation to make sure that all four phases have been considered and that there is a plan for each.

Prepare the Learner

Most learning initiatives assign some sort of "pre-work," such as reading, completing an e-learning program, taking an assessment, and so forth. We try (not entirely successfully) to avoid using the term "pre-work" for Phase I learning since it implies that it is less important than the "real" work to follow. In fact, Phase I is as much a part of the work of learning and as important as anything that follows.

The most common purpose of Phase I learning assignments is to establish a common base of knowledge. The potential uses are much broader, however, and include stimulating interest, creating learning and results intentionality, and gathering data to tailor instruction (Pollock, Jefferson, & Wick, 2014, p. 189).

Establishing a common base of knowledge is important, because all learning can be defined as the process of connecting new ideas and skills to existing mental frameworks (Sousa, 2011). Making sure that participants have the relevant background (education and experiences) they need to make sense of and meaning from the guided learning improves both effectiveness and efficiency. It helps avoid talking over the heads of some while boring others.

With every group you train, you have to start at the place where the group is at the time of training. When you assume that the group knows all the basics, that assumption will jump up and bite you every time.

Conklin, 2012, p. 103

An even more important goal of Phase I is to ensure that participants are primed with the right attitudes and expectations. Employees do not arrive at a corporate learning program like blank sheets of paper. Most have already formed an opinion of its probable value for them and, therefore, whether they are going to invest time and energy learning or just "go through the motions."

Tversky and Kahneman demonstrated the power of the "priming effect" in a brilliant series of experiments that contributed to their winning the Nobel prize in 2002. Perhaps the most chilling example was the finding that simply rolling a pair of dice influenced judges' subsequent sentencing decisions (Kahneman, 2013, p. 125). A more light-hearted example is Ariely's (2010, p. 202) demonstration that which beer students preferred depended on whether or not they were told, in advance, the identity of the "secret ingredient" he had added (Figure D2.5).

Kelley's classic experiment at MIT provides an example directly applicable to training. Changing just *two words* in the description of the instructor distributed prior to class significantly influenced how the students rated the experience (Kelley, 1950).

> Expectations strongly influence an employee's decision to participate in learning.

FIGURE D2.5.   THE SAME STIMULUS PRODUCES DIFFERENT RESULTS DEPENDING ON EXPECTATIONS

Interestingly, Colonel Barnard Banks of the United States Military Academy reported a similar finding about the power of just two words to influence expectations:

> In the fall of 2011, we changed the wording of one of the two main goals of PL 300 [Military Leadership] to: "Cadets will apply relevant frameworks, concepts, and theory to current leadership situations" (rather than can apply). Although we only changed two words in the purpose, moving from "can apply" to "will apply" and adding "current" to leadership situations changed the way both the instructors and students approached the course.
>
> Banks, 2014, p. 413

If just two words can sway learners' experiences, it is clear that participants' attitudes coming into a corporate learning initiative will influence both their experience and the ultimate outcomes. Tharenou (2001) showed that expectations—especially regarding the practical utility of the program—strongly influence an employee's decision to participate and engage. The priming effect is so strong that learning and development planners ignore it at their peril.

What determines the attitude that participants bring to class? Many things, chief among them:

- Their prior experience with learning (both in school and at work);
- The signals that their manager sends—intentionally or unintentionally;

- How the program is described; and
- What they have heard about the program from colleagues.

Prior Experience If participants have had great learning experiences before, they will come to class with a more positive attitude than if their prior experience has been bad, either in school or previous corporate programs. Unfortunately, bad experiences, in general, have greater impact and are remembered longer than good ones (Amabile & Kramer, 2011). That means that training and development organizations cannot afford to *ever* deliver an ill-conceived or poorly executed initiative. The negative impact of boring e-learning, a badly planned class, or training that fails to address the real issue extends long after the specific experience. It "poisons the well" for future learning initiatives and adversely impacts their value and effectiveness.

Also, it's hard for university-trained designers and facilitators to remember that not everyone enjoyed school. As the head of training for a power company in Canada told us: "Our power line workers are very skilled employees who have to know a lot to do their jobs safely and well. But many had bad experiences with the educational system and did not especially like school. Putting them back in a typical classroom setting stirs up a lot of negative emotions and defensiveness. So we avoid classrooms for these workers. We concentrate on hands-on training in the field and other non-school-like approaches."

 Practical Application

- Consider the background of the learners; teach in the ways they prefer to learn.
- Ensure that every learning initiative is relevant and useful; a bad experience makes creating value from future programs more difficult.

Signals from Their Managers Employees take their cues about what is important from their managers. If an employee's manager speaks disparagingly about an upcoming learning opportunity ("You have to be away from work *again*?"), that undermines its value. The employee will be less willing to engage. When a manager says nothing about training, employees assume it is low on his or her list of priorities, and therefore it is low on theirs. "Holding back information, failing to enter into a dialogue, or being less than proactive still sends a message—albeit certainly not the right one" (Crozier, 2011, p. 52). Conversely, when a manager signals that the training is important ("I really want you to pay attention and I want to hear how you plan to use it when you get back"), then employees are more likely to attend with the intent to learn and apply.

Brinkerhoff and Montesino (1995), for example, found that participants who had discussions with their managers before and after training reported significantly higher levels of skill application. Feldstein

> Employees take cues about what is important from their managers.

and Boothman (1997) found that half the factors that characterized high-performance learners were related to the influence of their managers. Seventy-five percent of the high-performance learners reported that their supervisors had expressed expectations of improved performance, whereas only 25 percent of low performers did. When a process was implemented to increase the pre- and post-course interaction with managers, both the learners and their managers reported much higher rates of transfer. More recently, Newton (2014) found a strong correlation between a pre-training discussion and the manager's opinion of the impact three months later.

The ultimate responsibility for learning, of course, rests with the employee. As Peter Drucker famously wrote: "Development is always self-development. For the enterprise to assume responsibility... is an idle boast. The responsibility rests with the individual" (1974, p. 427). At the same time, it is both unfair and unwise to expect individuals to devote effort to learning when the unambiguous signal from their managers is that it is not important. Given the impact of managers in shaping learners' attitudes, the most effective organizations facilitate pre-training discussions between managers and their direct reports. Some even require such a discussion as a prerequisite for attendance.

 Practical Application

- Encourage participants' managers to have short, focused, supportive discussions with their direct reports prior to the training.
- Educate managers on the value of doing so, and provide simple guidelines and scripts to facilitate the process.

How the Program Is Described How participants perceive a learning opportunity is shaped by the way it is communicated and positioned.

Marketing departments spend a great deal of time and money managing each product's *positioning* and *brand promise*—what they want customers to think of when they hear the product's name. The goal is to create a positive association between the brand and something the customer desires and to embed that association deep in customers' psyches.

But what do employees desire from training? Knowles's principles of adult learning, as well as studies of why employees attend training, indicate that adults are motivated to learn things that they believe will be of practical benefit in their lives and careers (Knowles, Holton, & Swanson, 2011). That's why in D1: Define Business Outcomes we stressed the importance of clarifying the program's *benefits*—how it will help the participant and the organization. To secure buy-in and garner support for learning programs, you need to be explicit about the "why"—the advantages that will accrue to the participants—by describing *benefits* (what it will do for them) and not merely its *features* or attributes. As our colleague Ray Phoon of PowerUpSuccess likes to say, "Features tell, benefits sell." Nevertheless, "too many people state the features of their offering and expect the buyer to join the dots and understand the value or benefit" (Dugdale & Lambert, 2007, p. 163). Many can't or won't connect the dots and as a consequence undervalue the opportunity.

The importance of explaining benefits is a part of every sales training curriculum. Yet, most course descriptions focus almost entirely on the

> Features tell; benefits sell.

features (length, facilitator, learning objectives), with little or no mention of the individual and enterprise benefits. Here is a typical example taken from an online course catalog:

> Strategic Cost Management is a two-day course that combines instructional and hands-on learning techniques through the use of case studies. You will:
>
> - Learn how to identify data sources for building cost models.
> - Gain an understanding of the cost structure of purchased services and materials.
> - Distinguish between managing price and managing cost.
> - Understand and apply a set of cost-management tools.
> - Learn to apply cost models effectively in negotiations.
> - Learn to exercise pricing discipline in long-term contract negotiations.

It is left up to the reader to translate those features into benefits. In contrast, here is an example that does a much better job of explaining why you should attend in terms of the WIIFM (What's in it for me?):

> Take the strain out of composing any kind of document! Would you like a quick and easy method for composing documents—letters, memos, reports, proposals, and performance appraisals—in an organized format? This seminar provides you with basic formats and formulas for tackling any kind of writing task—and communicating to your readers what they need to know. You'll streamline your writing process and save time by focusing on what to write instead of how to write it. Bring a current project and get one-on-one feedback.

Note how the benefits were stated clearly and how questions were used to draw you into agreeing that you would benefit from attending such a program. The power of focusing on benefits was demonstrated by one of the participants in a workshop we led in Asia. Following our discussion, she re-wrote all of the course descriptions in her division to emphasize the business and personal benefits (outcomes), rather than just the features (activities, outputs). Interest in the programs from potential participants and their managers increased dramatically ... even though the programs themselves *had not changed at all*—only the way in which they were positioned and described.

Although we have focused here on course descriptions, the same can be said for invitations to attend training programs. Most "invitations" to corporate learning initiatives that we have seen—especially those gener-

> Most "invitations" to training sound more like a prison sentence.

ated automatically by learning management systems—read more like a prison sentence than an opportunity to participate in a valuable learning experience (Figure D2.6). First impressions matter. Be sure the first impression of your learning initiative is positive.

Consider more enticing ways of communicating the invitation, especially for strategically vital programs. Some companies use a personal

FIGURE D2.6. BE SURE THE "INVITATION" TO A TRAINING PROGRAM DOESN'T READ LIKE A SENTENCE TO PRISON

invitation from a senior leader. Others are more creative: UBS Bank repurposed a marketing video, redubbing it with a high-energy invitation to a key leadership program. Wanda Hayes, director of Learning and Organizational Development for Emory University, uses video testimonials from prior participants to effectively communicate the benefits, as well as the time commitments and expectations of the University's Excellence Through Leadership Program (Hayes, 2014). If you don't want your program to be viewed as just another boring task, don't promote it that way.

 Practical Application

- Review your course descriptions and invitations.
- Make sure they stress the benefits to the attendee and not just the features of the design.

What Others Are Saying We are all influenced by others' opinions. If colleagues and friends speak positively about a movie, we are likely to make an effort to see it; if several pan a new restaurant in town, we are less likely to try it. Online reviews of products and services increasingly influence our purchasing decisions. Learners' attitudes about corporate learning initiatives are similarly shaped.

In this age of social media, employees are more connected than ever and more in tune with "the buzz." Whereas, in the past, peer-to-peer influence was confined mostly to co-workers with whom one was likely to have a conversation, nowadays opinions can "go viral" and spread rapidly across an entire organization in hours.

What people hear about a program influences their expectations. Expectations, in turn, affect their motivation to learn and apply ("Will I?"). As learning professionals, we need to pay more attention to the "word on the street." If a particular program is developing a bad reputation as "useless," "boring," or "a waste of time," it's essential to understand the root cause and address it. Ignoring such issues damages learning's brand and future prospects in the same way that ignoring product defects hurts a company more than a prompt recall and correction.

 Practical Application

- Pay attention to the "word on the street" about learning initiatives; it impacts their effectiveness.
- Take action to understand and fix the problem if the buzz is not positive.

Resetting Expectations

Learning professionals have been indoctrinated to think of learning in terms of "events"; so have learners. The corporate training programs employees have attended have rarely had any requirements beyond show-

> The most information ever collected was how I rated the instructor.

ing up and perhaps passing a test. Attendees rarely, if ever, have been held accountable for application, even in those programs that included "action planning." Peter Gilson, former chairman of Swiss Army Brands, Inc., described typical practice: "As a young corporate executive, I attended dozens of development programs, but no one ever once followed up with me to see what I had done with what I learned or how I had used it. The most information ever collected was how I rated the instructor."

Case in Point D2.2
Resetting the Finish Line

Home Depot conducted a series of large-scale learning events to help its store managers run more efficient and effective operations. At the end of the three-day forum, participants were presented with a very handsome crystal trophy. The then-president of Home Depot Canada, Annette Vershuren, realized that doing so sent entirely the wrong message. The award should be for *implementing* ideas that actually improved store operations, not just for showing up. So, in her unit at least, store managers received their trophies only when they could document at least one action they had taken as a result of attending the Store Managers' Forum that demonstrably improved store performance. That's a good example of redefining what it means to complete a course of learning.

An important part of the 6Ds approach to preparing the learners is to reset their expectations by redefining the "finish line" for company-sponsored learning as successful application on the job (Figure D2.7), not just getting to the end of a module, game, simulation, or workshop (Wick, Pollock, & Jefferson, 2009). Credit, certificates, tchotchke, and other indicators of "completion" should be awarded only after there is some tangible evidence of on-the-job application to reinforce the message that the ultimate goal is improved performance (see Case in Point D2.2).

There are many ways in which the new finish line can be defined and assessed; the appropriate timing and criteria depend on the nature and the goals of the program. Table D2.1 provides some examples of the ways in which companies have redefined the finish line for their learning initiatives.

FIGURE D2.7.   THE REAL FINISH LINE FOR LEARNING IS IMPROVED PERFORMANCE

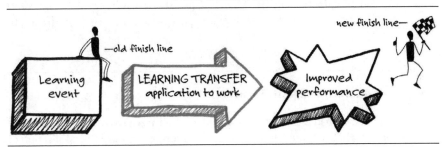

TABLE D2.1. EXAMPLES OF REDEFINING THE FINISH LINE

Goal of Program	New Finish Line	Organization and Reference
Improve use of PowerPoint slides	Submit three redesigned slides 90 days following training. Only if the slides pass the "glance test" (a standardized scoring scheme) do the participants receive their certificates.	KLA-Tencor (Hughes, 2014)
Enhance coaching skills to improve leadership effectiveness	Complete a computer-based training module that reinforces key concepts and tests knowledge of coaching principles, and engage in a SharePoint discussion about their application goals and progress with class cohorts.	Methodist-Bonheur Healthcare (Keeton, 2014)
Increase quality and lower cost by applying lean manufacturing principles	Complete, evaluate, and report on an improvement project that required application of lean principles.	Hypertherm, Inc. (Jaccaci & Hackett, 2014)
More effective leadership	Tell an achievement story about your leadership development, including application actions and improvements you are most proud of.	U.S. Military Academy at West Point (Banks, 2014)

Course descriptions and communications to participants should be explicit about what is expected. Trainees should arrive with the clear understanding that the *privilege* of attending an educational program carries with it the *responsibility* to apply it to improve their performance and that their work is not done until they have put what they learn to work. The timeline for every initiative should include the time needed for application (Figure D2.8). Agendas should be written so that they encompass the complete learning experience, not just the instructional event.

 ### Practical Application

- Reset participants' expectations about what it means to complete a course of study.
- Be sure that all materials and communications emphasize the application of learning and avoid wording that implies "event."

FIGURE D2.8.   A PROGRAM TIMELINE THAT ILLUSTRATES THE COMPLETE LEARNING EXPERIENCE

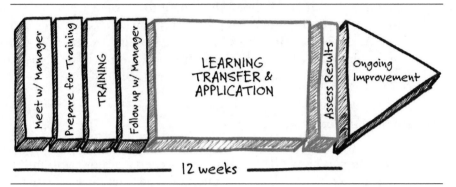

Readiness for Change Prochaska and DiClemente (1983) proposed a Stages of Change model that has become one of the most influential concepts in the field of behavior modification. They proposed that behavior changes occur in five stages: pre-contemplation, contemplation, preparation, action, and maintenance (DiClemente & Prochaska, 1998). Relapse can occur at any stage in the process (Figure D2.9).

Change efforts fail when they try to skip steps in the process—for example, trying to get people who are not even thinking about changing (pre-contemplation) to move straight to action. They also fail if they neglect to put in place support mechanisms (D5) to help maintain the change and prevent relapse. The model is relevant to corporate learning initiatives, as these are all, at some level, efforts to help employees change behaviors. Thus, an important aspect of Phase I is to move employees from pre-contemplation to the contemplation and preparation stages.

FIGURE D2.9.   PROCHASKA AND DICLEMENTE'S STAGES OF CHANGE MODEL

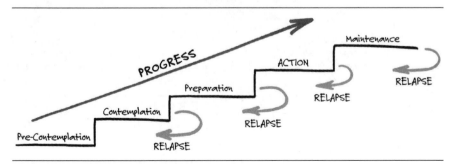

Bottom Line Companies can improve the impact of their learning initiatives by devoting greater effort and attention to shaping participants' "going-in" attitudes, because these tend to become self-fulfilling prophesies. Participants get out of a program pretty much what they expect they will. If they expect it to be a high-value learning experience, then that is most often what they experience. If they expect it to be a waste of time, then it usually is, at least for them (Figure D2.10).

Prepare the Environment

As we will discuss in more detail in D4, the transfer climate—that is, the employee's work environment—exerts a powerful influence on the answer to the "Will I?" question and therefore whether learning creates value or scrap. As Geary Rummler famously quipped, "Pit a good performer against a bad system, and the system will win almost every time" (Rummler & Brache, 2012, p. 11).

FIGURE D2.10. EXPECTATIONS INFLUENCE HOW MUCH PARTICIPANTS BENEFIT FROM THE SAME LEARNING EXPERIENCE

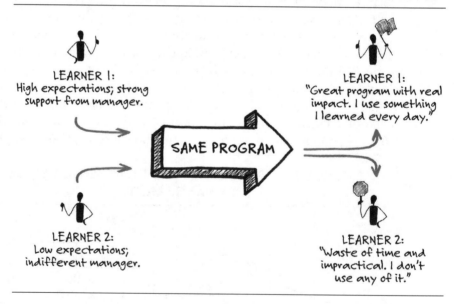

LEARNER 1:
High expectations; strong support from manager.

LEARNER 2:
Low expectations; indifferent manager.

SAME PROGRAM

LEARNER 1:
"Great program with real impact. I use something I learned every day."

LEARNER 2:
"Waste of time and impractical. I don't use any of it."

The best time to start thinking about and preparing the transfer climate is during the analysis and design phases. That's the purpose of asking, "What else needs to be in place?" as

> The transfer climate exerts a powerful influence.

part of the D1 Planning Wheel discussion. Unless the environment—the incentives, language, rewards, consequences, leadership actions, and culture—that surrounds the learning initiative is in alignment with the desired behaviors, the initiative is likely to fail.

Key questions to ask include:

- Does senior management visibly support the initiative in both word and action?
- Do the immediate supervisors of participants know their role in supporting application?
- Do managers have the skills and tools they need to coach effectively?
- Are they held accountable for doing so?
- Does the performance management system reward the behaviors being sought?
- Are there incentives for performing in the manner that will be taught?
- Are there negative consequences for *not* performing in the new way?

If the answer to any of these questions is "no," then it will undermine—or in some cases completely negate—the intervention's effectiveness. Learning professionals need to make a clear-eyed assessment of the environment, then work with management to reduce any impediments to progress. Such issues take time to correct. Therefore, preparing the environment needs to begin in Phase I.

 Practical Application

- As part of the analysis and design phase, critically evaluate the work climate to which the participants in a learning program will return.
- Work with management to prepare an environment that is conducive to learning transfer.

Phase II: Guided Learning

We will discuss Phase II, the guided learning period, in detail in the next chapter (D3: Deliver for Application). Regardless of the method or medium—facilitator-led instruction, e-learning, action learning, on-the-job training, discovery learning, or any combination thereof—the critical issues are to:

- Ensure congruence between the guided learning experiences and the ultimate business outcomes sought.
- Build on and reinforce the Phase I learning assignments.
- Use instructional approaches that are appropriate to the required behaviors and skills.
- Honor principles of adult learning.
- Ensure that participants are able to apply what they have learned to their work ("Can I?").
- Convince them of the benefits of doing so ("Will I?").
- Make the transition between Phase II and Phase III (Transfer and Application) strong and seamless.

Phase II is the most well-studied phase of corporate learning. There are numerous books, courses, and research papers on instructional design. Even so, learning in this phase can be enhanced by greater focus on the business goals, selecting methods of instruction that are congruent with the performance required, making sure that there is adequate time for practice, and that participants understand the relevance and utility of what they are being asked to learn. The latter is important. Adults are more motivated to learn and do so more effectively when the relevance of what they are learning is clear (Knowles, Holton, & Swanson, 2011).

An expanded logic model—the value chain for learning (see page 140)—can help ensure that the content and instructional methodologies are logically consistent with the desired outcomes. Use business objectives as the criteria for deciding what to include and what to leave out. Use the required performance to decide the best way to structure the learning. When learning initiatives are designed this way—with business outcomes always as the end in view—it is much easier for participants to see their relevance and answer "yes" to the "Will I?" question.

> Adults are motivated to learn when the relevance is clear.

Phase III: Transfer and Application

Phase III—learning transfer—is where the "rubber meets the road" and where most programs founder. What happens (or fails to happen) in this step of the process is the main arbiter of whether learning creates value or scrap. No matter how much learning occurs in Phase II, it is only a cost to the organization unless it is used in a way that improves performance (Figure D1.2, page 41). The whole value of learning—and therefore of the learning organization—depends on the effectiveness of transfer. As such, we strongly encourage learning professionals to take greater ownership of Phase III and influence the post-course environment.

Today, learning transfer and application—the third phase of the learning-to-performance process—is the weakest link in corporate learning initiatives (Figure D2.11). Thus, improving transfer represents the greatest opportunity to increase the overall effectiveness of corporate learning. Strengthening learning transfer is in everyone's best interest: the individual, the learning and development organization, the participant's manager, and the company as a whole. It deserves much greater attention than it has received in the past.

If transfer is so important, why haven't corporate learning organizations done more to manage this critical phase? We believe there have been three main impediments:

1. The prevailing paradigm treats training as an event and relegates instructional designers to little more than event planners.

FIGURE D2.11. PHASE III, LEARNING TRANSFER, IS THE WEAKEST LINK IN MOST LEARNING PROGRAMS

Copyright © Grantland Enterprises; *www.grantland.net*. Used by permission.

2. The post-event period is a "no-man's land" between the learning organization and day-to-day management; neither accepts ownership for learning transfer and results.

3. The historical lack of systems for managing the process.

We will address these issues in greater detail in the chapters on D4: Drive Learning Transfer and D5: Deploy Performance Support. The point here is that planning for Phase III—learning transfer and application—is a critical practice of the discipline of designing the *complete* experience. Indeed, the success of the whole initiative hinges on it. Smart learning organizations dedicate resources to influencing this vital, but neglected, aspect of turning learning into results.

Phase IV: Achievement

Phase IV is the new finish line for learning. It completes a learning cycle by acknowledging the progress that participants have made. There are three solid reasons for including recognition of achievement as part of the complete learning experience:

1. It is powerfully motivating.
2. It establishes a clear finish line.
3. Assessment is itself a learning experience.

Acknowledgment and "Will I?"

It turns out that having one's efforts acknowledged is powerfully motivating. For participants to answer: "Yes, I will make an effort to change," and to sustain their efforts over time, they need to feel they are making progress and have that affirmed. When Amabile and Kramer (2011) analyzed thousands of daily work logs, they discovered that a sense of making progress in meaningful work was associated with greater productivity, creativity, and commitment to the work.

Conversely, when workers felt they were not making progress, or when the work was meaningless, they were less motivated, less creative, and less productive. Unfortunately, Amabile

> A sense of making progress increased productivity, creativity, and commitment.

FIGURE D2.12. A SENSE OF MAKING PROGRESS IS VITAL TO SUPPORT BEHAVIOR CHANGE

and Kramer also found that: "Far too many managers are unaware of the importance of progress and therefore neither worry about or act to support it" (p. 158).

The sense of making progress is vital to sustaining any behavior change (Figure D2.12). Studies at the National Registry of Weight Control, for example, found that people who weighed themselves regularly were more successful at losing weight and keeping it off than those who didn't (National Weight Control Registry, n.d.). "The small win of dropping even half a pound can provide the dose of momentum we need to stick with a diet. We need to see small victories to believe a long battle will be won" (Duhigg, 2012, p. 278).

If we want to motivate employees to continue to learn on the job, then we need to find ways to tap into their intrinsic motivation by giving them a sense that they are making progress and that the work of applying learning is meaningful. Daniel Pink surveyed the literature on motivation in *Drive: The Surprising Truth About What Motivates Us* (2008) and concluded that, for most people, the intrinsic drive to achieve self-efficacy and self-satisfaction is more motivating than extrinsic rewards like money and position.

Dan Ariely provided evidence that the inverse is also true: having your efforts ignored is powerfully de-motivating (Ariely, 2011). He compared three groups: those whose work was acknowledged, those whose work was ignored, and those whose work was placed in a paper shredder as soon as it was completed. The surprising finding was that the group whose work was ignored quit almost as quickly as the group whose work was shredded.

In other words, lack of acknowledgment destroys intrinsic motivation almost as much as having your work trashed.

The key lesson for learning professionals is that if we want people to make the effort to apply what they learn, then we need to make certain that there is some acknowledgment of their efforts and some recognition for

> If we want people to apply what they learn, we need to acknowledge their efforts.

their accomplishments. That can be as simple as a self-assessment or awarding credit or a certificate for completion based on demonstrable application to the job. Or it could involve a more potent incentive, such as having to report your efforts and accomplishments to senior managers (see Case in Point D2.3).

Historically, training departments have not done enough to harness intrinsic motivation by ensuring that trainees receive recognition when they make the effort to apply what they learned back on the job. That is why we consider Phase IV—acknowledging achievement—an integral part of the complete learning experience.

 ## Practical Application

- Develop a process that ensures employees have a sense of making progress as they try to adopt new skills, even if this is just a self-assessment.

Case in Point D2.3
Delivering Value from Learning at DuPont

For more than 200 years, the DuPont Company has brought world-class science and engineering to the global marketplace through innovative products, materials, and services. DuPont introduces thousands of new products every year in markets as diverse as agriculture, nutrition, communications, construction, transportation, and safety.

DuPont employs a strategic marketing approach—DuPont Marketing Excellence (DMX)—to ensure successful product introduction and global market reach. Rand Mendez, director of DMX, is charged with ensuring that the foundational principles of DMX are taught in a way that leads to application and business impact.

The DMX for Project Teams program is a capability-development initiative that leverages experiential and project-based learning. Four high-priority growth projects are chartered, each of which needs a strategic marketing plan to succeed. The real work of these projects becomes the basis for learning during the course of the DMX for Project Teams program.

The 6Ds principles were used to design the process. The DMX team first established a solid D1 foundation to ensure clarity about expected outcomes. They also use the D1 process to identify and develop each of the project charters. Each project must pass a rigorous business review process before it becomes the subject of a DMX action learning experience.

Instructional modules and intersession assignments are designed to support learning transfer and application. Cross-functional participants are brought together for three three-day programs spread over six months in which they learn the fundamentals of strategic marketing and apply that learning to the high-priority project that is part of their ongoing work. "Achieving learning transfer was much easier when the participant's learning and priority work were inseparable," Rand told us. To further assure transfer, the DMX team deploys coaching and leader support throughout the process. The "finish line" for the program is presentation of the strategic marketing plan to the management team and its incorporation into the value stream of the DuPont sales process.

"One indicator of the success of the program is that the business does not bother to ask for return on investment metrics. They have already seen the value created from the successful implementation of plans developed in the program."

Rand credits the success of the program to the team's thoroughness in ensuring that all six disciplines and critical success factors were considered and planned for when creating the program, as well as his team's commitment to continuous improvement.

Staple Yourself to the Learner

Finally, you must ensure that the participant's experience across all four phases of learning is consistent and coherent. We have found the concept of "stapling yourself to the learner" (Figure D2.13) to be a useful exercise.

The idea grew out of an article by Shapiro, Rangan, and Sviokla (1992) in the *Harvard Business Review*. They argued that the only way to really understand your customer's experience (and how to improve it) was to figuratively "staple yourself to an order." In their case, that meant to follow an order through all the steps in their company to see how many times it was handled, how often it was set aside, how hard it was to find its status, where mistakes occurred, and so forth.

The application of this idea to learning and development is to imagine yourself stapled to a learner throughout all four phases, from first hearing about the opportunity, through the structured learning, to the on-the-job

FIGURE D2.13.   CHECK THE PROGRAM DESIGN BY IMAGINING YOURSELF STAPLED TO A LEARNER THROUGHOUT

application in the ensuing days and months, to achieving better performance. At each stage, imagine yourself as the learner, and ask:

- Would I understand what is expected of me?
- Is the expected business outcome clear and compelling?
- Would I understand how this initiative relates to all the other systems, slogans, and corporate initiatives?
- Is it clear how the learning initiative relates to my work?
- Would the instruction allow me to say, "Yes, I can perform in the new way?"
- Where would I turn for help if I needed it?
- Can I see the benefit for me personally?
- Would I answer "Yes, I will!" and make the effort to do so?
- Will anyone know or care whether I use this stuff?
- What does my manager think? Does she support it? How do I know?
- Would the way I am evaluated on the job reinforce what I learned, or work against it?

Whenever we have done this exercise with clients, they have discovered opportunities to make improvements that strengthened the overall experience and impact. The checklist in Exhibit D2.1 will help you make sure that your design encompasses the complete experience.

 Practical Application

- Review the *complete* learning experience to be sure that all the elements work together to ensure both "yes, I can" and "yes, I will."

Summary

The Second Discipline practiced by the most effective learning providers is that they design and manage the learner's *complete* experience—from how the program is positioned in the invitation, to the preparation expected in Phase I, to the instructional design of Phase II, to the accountability and support of Phase III, to how progress will be assessed and recognized in Phase IV. Their plans also include how elements of the transfer climate will be enhanced and coordinated.

Designing the complete experience goes well beyond the traditional scope of corporate learning professionals. It will require learning new skills and abandoning long-standing paradigms. It is, in our experience, the only way to achieve a real breakthrough.

> The complete experience goes well beyond the traditional scope of corporate learning.

Adopting this holistic approach to learning and learning transfer dramatically increases both the perceived and real value of educational efforts. Redefining the finish line as improved performance, rather than the last day of class, is an invigorating challenge that offers substantial rewards.

Exhibit D2.1
Checklist for D2

Use the checklist below to ensure that the design of a learning initiative contemplates the "complete experience."

PHASE I—Preparation		
	Element	**Criterion**
❏	Selection	The selection or enrollment process makes sure the "right people are on the bus"—meaning those who have the experience and responsibilities to benefit from the program.
❏	Invitation	The invitation is clear and compelling. It explains the benefits of attending and sets expectations for on-the-job application.

❑	Preparation (participants)	There is meaningful preparatory work—reading, experiential learning, simulations, feedback, etc.—that will help maximize the value of the time spent in the learning program itself.
❑	Preparation	A pre-program meeting between the participant and his or her manager is strongly encouraged (ideally, required). Guidelines and worksheets are provided.
❑	Preparation (managers)	Managers are provided with an overview of the program, its objectives, the business needs being addressed, and guidelines for maximizing its value.

PHASE II—Guided Learning (See D3)		
	Element	**Criterion**
❑	Use of Pre-Work	The preparatory work is utilized extensively in the program—so much so that those who did not complete it are at a disadvantage (or ideally, not allowed to attend).
❑	Logic Model	There is a clear understanding among the designers and facilitators of how each activity relates to the desired behaviors, capabilities, and expected business outcomes. These links are communicated to the learners.
❑	Relevance	Relevant examples, stories, simulations, discussions, and so forth are included to help learners see how the material applies to their jobs. Current practitioners and/or prior graduates of the program are used to help underscore its utility.
❑	Practice	The agenda provides adequate time for learners to practice the desired skills and behaviors with supervision and feedback.
❑	Process Check	End-of-course evaluations include assessment of whether learners perceived the utility and relevance of the program and feel prepared to use it to advantage in their work.

PHASE III—Transfer and Application (See D4 and D5)		
	Element	**Criterion**
❑	Performance Support	Job aids or other materials and systems are included as part of the learning plan to ensure that learners have help when they need it.
❑	Manager Involvement	Participants and managers are strongly encouraged to meet following the course. Guidelines are provided for that meeting. Ongoing manager involvement is facilitated.

❑	Accountability	Processes are in place to periodically remind participants of their obligations, hold them accountable for progress, and recognize superior effort and accomplishment.
❑	Process Management	A process and systems are in place to allow learning professionals to monitor, support, and manage the learning transfer process.
PHASE IV—Acknowledge Progress		
	Element	**Criterion**
❑	Completion	The "finish line" for the initiative is defined as on-the-job application. An assessment plan is in place, and participants know what it is.
❑	Progress	The plan includes a process to help participants get a sense of making progress.
❑	Recognition	There is a process to recognize superior effort and accomplishments.

Recommendations

For Learning Leaders

- Review the programs for which your group is responsible to ensure that the designs truly encompass the complete experience from the learner's point of view.
- Draw a logic map that includes activities in all four phases of learning.
- Be vigilant for mixed messages—where what is taught in the program and what is practiced in the business are inconsistent or do not support one another.
  - Such inconsistencies discourage participants from trying to transfer their knowledge and, if glaring, lead to cynicism.
- Review course descriptions and invitations to be sure they emphasize benefits and not just features.
- Emphasize to business managers the importance of their support in all four phases of the program to achieve optimal return on investment.
- Redefine the finish line; award credit, certificates, and so forth only after learning has been applied.
- Make sure descriptions, agendas, and other communications do not inadvertently reinforce the "learning-as-event" paradigm.

- Be sure there is a mechanism to give participants a sense of progress during the application phase and to acknowledge improved performance.
- Check back with participants: How did they answer "Can I?" and "Will I?" at work, and why?

For Line Leaders

- Ask learning leaders to draw a logic map for a strategically important program.
  - Review it to be sure there is a plan for all four phases of learning.
  - Are the business goals clear? Do the activities make sense?
- Listen to the way you and other managers speak about learning. What messages are you sending? Are you inadvertently reinforcing the event mindset?
- Ask your line managers what they are doing to ensure that development programs are reinforced so they "stick."
- Devise systems to hold line managers accountable for their roles in obtaining results from learning and development.
  - Measure and reward managers' active engagement in the process.
  - Ensure that "the video matches the audio." That is, be certain that what management says, what managers do, and what the system rewards, are in alignment. If not, you are wasting time and money in training.
- Make sure that there is a process to assess, recognize, and reward accomplishments.
  - Remember that it takes a village; acknowledge the contributions of managers and participants as well as training professionals to successful initiatives.

DELIVER FOR APPLICATION

"If the trainees do not apply what they learned, the program has been a failure even if learning has taken place"

—DON AND JIM KIRKPATRICK

THE FUNDAMENTAL RATIONALE for any corporate learning initiative is to improve business results by helping employees do their jobs more effectively (Figure D3.1). How well trainees first learn, and then utilize, new methods determines training's ultimate value. A return on the investment requires effective as well as efficient learning.

In a corporate setting, the *effectiveness* of learning equates to its *applicability*. Learning and development programs must do more than simply impart new knowledge and skills; they must do so in ways that facilitate their *application* toward organizational goals.

How instruction is delivered—the sequence, methods, structure, timing, assessments, feedback, medium, and so forth—impacts how participants answer the "Can I?" and "Will I?" questions and, therefore, whether the initiative creates value or is scrap. "Every training solution must be based on the way the learner processes information, or it just will not work" (Hodell, 2011, p. 64).

Because learning only adds value when it is applied, the Third Discipline (D3) of breakthrough learning is to **Deliver for Application**, that is, to utilize instructional strategies that maximize the applicability (transferability) of learning to the work of the individual and firm.

In this chapter, we focus on those aspects of instruction that help employees learn new material and then apply it across the learning-doing

FIGURE D3.1. THE FUNDAMENTAL LOGIC FOR TRAINING: PERFORMANCE IMPROVES WHEN EMPLOYEES LEARN AND THEN APPLY NEW KNOWLEDGE AND SKILLS

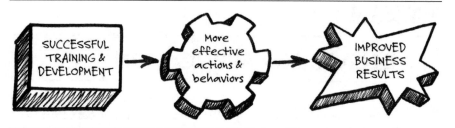

gap. We highlight the problems we encounter most frequently in corporate learning and development programs and suggest solutions. Topics covered include:

- Learning is a means to an end
- How people learn
- Bottlenecks and roadblocks in the learning process
- Ensuring "Yes, I Can"
- Encouraging "Yes, I Will"
- A checklist for D3
- Recommendations for learning and business leaders

 ## Learning as a Means

A central theme of *The Six Disciplines,* and especially of D3, is that business-sponsored learning is a means to an end: improved performance. While learning is an essential step in the performance-improvement process, it is not the ultimate goal (Figure D3.2). In this respect, corporate training differs from, for example, university education. Corporate-sponsored learning needs to maximize *application,* not just theoretical insight or understanding.

A focus on application requires a pragmatic approach to instruction that emphasizes skill development and practice. It also requires that assessments evaluate the learner's ability to *apply* new skills and knowledge in

FIGURE D3.2.   LEARNING IS AN ESSENTIAL STEP IN PERFORMANCE IMPROVEMENT, BUT IT IS ONLY AS A MEANS TO AN END

the work environment—as opposed to simply being able to recall facts and theories.

Effectively applying new knowledge and skills is a three-step process (Figure D3.3). The first step is recognizing a relevant opportunity. The situations in which employees need to perform are rarely, if ever, exactly like those presented in training. As such, employees need to be able to identify the salient features (cues) of the current situation and correctly relate them to something they have learned. They then must be able to retrieve the appropriate information and skills, and finally, adapt them to the new situation, a process that learning theorists call "far transfer" (Royer, 1979).

How the information was learned affects the employee's ability to perform each of these three steps and, therefore, whether or not the learning

FIGURE D3.3.   THE THREE STEPS IN EFFECTIVELY APPLYING NEW KNOWLEDGE AND SKILLS

will be successfully applied. Optimizing training's effectiveness requires selecting instructional methods and strategies based on research about how people learn, remember, and perform. Many current practices in corporate training are suboptimal or even directly contrary to what is now known about how people learn best. To explain that assertion requires a brief examination of the neuroscience of learning.

How People Learn

Progress continues to be made in our understanding of how people learn and what educational approaches are most effective. A number of excellent summaries of the research and its implications are available, such as *How the Brain Learns* by Sousa (2011), *Make It Stick: The Science of Successful Learning* by Brown, Roediger, and McDaniel (2014), *Cognitive Psychology and Its Implications* by Anderson (2010), *Evidence-Based Teaching* by Petty (2009), and *Evidence-Based Training Methods* by Clark (2015). Unfortunately, many of the insights in these accounts have yet to be incorporated into corporate learning initiatives.

When Medina (2014) reviewed the literature on learning and the brain in his engaging book, *Brain Rules,* he summed up his findings this way: "Taken together, what do the studies in this book show? Mostly this: If you wanted to create an educational environment that was directly opposed to what the brain was good at doing, you would probably design something like a classroom" (p. 5).

That is not to say that e-learning, at least as typically executed, is the solution either. According to Michael Allen, "Even e-learning ... tends to be laden with text-heavy presentations delivered in page-turning format. This

> Boring instruction is costly, damaging, ineffective, and wasteful.

type of learning is tiresome and boring. And sadly that's not the worst part. Boring instruction is costly, damaging, ineffective, and wasteful" (Allen & Sites, 2012, p. 4). Why is boring (whether live, digital, or virtual) so bad? Because we can't learn what we don't attend to (see Bottleneck 1 below) and we don't pay attention to boring things.

Understanding how people learn, remember, transfer, and apply knowledge will enable you to deliver learning in ways that are more readily put to work and that produce greater value. Therefore, the next section provides an overview of the learning process and the implications for training and development.

An Overview

A simplified model for how people learn is given in Figure D3.4. The process starts when some input stimulus (1) attracts the brain's attention. The stimulus can be external—involving any of the five senses—or internal, such as hunger, pain, desire, or even imaginings generated by other parts of the brain.

Input to which we choose to attend (2) is passed to short-term, working memory (3), which holds it briefly while the brain tries to make sense of it. If it is sufficiently meaningful and interesting, it is then encoded (4) for consolidation into long-term storage (5). Later, given the right trigger, the brain retrieves (6) the relevant information (which often includes procedural as well as declarative knowledge and even emotions), adapts, and applies it (7).

The entire sequence must be completed—including appropriate retrieval and application—for learning to add value. Unfortunately, there are several bottlenecks in the process and numerous potential points of failure. The effective practice of the Third Discipline—delivering for application—requires that instructional designers and facilitators be aware of the most common points of failure and take steps to circumvent them.

The critical aspects of each step in the process are discussed below, together with the practical application of research insights to corporate training and development.

FIGURE D3.4.   A MODEL OF THE KEY STEPS IN LEARNING AND APPLICATION

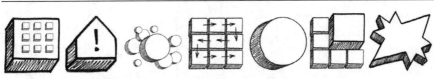

INPUT   Attention Short-Term Encoding/ Long-Term Retrieve   APPLY
                    Memory   Consolidation Memory

Bottleneck 1: Attention

Our attention span—in both breadth and duration—is strictly limited. At any given moment, the brain receives far more input than it can attend to (Figure D3.5). Most of the incoming information—unless it poses a threat or is especially interesting—is simply ignored and never processed further. A simple example is that you receive a constant stream, 24/7, of information from the sensory neurons in your feet. But unless your shoes are uncomfortable, your feet are cold, or you have sprained your ankle, the input from your feet rarely rises to the level of conscious thought (although it did just now, as soon as we called attention to it).

Even most of what you see and hear is ignored, unless you consciously choose to pay attention to it, or it is something that your subconscious perceives as a threat and which it therefore forces up to the level of

> Attention is the most significant bottleneck in the learning process.

awareness. We are programmed by nature to pay attention to certain sounds—like a crying baby—whether we want to or not. That explains why it is so stressful to be seated near one on an airplane.

Attention is the most significant bottleneck in the whole learning process. The instruction must gain—and hold—the learner's attention. Otherwise, it will not be processed and little will be learned. That's why Gagné made "gain attention" the first of his Nine Steps of Instruction (Gagné, Wager, Golas, & Keller, 2004). See Table D3.1.

FIGURE D3.5.   THE BRAIN RECEIVES MORE INPUT THAN IT CAN PROCESS; MOST INPUT IS FILTERED OUT AND IGNORED

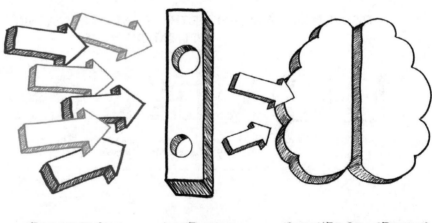

SENSORY INPUT   ATTENTION   FURTHER PROCESSING

TABLE D3.1. GAGNÉ'S NINE STEPS OF INSTRUCTION ANNOTATED FOR CORPORATE LEARNING

1. Gain Attention	A first and critical step in instruction is to gain people's attention. Techniques include posing a question, relating a surprising fact, doing a demonstration, playing a video, giving a quiz, and so forth.
2. Explain the Objectives	Adults, in particular, want to know *why* they should learn something before they will willingly engage. State the objectives of the program in a way that explains the "What's in it for me?" (WIIFM) for the audience.
3. Stimulate Recall of Prior Knowledge	All learning builds on prior learning. The better the audience can connect the new material to things they already know, the easier it will be to learn and the more durable the learning will be. Start by having them recall something they already know or expand on a familiar concept or personal experience. Analogies are particularly valuable in this regard.
4. Present New Content	Present new information or approaches in ways that build on the audience's prior knowledge and experience. Link new terms and concepts to familiar ones. "Chunk" the material into manageable segments and avoid cognitive overload caused by providing too much information too quickly.
5. Provide Learning Guidance	Help the learners transfer the material to long-term memory by providing guidance in the form of examples, mnemonic devices, analogies, mental models, and opportunities for discussion and questions.
6. Practice/Elicit Performance	Provide time for learners to practice using the new material or skills and require that they do. Practice is vital to mastery. Repetition increases retention. Start with simple scenarios and work to more complex or difficult. Opportunities for practice include self-check questions, games, role plays, problems to solve, simulations, and many others.
7. Provide Feedback	Feedback is essential to improve performance, both in training and on the job. Ensure that there is adequate time and a mechanism for learners to receive feedback on their answers/performance in the practice sessions. Use rubrics or checklists to ensure consistency.
8. Assess Performance	Use some form of assessment to ensure that the participants have achieved the learning objectives. Make certain that the questions or exercises fulfill the alignment principle, that is, they reflect both the learning goals and the real-world needs. Avoid questions that require only simple recall of rote memorization.
9. Enhance Retention and Transfer	Provide job aids, tools, templates, and other forms of performance support that will help participants transfer what they learned to their jobs. Provide managers with specific pull-through plans and activities to enhance retention and transfer.

Practical Application

- Design programs to grab learners' attention immediately. Don't waste time on long, boring introductions; you will lose them.
- Capture their attention by explaining (or better, illustrating) the benefits for them personally; answer the "What's in it for me?" question.

Special Challenges for Corporate Learning Two aspects of attention present special challenges for corporate learning programs. First, humans can attend to a very limited number of inputs at any given time. Second, paying attention is hard work; it cannot be sustained indefinitely.

Multi-Tasking Is a Myth The first challenge is attention's limited bandwidth. Despite the widespread belief among young people that they can effectively multi-task, multi-tasking is a myth. People can switch rapidly between tasks, but every time they do, there is a momentary but measurable blackout period in which they are attending to neither (Medina, 2014, p. 117). That explains why trying to drive and text—or even talk on a cell phone—increases your chances of an accident many-fold (Seppa, 2013). "Multi-tasking is merely the opportunity to screw up more than one thing at a time" (Steve Uzzell, quoted in Keller & Papasan, 2013, p. 44).

The relevance to corporate learning is that participants cannot truly attend to the program if they are simultaneously reading their email or text messaging. The temptation to "multi-task" during webinars ("I'll just have a quick look at email") reduces their effectiveness. In a frequently quoted study at Stanford University, students who characterized themselves as high multi-taskers performed worse on a variety of tests. One of the study's authors, Clifford Nass, told *The New York Times*: "Multi-taskers were just lousy at everything" (Pennebaker, 2009). Unfortunately, despite the demonstrably detrimental effects, the myth of multi-tasking is still alive and well in the business world, widely practiced, and even encouraged.

There are numerous lines of evidence that people cannot truly attend to more than one or two input streams at a time. The issue appears to be a bottleneck in processing, rather than in the sensory organs themselves (Anderson, 2010, p. 63). For example, when

> Multi-tasking is the opportunity to screw up more than one thing simultaneously.

you are engaged in an interesting conversation, you are able to "tune out" other voices in a crowded and noisy room. Even though the other conversations are clearly audible, you barely notice them as long as you are truly attending to the conversation you are in, until something—like overhearing your own name or a voice raised in anger—commands your attention. Of course, as soon at that happens, you lose the thread of the original conversation.

Another example of "attention as gatekeeper" that is familiar to many learning professionals is the classic work of Simons and Chabris (1999). They demonstrated that when people were asked to closely attend to a specific action in a video, half completely failed to notice a man in a gorilla suit who walked into the center of the action and beat on his chest! The point is that, whenever we choose to attend to one thing, we necessarily ignore something else.

Practical Application

- Discourage multi-tasking, especially the use of smartphones and email during training.
- Demonstrate the downside of multi-tasking with the "Gorillas in Our Midst" or similar videos to make the point.
- Recognize that "being out of touch" is a source of stress for many; provide enough breaks and time for people to check their email, etc.

Paying Attention Is Hard Work Attention is not only narrowly focused, but short-lived and easily diverted. A single instance of a ringing cell phone, for example, demonstrably reduced the amount learned (McDonald, Wiczorek, & Walker, 2004). Interestingly, learning by reading has an edge over learning by listening, because "when listening to new information, extraneous sounds can divert the brain's attention. But reading is a much more focused activity, thereby reducing the effect of distractions" (Sousa, 2011, p. 121).

When people are intensely motivated and immersed in a task, they can spend hours thinking and working on it—Csikszentmihalyi's concept of "flow" (Csikszentmihalyi, 2008)—but for most tasks, paying attention is hard work. It requires willpower: executive control by the pre-frontal cortex.

Numerous experiments have shown that, in the short term, willpower can be exhausted—for example, by having to eat radishes while seated in front of a bowl of freshly baked chocolate chip cookies

> Corporate training expects people to pay attention longer than is possible.

(Baumeister, Bratslavsky, Muraven, & Tice, 1998). "There's been more than two hundred studies on this idea since then, and they have all found the same thing. Willpower isn't just a skill. It's a muscle, like the muscles in your arms and legs, and it gets tired as it works harder, so there's less power left over for other things" (Mark Muraven, quoted in Duhigg, 2012, p. 137).

The less engaging the presentation, the more difficult it is for learners to maintain attention. "As you no doubt noticed if you've ever sat through a typical PowerPoint presentation, people don't pay attention to

> Regardless of the learning modality, the brain needs a break now and then.

boring things" (Medina, 2014, p. 2). An extensive meta-analysis of safety training found that "as training methods became more engaging (i.e., requiring trainees' active participation), workers demonstrated greater knowledge acquisition, and reductions were seen in accidents, illnesses, and injuries" (Burke, Sarpy, Smith-Crowe, Chan-Serafin, Salvador, & Islam, 2006). Adults also tend to be very pragmatic; they don't pay attention to training that does not seem relevant to them or readily applicable to their work.

Most corporate-sponsored learning expects participants to pay attention longer than is humanly possible. The constraints imposed by attention span are the driving force behind the interest in moving to "bite-sized" learning—breaking instruction into ninety-minute or shorter episodes. Commercial studies suggest the short-segment approach is at least, if not more, effective than day- or multi-day-long programs (MindGym, 2013).

Regardless of the overall duration, Medina (2014) recommends breaking all instruction into ten-minute segments—because that is about when most learners' attention begins to wander—and using "hooks" to recapture their attention. Effective "hooks" are relevant to the topic and evoke some sort of emotion—laughter, anxiety, disbelief, surprise, and so forth. Well-chosen stories and anecdotes can be especially efficacious in this regard.

The critical point is that people have to attend before they can learn, so a key task of instruction is to capture, hold, and periodically recapture attention. "To learn, a person needs to be engaged" (Kapp, Blair, & Mesch, 2013). Part of the continuing popularity of Thiagi's learning games (Thiagarajan, 2006) and, more recently, gamification in general, is that game elements help sustain attention, engagement, and interest—which are prerequisites to learning.

Practical Application

- Give audiences a break from the fire hose of information every ten minutes or so; use some sort of "hook" to recapture attention.
- Use game elements judiciously to engage learners.

Bottleneck 2: Working Memory

Information that is attended to is passed to working (short-term) memory, which has a very limited capacity. When too much content is delivered too quickly, it overwhelms your working memory's capacity to adequately process and make sense of it. Everyone has, at some point, felt like the student in Gary Larson's *Far Side* cartoon who asks to be excused from class because his "brain is full." That's cognitive overload: so much information coming in so fast that your brain is overwhelmed and cannot adequately process it. According to Geoff Petty, "teacher talk can deliver material at least twenty times faster than it can be learned. If content is delivered too fast, the working memory and short-term memory soon get swamped. Key points, relations, and subject principles get obscured by the detail" (Petty, 2009, p. 25).

In other words, there comes a point at which including additional content actually *decreases* the total amount learned (Figure D3.6). It's not just that learners don't remember the "nice-to-know"—too much

FIGURE D3.6.   BEYOND A CERTAIN POINT, ADDING MORE CONTENT ACTUALLY *REDUCES* THE AMOUNT LEARNED

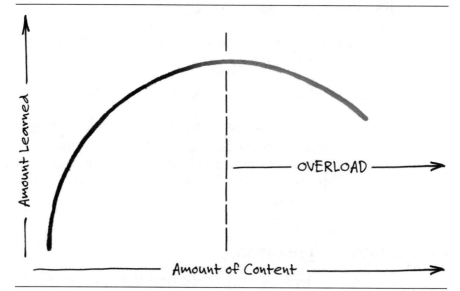

content delivered too quickly interferes with learning the basics. It also leads to superficial learning; when participants aren't given the time they need to process the material, they will fail to grasp its underlying structure.

Key points, relationships, and principles can be obscured by too much detail.

The most common error we see in corporate training is the tendency to overstuff students with information, with not enough time allotted to "connecting the dots." An over-emphasis on content also reduces the time available for active engagement and practice—essential elements of the learning process.

Another common cause of cognitive overload is too many simultaneous streams of information (graphics, text, audio) in e-learning programs. Cognitive load is intensified when two streams of information compete for the same processing capacity—for example, trying to read text on slides and simultaneously listen to the presenter, both of which require language processing. Conversely, images and words can be complementary, since they are processed separately, as long as the images are relevant. Extraneous images added "for interest's sake" actually diminish learning by distracting attention away from the salient features (Clark & Mayer, 2011, p. 161).

Practical Application

- Pay attention to the cognitive load in learning initiatives.
- Avoid the temptation to use extraneous audio, graphics, and so on; if something does not contribute to understanding, leave it out.
- Avoid excessively wordy "slideuments"; they compete with the presenter for language processing capacity.

Bottleneck 3: Encoding and Consolidation

Encoding is the process of converting information and experiences into meaningful memory traces. Consolidation is connecting those new memory traces to existing knowledge structures so that they can later be retrieved (Brown, Roediger, & McDaniel, 2014, p. 73). It is the essence of learning. The more firmly and elaborately the new information is encoded and connected, the easier it is to access it later. Because each person's life experience is unique, each person's mental framework is unique, and therefore, the way that each person encodes and consolidates new learning is unique. It is work each individual has to do for him- or herself; the instructor cannot provide it ready-made.

Rich encoding and connectivity are important because the process of responding to a stimulus requires retrieval from memory at multiple points (Figure D3.7). The ability to recall the cues, insights, and skills gleaned from a learning experience is prerequisite to their adaptation and application. An important part of the practice of delivering for application (D3), therefore, is to utilize instructional methods that enhance encoding, foster long-term memory, and facilitate subsequent retrieval. Topics need to be

FIGURE D3.7. SEVERAL DIFFERENT KINDS OF MEMORY ARE NEEDED TO RESPOND APPROPRIATELY TO A STIMULUS

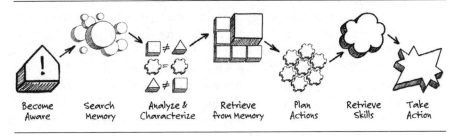

Become Aware — Search Memory — Analyze & Characterize — Retrieve from Memory — Plan Actions — Retrieve Skills — Take Action

presented in ways that are *memorable*—so that they come to mind later to guide action at work.

Humans are best able to remember new information when it is associated with and linked to ideas, patterns, and knowledge already stored in long-term memory (Buzan & Griffiths, 2013). Concepts that extend or enrich existing knowledge are much easier to recall—and therefore use—days, weeks, or months later than those that are free-standing or disconnected. The richer and more relevant the network of connections between new and existing knowledge, the easier it is to recall and use. The more deeply learners encode and consolidate learning, the better they are able to retrieve and use it back on the job.

The encoding and consolidation process can be enhanced through the use of "advance organizers" (Petty, 2009, p. 197). These are conceptual overviews of the material to be covered—ideally in graphic form— that are presented prior to the specific

> The better the learning is encoded, the easier it is to retrieve.

content. They provide a framework on which to attach new information and insights. Visual depictions of workflows, for example, can help employees establish effective mental models to which they can then relate specific skills and know-how (Gottfredson & Mosher, 2011, p. 65). Relevant visual images aid retention because the brain's visual memory system has enormous capacity for storage and detail (Konkle, Brady, Alverez, & Oliva, 2010).

Encoding and consolidation are also enriched when learners talk to others about something they just learned or experienced. That is one of the reasons that "teach-backs" (reciprocal teaching) are an effective instructional tactic. Describing an event or concept greatly strengthens its connections and the ability to recall it later (see Case in Point D3.1). Every time you relay information to another person—a process known as elaborative rehearsal—you strengthen and enrich the memory trace (Medina, 2014, p. 149).

The connections each individual generates for him- or herself are much stronger and more meaningful than those supplied by the instructor (Petty, 2009). That is why "generation" (meaning self-created connections) is one of the four key elements of the AGES mnemonic for improving learning retention (page 128). It is also why generative learning—asking and attempting to answer questions about a topic—is a much more effective study strategy than merely re-reading the text (Brown, Roediger, & McDaniel, 2014, p. 94).

Case in Point D3.1
Elaborative Rehearsal

Glenn Hughes is senior director of learning and development for KLA-Tencor, the world's leading supplier of process control and yield management solutions for the semiconductor and microelectronics industries. When we asked Glenn about what learning strategies have the highest payoff, he thought immediately of elaborative rehearsal.

"I realized that that's probably my preferred learning tool. People have often remarked at my memory and how I can remember the names of Japanese temples I went to twenty years ago. I remember courses, events, and conversations in much the same way, and I could never really understand why until I read about elaborative rehearsal. Then I realized that the first thing I do when I walk out of a learning experience is I go and explain it to someone.

"I come home and I tell my wife, 'Hey! I was just at this class today, here's what I learned.' And I go through it. That weekend, when I call my dad I tell him, 'This is really an interesting class,' and then I tell him about slide:ology or the 6Ds or whatever I was just learning about. I'll come into work and I'll get out my pen and I'll diagram it on the board and tell my colleagues what it was I just learned.

"And people challenge me and ask me questions; they force me to be clear about my thinking. They add their own applications. And, of course, the whole while I'm telling them about it, I'm tapping it into experiences that the two of us have in common. So I'll say, 'Hey, you know, remember three months ago when we were talking to this leader and he said . . . . Well, I think I might have found the answer.'

"That's the sort of web I weave within say forty-eight hours of any critical learning experience. I weave a web that involves a lot of other people and even different media and tools, and how it relates one idea to another. And what's interesting is, from that network of people, the number of application points multiplies exponentially, because they all see ways that it can be used, too. And so then it becomes very easy to take something and apply it.

"That's probably the most important thing I do when I come out of a learning experience. I go through the whole elaborative rehearsal process."

Elaborative encoding—the sort that makes for strong and more readily retrieved learning—requires active engagement on the part of the learners; they have to think about the meaning of the material and its connections to their own experiences and prior knowledge. Learning activities need to be designed to ensure that people have adequate time and encouragement to actively process the experience. Consolidating memories involves forming new physical connections among cells in the brain. That takes time and—interestingly—adequate sleep (Maas & Robbins, 2011, p. 36).

A final consideration is that encoding is not selective. A lot of information is encoded that is not necessarily relevant, but nevertheless affects the ease of recall (see review by Thalheimer, 2009). That explains why scuba divers trained underwater performed better when tested underwater than when tested on land nearby (Godden & Baddeley, 1975) and why students score better when tested in the same room in which they learned the material.

The relevance to corporate learning is that retrieval of work-related learning is enhanced when the cues that the learner will encounter in the work environment are encoded along with the new knowledge or skill (Gottfredson & Mosher, 2011, p. 82). Learning to recognize and correctly categorize situations is pre-requisite to appropriate application. According to a study at Indiana University, management training focuses too much on content and skill development and not enough on teaching managers to recognize the situations in which to apply them (Baldwin, Pierce, Joines, & Farouk, 2011).

The point is two-fold: (1) on-the-job training has the advantage of embedding relevant environmental cues into the learning and (2) teaching and then testing in the same classroom environment may over-estimate actual ability (Thalheimer, 2009).

Practical Application

- Encourage deep and elaborative processing by asking learners to come up with their own examples, connections, and analogies or to explain concepts to others.
- Provide enough time to think; it takes time to construct personal meaning.

Long-Term Memory

Long-term memory is sometimes compared to a computer's hard drive, in that it stores data for retrieval days, weeks, or even years later. But the analogy should not be interpreted too literally. Memories are not stored as discrete, verbatim files or images like those on a hard drive. Rather, human memories are vast interlocking webs of data distributed across the brain (Davachi & Dobbins, 2008). You can demonstrate this by thinking of a single word, such as "automobile" or "manager." You immediately become aware of a host of other associations. You might recall your first car, for example, or your first accident, your favorite boss or a manager you intensely disliked. Each person's associations to a given concept or incident are unique. The thicker and more branched the web of associations (the more entry points attached to the information), the easier it is to retrieve a memory later.

Memories are actually "constructed." That is, they are assembled from bits and pieces at the moment of recall, not merely replayed like a video recording, even though it seems that way to us. The brain fills in missing bits it assumes should be there, whether they are or not. That is one reason that eye-witness testimony is demonstrably unreliable. It is also why it is quite hard to memorize a long passage or poem verbatim; your brain tends to fill in the words it "expects" to be there, not necessarily what the author wrote. In general, people are better at remembering the "gist" of things, rather than the precise details—a point to which we will return in D5.

Whether or not items are encoded and consolidated into long-term memory depends on the answers to two questions: "Does this make *sense* to me?" and "Does this have *meaning* for me?" (Sousa, 2011, p. 52). If we want people to remember things they learn, then we must ensure that it is explained in a way that is understandable (makes sense) *to them*. We must simultaneously ensure that there is personal relevance for the learners (it is *meaningful* to them). Sense and meaning are independent and synergistic (Figure D3.8). That means that, even if something makes sense to me, but it has no personal relevance, I am not likely to retain it (see Exhibit D3.1: Relevant Principles of Adult Education, below).

> Only that which makes sense and is meaningful is moved to long-term memory.

Retrieval

The ability to remember and act on prior experience has great survival value. If you ate a certain kind of fruit and nearly died because it turned out to be toxic, then it is very useful to remember the experience and to be able to recognize the plant again so you do not make the same mistake in the future. Everything hinges on "recognize again"—that is, be able to retrieve the relevant memory at the appropriate time. It doesn't do much good to "know" something if you cannot access the memory when you need it.

Retrieval is thus another potential point of failure in the learning process. How well people can retrieve information at the moment of need

FIGURE D3.8.   THE MORE THAT LEARNING IS PERSONALLY MEANINGFUL AND MAKES SENSE, THE MORE LIKELY IT WILL BE REMEMBERED

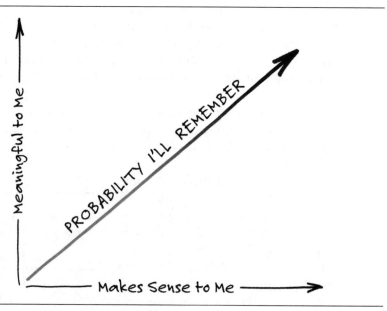

determines its value. Of course, the situation in which the information must be retrieved will never be exactly like the situation in which it was learned. Sticking with the poisonous fruit example, the real value is being able to *generalize* the information from that experience so that you avoid all instances of that particular plant, not just the one bush that made you sick. At the same time, you must *discriminate* between poisonous and edible fruits; if you generalize too much ("all fruits are bad"), you will starve to death. Discrimination requires learning the salient features (like leaf, plant, and fruit shape), while ignoring the irrelevant aspects (specific location or day of the week, for example).

Learning in a corporate environment is similar. People need to be able to remember what did and did not work (whether by direct or vicarious experience) and then retrieve and transfer that knowledge to a similar—but not identical—situation in the future. That suggests that practicing discrimination with a variety of examples should be included in any learning initiative. It may also explain why exercises that include the likelihood of making errors result in superior learning compared to those in which participants are almost always successful (see meta-analysis by Keith & Frese, 2008).

Several important features of the retrieval process are well known and relevant to corporate training. The first has been mentioned above: the more elaborate the encoding, the

> The more often learning is used, the easier it is to recall.

easier and more reliable the retrieval. The second is the long-established principle that retrieval occurs more readily when the features considered at retrieval match those during learning (Morris, Bransford, & Franks, 1977). The third is that the more often a memory is retrieved, the easier it becomes to retrieve subsequently. Indeed, repeated retrieval practice is several times more effective than either rereading the material or creating concept maps (Karpicke, 2012). "Every time we recall information from long-term storage into working memory, we relearn it" (Sousa, 2011, p. 134).

 ## Practical Application

- Use stories, cases, simulations, and role plays that are relevant to your organization and business so that they are easier to recall later.
- Include discrimination practice—that is, ask learners to differentiate case from non-case examples—since it is as important to know when *not* to use a specific approach as when to use it.

Application

 The final step in the process of using learning to guide action is to apply the relevant insights or methods to the situation at hand. This usually requires the learner to adapt the approach somewhat, a process that is greatly aided by experience with a number of situations and scenarios and, surprisingly, by interleaving different subjects rather than studying one at a time (Brown, Roediger, & McDaniel, 2014, p. 49).

Application is the point at which the process shifts from a question of "Can I?" to one of "Will I?" Even if the person is adept at recognizing the critical elements of the situation and retrieving the appropriate repertoire of actions, he or she must make the voluntary decision to *act* on the information.

Practical Application

- Provide practice retrieving the information in a variety of contexts to assist learners with far transfer and adaptation.
- Build in "desirable difficulties" (like the probability of making mistakes) that make the learners work harder and therefore learn more effectively.

A Useful Mnemonic

Davachi and her colleagues at the Neuroleadership Institute proposed AGES (Table D3.2) as a useful mnemonic for remembering four key variables—**A**ttention, **G**eneration, **E**motions, and **S**pacing—that impact learning though their effects on the hippocampus, a brain structure that plays a central role in memory (Davachi, Kiefer, Rock, & Rock, 2010).

TABLE D3.2. KEY ELEMENTS OF THE AGES MODEL

Attention	People can only learn what they pay attention to
	Multi-tasking (divided attention) reduces learning
	Attention span is limited; do not expect people to pay attention for prolonged periods without a frequent change of pace
Generation	Learning is the process of linking new information with existing knowledge
	Each learner must generate his or her own meaning
	Elaborative rehearsal aids retention
	The connections a learner creates for her- or himself are more meaningful and more durable than those provided by instructors
Emotions	Emotions have powerful direct and indirect impacts on learning
	A mild degree of stress (anxiety) improves learning; high stress interferes with learning
	Positive emotions like joy, humor, and satisfaction aid learning
	Negative emotions, especially fear and stress, suppress creative thinking, elaborative processing, and learning in general
Spacing	Revisiting a topic at intervals generates greater learning than "one and done"
	Repeated retrieval practice (trying to answer questions about the material) is superior to re-reading
	Spacing is particularly beneficial if long-term retention is the goal

Adapted from Davachi, Kiefer, Rock, and Rock, 2010.

We discussed the crucial role of attention (the A in AGES) in the general learning model above. Generation (G in the AGES model) means having learners generate their own connections between new information and their existing knowledge structures—for example, by asking participants to "formulate, organize, or add their personal experiences." Such self-created relationships are more meaningful and more durable than the associations supplied by others (instructors, e-learning, etc.). Deep learning "requires that the learner give not only conscious attention, but also build conceptual frameworks that have sense and meaning for eventual consolidation into the long-term storage networks" (Sousa, 2011, p. 91).

The "E" in the AGES acronym is to remind learning professionals that emotions have a powerful effect—positive or negative—on learning, both directly and indirectly. For example, how people feel about the learning situation affects the amount of attention they devote to it (Sousa, 2011, p. 48). Positive emotions, like humor or a feeling of social connectedness, enhance learning (Medina, 2014). Negative emotions—such as fear or perceived threat—increase attention, but narrow its focus, inhibit creativity and innovation, and suppress the reflection necessary for elaborative encoding (Subramaniam, Kounios, Parrish, & Jung-Beeman, 2009). Unfortunately, it is easier to generate negative emotions than positive ones, and negative emotions, in general, have greater and longer-lasting effects.

Stress is not all bad for learning … up to a point. Hunter (2004) suggested that a moderate "level of concern" stimulates optimal learning. If learners have no level of concern, then they expend little or no effort to master the material. At the other end of the scale, learning suffers when the level of concern is too high (Figure D3.9). Learners who have a high fear of making errors devote a significant portion of their working memory to self-monitoring, which interferes with both learning and performance (Brown, Roediger, & McDaniel, 2014, p. 91).

What that means for corporate learning is that we need to raise the level of concern by showing employees how the topic or behavior is vital to their success or personal safety. At the same time, we cannot make the consequences of failing to master the material so high that people become too "stressed out" to concentrate on learning.

The "S" in the AGES mnemonic stands for spaced learning: revisiting a topic at intervals with breaks between. Spacing out learning over time reduces cognitive load, encourages more elaborative encoding, and

FIGURE D3.9.   THE AMOUNT OF LEARNING VS. DEGREE OF
CONCERN

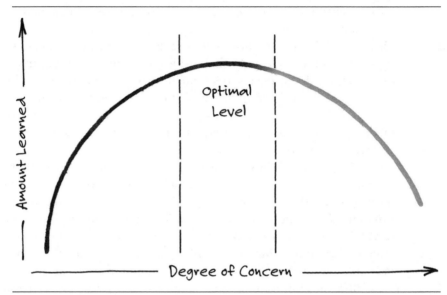

After Sousa, 2011, p. 72.

produces learning that is both more durable and richer than when a topic is presented only once, *even if the total amount of time spent is identical* (see review by Thalheimer, 2006). Karpicke (2012), for example, reported a four-fold greater recall rate among students who practiced rereading and retrieval at intervals, compared to those who studied all in one block. Most corporate training programs continue to present information in single, large blocks, despite the evidence of the inefficiency of this approach. Part of the rationale for "micro-learning"—providing very short, stand-alone lessons—is to take advantage of the spacing effect.

 Practical Application

- Use the AGES mnemonic as a quality check on instructional design.
- Ensure that participants are given the time and encouragement they need to generate connections that are meaningful to them personally.
- Pay attention to the stress level. A moderate stress (such as knowing there will be an assessment) aids learning; fear or intimidation is counter-productive.
- Space out the learning and revisit topics more than once to aid retention.

Additional Success Factors

Three other factors that are especially important in the practice of delivering for application (D3) are often underdeveloped in corporate training programs:

1. Providing know-how
2. Ensuring adequate practice and feedback
3. Engaging the heart as well as the mind

Provide Know-How

For learning to improve performance, employees have to answer "yes" to the "Can I?" question. That requires that they take away more than just information and theory; they have to *know how* to use the information and how to *apply* their new skills to their work. Delivering for application means providing know-how.

Corporate learning programs are often long on facts and concepts, but short on "this is how you actually perform the task." That may be in part because they rely on subject-matter experts for input. Experts often have a difficult time explaining how they think through problems or actually perform tasks because it has become so second nature to them. On the other hand, they can wax eloquently and at length on the facts and theories of their favorite fields.

The late Joe Harless, long-time contributor to the International Society for Performance Improvement, admitted "Early in my career, I set about determining what to teach based on the question, 'What do you want people to know?' The problem with asking subject-matter experts (SMEs) that question is that they'd tell me everything they knew" (Harless, 1989). And what they knew usually included things like the widget theory, the history of widgets, the greatest widget makers of the 18th century, widget policy, and so on and so on. "Once I realized my folly, I ... began to insist that SMEs answer the question, 'What do you want them to *do* on the job?'"

> Never ask a subject-matter expert "What do you want people to *know?*"

Keeping the focus of learning initiatives on *performance*, rather than *knowledge*, is a buffer against "they really oughta know about...." It also informs the appropriate choice of instructional method. For example, you would not give your child a PowerPoint lecture on how to swim and then throw him into the deep end of the pool. Providing know-how requires instructional approaches that give participants opportunities to practice the kind of thinking and actions they need to use on the job. If the objective is to improve the ability to deal with an irate customer, then participants need opportunities to practice irate-customer-handling skills during the program and receive feedback on their performance. It is not sufficient for the instructor to just talk about it.

Yet, in today's time-pressed business climate, interactive exercises and practice are often the first things jettisoned because they "take too much time." Marc Lalande, president of Learning Andrago, feels strongly that

> For learning to produce improvement, participants have to know how.

such reasoning is false economy. Doing something that's quick but doesn't work does not save time. When he was head of training for a pharmaceutical company and was asked to shorten a program, he would tell the sponsors: "You can eliminate anything you want from the agenda except the time for practice and role play. If you remove that, we might as well cancel the program."

Ensure Adequate Practice and Feedback

After reviewing some 200 research papers on training and development, Salas and colleagues (2012) concluded: "We know from the body of research that learning occurs through the practice and feedback components." As an example, assertiveness training failed to produce any behavioral effect when it incorporated only information and demonstration. However, when the training included a series of role-play exercises in which participants received feedback on their performance, they subsequently demonstrated significantly more situation-appropriate assertiveness behaviors (Smith-Jentsch, Salas, & Baker, 1996).

Hattie (2008), after synthesizing the results of 800 meta-analyses, came to the conclusion that "the single most powerful influence enhancing achievement is feedback" (p. 12). Relevant practice activities are required to provide the opportunities for constructive feedback.

> Feedback is the single most powerful influence on achievement.

The need to devote more precious class time to practice and less to content delivery is the driving force behind the "flipped classroom" concept. In a flipped classroom approach, "the typical lecture and homework elements of a course are reversed" (Educase, 2012). That is, instead of using class time to lecture and having students do assignments outside of class as homework, the content is delivered outside of class via e-learning, recorded lectures, and so forth. Class time is devoted to having students work through problems and cases with help from the instructor and each other.

Empirical research on the value of the approach so far is limited, but promising, with most studies showing significant gains in student achievement (Hamdan, McKnight, & Arfstrom, 2013). Success depends on careful preparation on both the part of the instructor and the students. If learners are used to spending their class time sitting passively listening to lectures, they may not do the preparation necessary to gain full benefit from the flipped classroom exercises. This is of particular concern for applying the concept in a business setting in which the completion of "pre-work" has traditionally been poor.

Some have argued that the "flipped classroom" is really nothing new and is how teaching should always have been conducted. Others have noted that it is really just an extension of blended learning, albeit with even greater emphasis on application in class. Polemics aside, the flipped-classroom movement underscores the growing recognition that effective learning requires more doing and less passive listening.

For skills development, practice should include hands-on practice in environments as close as possible to the actual work. Ann Schwartz, vice president of global learning and development at United Parcel Service, noted: "We thought those younger

> Everybody learns best when they have hands-on experience.

generations wanted to learn everything on the computer. What we actually found out is that they prefer to learn hands-on" (quoted in Margolis, 2010). So UPS has a training facility with real truck bodies so their drivers can learn by doing and experiencing. They found that it is not just younger workers who benefit from hands-on practice, "everybody learns best if they can have a hands-on experience and then demonstrate it and go back and apply it" (p. 27). The investment in hands-on practice has paid off handsomely for UPS in measurably better performance on the job.

The main point to be made here is the growing recognition that people learn best by doing. In the context of corporate-sponsored learning, that means reducing the amount of content and increasing the amount of time people spend practicing in situations as close to the actual work environment as possible, with meaningful feedback on their performance.

 Practical Application

- Measure the actual time devoted to active practice and application versus absorbing content.
- Commit two-thirds or more of learning time to practice with feedback.

Engage the Heart

The discussion of delivering for application (D3) up to now has been chiefly concerned with ensuring a positive response to the "Can I?" question. However, as we discussed in the Introduction (page 13), participants must also answer "yes" to the "Will I?" question if the learning is to have impact. Improving performance requires changing behaviors and, as anyone who has had a teenage child knows, simply talking at people has little impact on behavior. "If you want people to change … drop verbal persuasion and come up with innovative ways to create personal experiences" (Patterson, Grenny, Maxfield, McMillan, & Switzler, 2008, p. 53). In other words, you have to engage learners' hearts as well as their minds.

Beverly Kaye, founder of Career Systems International and a thought leader in the area of employee development and retention, put it this way:

To ensure that people get the maximum value from learning and development, we need to engage their hearts as well as their heads. We design and deliver every program so that when participants walk out the door they feel empowered and prepared to take action with a "can-do" attitude. We intentionally work to get participants' adrenalin going. We engage their hearts so they have a passion to apply what they learn. They leave with an understanding that no one can take charge of their development and job satisfaction but themselves. So learning about taking charge of your own development is more than a cognitive exercise.

Kaye, 2005

Praise Mok, principal consultant for ROHEI in Singapore, echoed that sentiment: "To produce a lasting change, we had to create an experiential learning environment that would engage participants' emotions as well as their intellect" (Mok, 2014).

Practical Application

- Make sure learning is more than an intellectual exercise; include experiences that engage learners' emotions as well as their reason.

 ## Motivate Learning

For most people, mastery of a concept or skill is its own reward. Beginning as infants, human beings exhibit a strong, intrinsic motivation to learn (Pasupathi, 2013). The urge to learn persists: adults continue to do so throughout their lives; there seems to be no upper age limit for learning. Adults, however, tend to approach learning tasks with a very pragmatic point of view (see Exhibit D3.1). "Adults need to know *why* they need to learn something before undertaking to learn it" (Knowles, Holton, & Swanson, 2011, p. 63).

Victor Vroom of the Yale School of Management developed the Expectancy Model as a way to explain what motivates employees (Vroom, 1994). Vroom proposed that effort is proportional to motivation (Figure D3.10) and that motivation in the workplace was the result of three factors:

- *Expectancy*—the expectation that the new approach will improve performance
- *Instrumentality*—the expectation that improved performance will be rewarded
- *Valence*—the relative value of the reward for the individual

Therefore, effectively delivering for application must include a clear answer to the WIIFM (What's in it for me?) question. It must "make the sale" (create expectancy) that learning and using the new approach will lead to superior performance.

FIGURE D3.10.   VROOM'S EXPECTANCY MODEL OF MOTIVATION

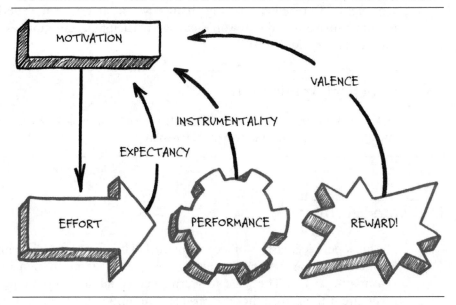

Exhibit D3.1
Relevant Principles of Adult Education

Many aspects of "delivering for application" reflect the principles of adult learning as summarized by Knowles, Holton, and Swanson in their classic *The Adult Learner* (2011). See also Caffarella and Daffron (2013), *Planning Programs for Adult Learners*. Principles that are especially relevant to corporate-sponsored learning include:

- Adults are *practical* and place high value on *relevance.*
  - They willingly engage in learning when it is personally meaningful to them.
  - They may not be interested in knowledge for its own sake, especially in a work setting.
  - They want a reason for learning something: "What's in it for me?"
  - The relevance of theories, concepts, examples, and exercises needs to be immediately apparent; concrete examples of application help.
- Adults are *goal-oriented.*
  - They prefer a problem-centric rather than content-centric approach.
  - They want to know how the class will help them attain their personal goals.
- Adults learn from *experience.*
  - Include opportunities (simulations, role play, problem solving) in which they can apply their new knowledge and practice skills in a safe environment.
  - Provide feedback that reinforces the correct actions and provides insight into missteps.

- Adult learners need to be shown *respect*.
  - Adults bring with them a rich tapestry of experiences and knowledge that should be honored and drawn out.
  - Treat learners as equals and encourage them to share their wisdom and opinions in class.
  - Never ridicule or "talk down to" participants.
- Adults are *autonomous* and *self-directed*.
  - They prefer to be actively involved in the learning process, rather than passive recipients of knowledge.
  - Instructors are most effective when they act as facilitators—guiding participants to their own knowledge and conclusions—rather than supplying them with facts.

The problem with many corporate learning events is that they dive into the *what* and *how* of the subject without adequately explaining the *why*—the benefits of learning and using the new approach. To motivate employees to *want* to learn, we need to give them a credible and personally meaningful reason to actively engage (see Case in Point D3.2). Likewise, if we want managers to encourage their direct reports to participate in learning initiatives and to support them afterward, then we must be able to clearly and succinctly explain the benefits that will accrue to the managers and their departments.

Case in Point D3.2
Start with Why

Two of the participants in a workshop we were teaching at Keurig Green Mountain had the challenging assignment of teaching the safety programs. Participation was lackluster, despite the obvious importance of the topic.

We suggested that the problem might be one of marketing and messaging, rather than the design or content of the course itself. Only half in jest, we proposed re-branding the program; instead of calling it "Safe work practices," we suggested rebranding it as "Going home to your loved ones as healthy as when you came to work."

The course directors took the concept and ran with it. They started making short videos of production workers talking about their families. One showed a picture of his wife and children around the Christmas tree, another talked about her dog as her family, another about his mom who depended on him for support. In every case, they were able to say from the heart: "This is why I want to work safe, so I can come home to the ones I love as healthy as when I left."

The videos were posted on the learning portal. The response was overwhelming. Instead of struggling to fill the safety classes, the programs were oversubscribed. Instead of having groups who were only attending out of compliance, facilitators had participants committed to improving safety for themselves and those around them.

The difference was they started with "Why?" They gave people a reason to attend that appealed to their hearts as well as their heads.

The need to understand "Why?" doesn't stop at the course level. Learners want to know the rationale for each topic and exercise, especially for those that are more challenging or more work (Figure D3.11). Margolis and Bell (1986) observed that the linkage between exercises and benefits

FIGURE D3.11.   LEARNERS WANT TO KNOW WHY THEY ARE BEING ASKED TO LEARN SPECIFIC TOPICS OR SKILLS

"Please, Ms. Sweeney, may I ask where you're going with all this?"

is often not clear to participants. That's a problem. When learners do not see the relevance (What's in it for me?) of a training exercise, they are less likely to take it seriously, participate actively, and learn from it.

A significant contributor to the disconnect, Margolis and Bell argue, is the way in which exercises are typically introduced, whether in the classroom or online. The tendency is to use an "administrative approach," starting with the *how* without first explaining *why*. A typical example sounds like this: "In the next ten minutes, I am going to break you into small groups...." or "In each of the following scenarios, pick the best next step."

The problem with introducing exercises in this way is that participants begin thinking immediately about whether they will have enough time and whether they like or hate this kind of activity, rather than about its

> Always introduce exercises by explaining the benefit for the learner.

purpose and potential payoff for them; the thread to the purpose is lost and so are the participants.

Margolis and Bell recommend that every exercise be introduced by first explaining the rationale and its relationship to job performance. "This sequence follows the logic of learning and the logic of motivation.... The introduction/rationale is a statement that answers a fundamental question for the learner: 'Why should I enter into this task or experience?' ... The rationale [should be] always stated from the learner's perspective, not the trainer's or the organization's perspective" (p. 63).

 ## Practical Application

- Always start with why—whether introducing a learning opportunity as a whole or a specific topic or exercise.
- Explain the rationale and the benefit before describing the process.

Map the Linkage

Four conditions must be met to optimize the effectiveness of guided learning:

1. The business outcomes and expected benefits have been clearly defined.

2. The performance required (skills and behaviors) has been determined.
3. The content has been winnowed down to only what is essential to do the job.
4. The instructional methods match the performance required.

Satisfying the first of these pre-conditions depends on a well-executed D1. Performance analysis satisfies the second. The third requires critical thinking about how much background knowledge is really essential to perform satisfactorily (which may require politely curtailing subject-matter experts' enthusiasm—see page 131). Satisfying the fourth criterion requires selecting the most effective instructional methods to achieve the required performance.

Extending the logic map (Figure D1.8, page 68) to create a value chain has proven to be a useful tool in ensuring that the four conditions are met and that there is coherence among them. A value chain for learning builds on three related concepts:

- Porter's value chain analysis (Porter, 1998)
- Brinkerhoff's impact map (Brinkerhoff & Apking, 2001)
- Logic modeling (Frechtling, 2007)

The value chain can be thought of as a "zoomed in" view of a logic map that illustrates the relationships between the detailed learning activities and the desired outcomes (Figure D3.12). While logic maps are usually drawn in time sequence from left to right—that is, with activities generating outputs that lead to outcomes—for planning learning experiences, we find it better to work "backward," from desired outcomes to planned activities.

In the value chain for learning, the expected outcomes are the business goals for the initiative—the first quadrant of the Planning Wheel (Figure D3.13). The expected outputs are the acquisition of new skills and knowledge. The activities include the specific learning experiences and support mechanisms designed to help people master the requisite skills and apply them consistently. As with Porter's Value Chain, competitive advantage is maximized when all the links in the chain are strong and each adds value.

A value chain for learning serves four purposes:

1. It makes the logical links between the planned learning activities and the desired outcomes explicit;

FIGURE D3.12. A VALUE CHAIN IS A "ZOOMED-IN" AND MORE DETAILED VIEW OF THE LEARNING TRANSFER ACTIVITIES OF THE LOGIC MODEL IN PARTICULAR

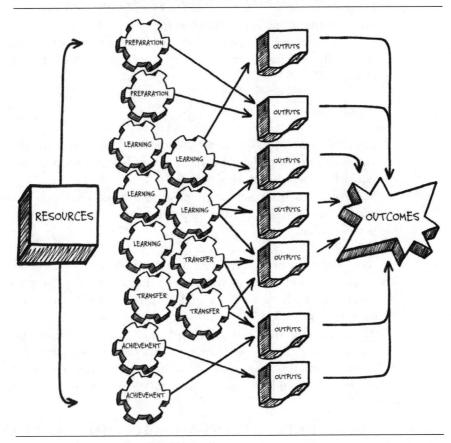

FIGURE D3.13. THE VALUE CHAIN FOR LEARNING ILLUSTRATES THE LINKAGE BETWEEN LEARNING AND BUSINESS GOALS

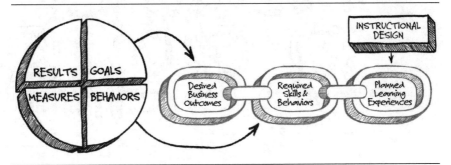

2. It helps facilitators and participants see the relevance of the learning all the way down to the level of the individual topic and exercise;

3. It serves as a guard against "scope creep"—the addition of "nice to know" content that is not really essential to performance; and

4. It helps the design team think creatively and critically about "Is this really the best instructional approach to achieve this particular outcome?"

To build a value chain:

1. List the key business outcomes the initiative is designed to achieve.
2. For each outcome, list the critical actions employees must be able to perform to achieve the desired result.
3. For each essential action, decide what combination of learning experiences will ensure that employees achieve the requisite level of performance.

The outcome of the exercise will be a fairly large tree structure in which every learning element is connected to a required skill or behavior and each of these is tied to one of the business outcomes (Figure D3.14).

In developing the third level (planned learning experiences), be sure to consider the *complete* learning experience (preparation, instruction, on-the-job learning, social learning, performance support, sense of achievement, and so forth) that will be required for participants

FIGURE D3.14. A COMPLETED VALUE CHAIN HAS A TREE STRUCTURE

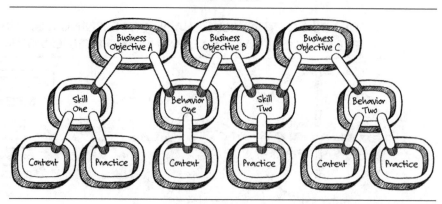

to achieve proficiency and be self-sufficient. The key questions to ask include:

- Is this really the best way to teach these skills?
- Have we truly considered the complete path to proficiency?
- Is this topic/content really essential to performance?
- Do we have the right balance of practice to content?
- Have we provided enough time for reflection, generation, encoding, and consolidation?
- Have we built in adequate scaffolding and advance organizers?
- Is the sequence logical?
- Are the linkages clear and defensible?
- Have we taken advantage of the spacing effect?

We find it helpful to work on the value chain as a group. The process benefits from a variety of perspectives and experience, sharing ideas, and constructively challenging designs. It is also helpful to use "sticky notes" so that elements can be easily moved around, added, deleted, replaced, and so forth. Emerson introduced the innovation of color coding the learning elements to distinguish between those that involved active engagement versus passive listening, which provides an immediate visual cue to this critical balance.

Creating a value chain helps ensure that everyone involved—participants, their managers and coaches, and facilitators—understand the purpose and rationale for each element of the program. It is also a good guard against the extraneous material that tends to creep in; if a topic or exercise has no link to a performance requirement, then it should be eliminated.

In theory, the whole value chain could be incorporated into the logic model for the initiative, but this level of detail would make the model unwieldy and compromise its value as a communication tool. We recommend developing a detailed value chain to guide the learning design and then incorporating just the high-level summaries of the key components into the logic model, as shown in Figure D3.15.

 Practical Application

- Draw a value chain when designing new learning initiatives to ensure that each element contributes value and is logically linked to a business outcome.
- Re-evaluate existing programs by trying to draw them as a value chain to ensure that every element is necessary and optimally designed.

FIGURE D3.15.   AN EXAMPLE OF A LOGIC MODEL WITH SOME KEY LEARNING ELEMENTS ADDED

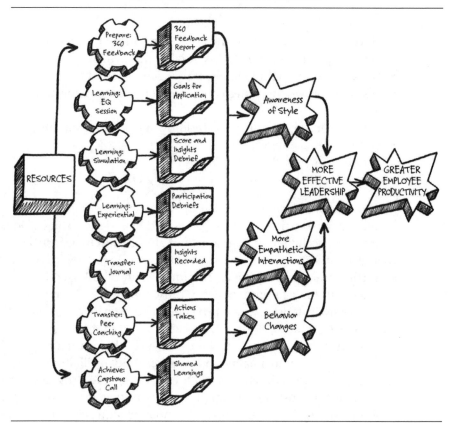

 ## Check the Process

The discipline of delivering for application (D3) is designed to ensure, that following a guided learning experience, participants are able to answer "yes" to the "Can I?" question. Making the business linkage explicit helps motivate employees to learn and then to apply new skills and knowledge ("Will I?").

But how do you know whether the process is working?

We recommend building in-process checks along the way, analogous to the in-process checks used in manufacturing to ensure that critical sub-processes are working as expected. Given the importance of relevance to adult learners (see page 136), it is particularly important to assess whether participants *perceive* the learning as relevant and useful.

At the end of instruction (Phase II Learning), ask participants to rate the degree to which they are motivated to use what they have learned, think they are able to apply it, and see its relevance (Exhibit D3.2). As we will discuss in more detail in D6: Document

> If employees don't perceive the learning as relevant, they won't even *try* to use it.

Results (page 234), most immediate post-course reaction data is of limited value. Positive reactions—no matter how glowing—simply do not predict whether learning will be transferred to work or that performance will improve. On the other hand, *low* scores on relevance and utility questions like those in Exhibit D3.2 can provide an early warning that something is amiss.

Exhibit D3.2
Suggested Questions for Gauging Participants' Perceptions of a Program's Utility

Rate the extent to which you agree or disagree with the following statements by circling the responses that best describe how you feel:

1. The learning was directly relevant to my job.

   Strongly disagree   Disagree   Neutral   Agree   Strongly agree

2. I feel well-prepared to use what I learned.

   Strongly disagree   Disagree   Neutral   Agree   Strongly agree

3. Using what I learned will improve my performance.

   Strongly disagree   Disagree   Neutral   Agree   Strongly agree

4. I feel motivated to put the learning to work.

   Strongly disagree   Disagree   Neutral   Agree   Strongly agree

---

Why? Because if employees do not *perceive* what they learned is useful or relevant, then they are very unlikely to make the effort to apply it ("I won't"). The initiative will be a failure in terms of improving performance. We italicized the word *perceive* to indicate that it is the perception—not the reality—that matters. People act in accordance with their *perception* of the situation, which may or may not be correct.

Obviously, an organization would not invest in a learning initiative that it did not think was going to be relevant and useful. But if, for whatever reason, participants do not perceive that relevance, the initiative is scrap. When the utility ratings for a program are low, steps must be taken to identify and address the source of the process failure. There could be any number of reasons: it might have been the wrong audience, or the right audience at the wrong time, or the design failed to make the relevance clear, and so on. The point is: it needs attention. Be sure to fix the problem, not the blame.

Measures of perceived utility are much more useful than typical reaction data, which are often mainly a question of enjoyment. It really does not matter whether participants "enjoyed" the program; what matters is whether they are convinced that what they learned is useful, that they are motivated to use it in their work, and that they feel they know how to do so.

 Practical Application

- If you do not already ask questions about perceived relevance and utility in post-learning evaluations, add them.
- Review the results regularly, investigate the cause of low ratings, and take action to address the root causes.

 **Summary**

In this chapter, we have emphasized the importance of designing and delivering learning so that it supports application of new knowledge and skills to the individual's and organization's work.

We briefly reviewed the neuroscience of learning and highlighted a number of key bottlenecks and points at which the learning process can go off track. In particular, we emphasized the primacy of attention: how it is limited, easily distracted, and quickly exhausted. We talked about the limitations of working memory and how too much content leads to cognitive overload and diminished learning. We discussed the importance of the way that new knowledge is encoded and the need to give learners time and encouragement to generate their own connections.

We stressed the importance of perceived relevance and utility for adult learners and why program designers and instructors need to help participants see the connections to their work and the WIIFM ("What's in it for me?"). We argued that every element of the learning experience should be selected and constructed in a way that supports the ultimate objective: improved performance. Each topic and exercise should map to a chain of value that links learning to requisite actions and, ultimately, outcomes. The links should be explicit and shared with participants and their managers. Instructional methods should reflect the manner in which the learning will be used.

Use the checklist in Exhibit D3.3 to assess your own practice of D3.

Exhibit D3.3
Checklist for D3

Use the following checklist to help you improve the transferability of learning. Aim to include as many of the factors that favor learning transfer and application as possible.

❑ *Motivate.* Program materials and instruction answer the What's in it for me? (WIIFM) question for participants.

❑ *Relate.* The links between the learning experiences and business needs/job responsibilities are clear. They are reiterated for each major exercise/topic.

❑ *Connect.* Participants are provided with adequate time and encouragement to connect new learning to their past experience.

❑ *Calibrate.* The amount of new information and skills is not so great as to cause cognitive overload.

❑ *Demonstrate.* Relevant examples of application are used throughout to help participants visualize its use.

❑ *Share.* Adult learning principles are honored by encouraging sharing of best practices and learners' experiences.

❑ *Practice.* The design includes sufficient time for meaningful practice with feedback.

❑ *Support.* "Job aids" are provided and used during instruction (see D5).

❑ *Monitor.* Participants' perceptions of the program's relevance and utility are solicited, tracked, and acted upon.

---

* * *

Recommendations

For Learning Leaders

- Create a detailed value chain that maps the links between each learning activity and the desired business outcomes.
- Add the major activities to the logic map for the initiative.
- Poll learners at the end of the learning intervention to assess their perception of their ability to perform ("Can I?").
  - Identify and fix cause of low scores.
- Include questions on the end-of-course evaluations regarding the participants' perceptions of the relevance and usefulness of what they learned ("Will I?").
  - If these are suboptimal, do a root-cause analysis and take corrective action.
- Measure the actual percent of time participants spend sitting passively versus actively practicing skills and solving problems.
  - Aim for two-thirds or more active learning.

For Line Leaders

- Review the key learning initiatives that affect your area of responsibility.
  - Are they structured in a way that makes sense to you, or does it seem like learning to swim with PowerPoint and no pool?
  - If you do not understand the rationale for the approach, ask for clarification and to see the logic map.
- Request reports on how learners rated the relevance and utility of what they learned (not just whether they liked it!).
  - If the learning organization does not collect this information, request that they do.
  - If the scores are poor, ask for a plan of action to address the issue.
- Ask the managers who report to you about whether they feel their direct reports are adequately prepared when they return from training.
  - If not, share their perceptions with the learning team and work together to rectify the issues.

DRIVE LEARNING TRANSFER

"Learning may be a means of achieving the performance results, but it is not the end."

—HAROLD STOLOVITCH

FOR CORPORATE LEARNING INITIATIVES to create value, employees have to transfer what they learned to their work roles in ways that improve individual and organizational performance. Learning itself—no matter how insightful, stimulating, and motivational—is scrap unless it is put to work. Unless employees answer both "Yes, I can" and "Yes, I will apply what I learned to my work," the time, effort, and resources invested in learning go to waste.

That is why the Fourth Discipline practiced by the most effective learning organizations is to **Drive Learning Transfer**. We chose the word *drive* intentionally to draw parallels to the way athletes drive to the finish line and companies drive to achieve objectives. Drive implies investing energy to propel something forward, as opposed to the laissez-faire approach to learning transfer that has been typical in the past (Figure I.8, page 23).

Learning interventions are created to engender more effective and efficient on-the-job behaviors to produce better business performance (Figure D4.1). Knowledge alone, however, rarely alters behavior (Grenny, Patterson, Maxfield, McMillan, & Switzler, 2013). "To change behavior and get the results you want, you need structure, support, and accountability" (Blanchard, Meyer, & Ruhe, 2007). Organizations that are most effective at turning learning into results are those that invest in the "structure, support, and accountability" needed to assure learning transfer and application on the job. They recognize that how employees answer the

FIGURE D4.1.   LEARNING IS EXPECTED TO CONTRIBUTE TO BETTER RESULTS

"Can I?" and "Will I?" questions is as much a function of their work environment (the "transfer climate") as it is of the learning itself. So they measure transfer rates, monitor progress, and strive to continuously improve transfer with the same care and rigor that they apply to other critical business processes.

Topics in this chapter include:

- Learning transfer defined
- Why great learning is not enough
- Learning transfer deserves more attention
- Who owns transfer
- What impacts transfer
- The transfer climate and how to improve it
- A checklist for D4
- Recommendations for learning and business leaders

 Learning Transfer Defined

Various authors define transfer in various ways. Learning transfer is often confused with knowledge transfer, as in the transfer of knowledge from an instructor to a student or from a more experienced worker to an apprentice. That is not what we mean here at all. Moving knowledge from one medium or person to another does not create business value; it is the transfer of learning and its *application to business tasks* that creates value.

In the educational literature, learning transfer refers to the ways in which "previous learning can facilitate the acquisition of current instruction" and how "skills and knowledge acquired in school can be used in solving and dealing with real-world problems and events" (Royer, 1979). The latter is the principal challenge for corporate training. Corporate trainees must accomplish what is known as *far transfer,* that is, "where information learned in school transfers to a real-world (out of school) problem" (Royer, 1979).

We believe that the appropriate definition of learning transfer in a corporate setting is "the process of putting learning to work in a way that improves performance" (Wick, Pollock, & Jefferson, 2010, p. 9). From this perspective, learning transfer is considered successful only if the learning is applied ("put to work") *and* if it is done in a fashion that produces an enduring uptick in performance—the raison d'être for the training in the first place.

Learning transfer is sometimes defined as "the percentage of training that was transferred to the job" (Mattox, 2010), but that doesn't seem like the appropriate measure. First, it would be extremely difficult to assess with any precision. Second, given the

> Learning transfer is the process of putting learning to work in a way that improves performance.

amount of material covered in even a relatively short class or e-learning program, it is unlikely that even the most effective students will actively utilize more than a small fraction of the total content covered.

In our view, a better and more straightforward measure of transfer effectiveness is the *percent of employees* who achieve an acceptable level of improvement following training (who meet the conditions of satisfaction). Thus, if four out of five employees achieved the on-the-job performance objectives defined in D1 following a learning intervention, then the effective transfer rate is 80 percent. When defined this way, most programs today appear to have transfer rates in the 10 to 50 percent range.

 ## Practical Application

- Define and measure learning transfer as the percent of employees who achieve performance improvement objectives.

Great Learning Is Not Enough

The results of a learning intervention are the product of the amount learned (Can I?) times the amount transferred (Will I?). The relationship is expressed by the formula:

$$Learning \times Transfer = Results$$

Two conclusions are immediately apparent: First, great learning is still essential. People cannot transfer what they haven't learned; that's why the Third Discipline—Deliver for Application—is so important. Second, it is clear that great learning alone is not sufficient: even when the learning is a "10 out of 10," if the amount transferred is zero, then the on-the-job impact is zero (Figure D4.2).

That truism notwithstanding, most corporate learning providers concentrate all their efforts on the learning event, and largely ignore transfer. They hope that if they create a sufficiently motivating and compelling training event, it will impart sufficient momentum to carry the participants through the hard work of turning learning into results. It's like trying to use a cannon to shoot an object into space, as Jules Verne did in his 1865 science fiction masterpiece, *From the Earth to the Moon*.

We know now, of course, that it is simply impossible to generate sufficient momentum in one big bang to accelerate an object to the velocity it needs to break free of gravity. Sooner or later, air resistance and gravity take over, the projectile loses momentum, and it falls back to earth (Figure D4.3).

FIGURE D4.2.   NO MATTER HOW GREAT THE LEARNING IS, IF TRANSFER IS LOW, THE RESULTS WILL BE POOR

FIGURE D4.3. THE PROJECTILES OF THE MOST POWERFUL CANNONS EVER BUILT ALWAYS FALL BACK TO EARTH

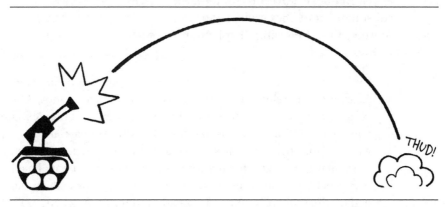

The problem for training and development is similar. No matter how much impetus the program imparts initially, resistance to change and the weight of old habits cause participants to lose momentum and fall back into pre-training routine (Figure D4.4)— "relapse" in the Stages of Change Model (Figure D2.9, page 95). Like launching a rocket, a continuing input of energy over time is needed to help participants achieve "escape velocity."

FIGURE D4.4. UNLESS ENERGY IS EXERTED TO DRIVE TRANSFER, CHANGE EFFORTS LOSE MOMENTUM

Why is so much energy required to prevent recidivism? John Izzo, consultant and best-selling author, shared the following explanation with us:

> Great learning alone is not sufficient to produce lasting change.

Learning is like sledding down a hill on a fresh field of snow. On your first try, you could take any number of paths. But the next time you go down, the sled tends to follow the path you have already established. The more times you slide down, the deeper you wear a particular groove and the harder it is to go a different way. That is very much how the brain works: the more you perform a particular action, the more it becomes automatic and harder to change. That's essential for survival; we'd be paralyzed if we had to think through every single action all the time. But it does mean that long-established habits—whether how to do a certain task or how to react to another person—take real effort to change.

Neuroscientists have confirmed Izzo's hypothesis. Frequent use produces physical changes in the brain; like a muscle, the brain becomes larger and stronger with exercise (Deutschman, 2005). Once habits are hardwired into the structure of the brain itself, it takes time and sustained effort to change them. That is why it is easier to learn a completely new skill than to try to change an old habit (Duhigg, 2012). A great learning experience by itself can introduce participants to a better way of doing things, but is rarely sufficient to produce lasting change.

The formula, Learning × Transfer = Results, also explains a common misunderstanding between learning professionals and business professionals. Learning professionals tend to define success by how much people learned; the business defines success by whether performance improved, which requires both learning *and* transfer. Business people

> It is easier to learn a new skill than to change an old habit.

don't differentiate between learning and learning transfer. If they invest in training, but see no change in performance, then their assessment is "the training failed," even though the real problem may well have been in the transfer step. From a business perspective, claiming that the learning was a success, even though performance did not change, is like saying "the operation was a success even though the patient died."

Do not underestimate the difficulty of changing behavior. A life-threatening illness ought to be the ultimate incentive for change. And yet, among people who have had coronary-bypass surgery, only 10 percent succeeded in changing their lifestyles in ways that would reduce the risk of a subsequent and potentially fatal attack (Deutschman, 2005). Even when the choice is "change or die," many people are unable to change.

There is tremendous organizational and personal inertia that resists change (Figure D4.5). And, in accordance with Newton's First Law of Motion, "an object at rest remains at rest unless acted upon by an external force," things will continue as they are until there is a sufficient motive force to overcome the inertia. The challenge is to supply sufficient motivation and propulsion to change behaviors and drive performance to a higher level.

 ## Practical Application

- Remember the formula "Learning X Transfer = Results" to be sure you plan and manage both for optimum results.
- Do not underestimate the difficulty of changing performance; learning alone won't suffice.

FIGURE D4.5. PEOPLE AND ORGANIZATIONS HAVE GREAT INERTIA THAT RESISTS CHANGE

Importance of Practice

There is an old saw about the tourist asking the policeman in New York City, "How do I get to Carnegie Hall?" to which the officer replies: "Practice, practice, practice." It turns out that the policeman is right. Recent research suggests that in every field of human endeavor—from chess, to business, to sports, to the performing arts—what really separates world-class performers from everybody else is the amount that they practice. When we think of top performers—Jack Welch in business, Venus and Serena Williams in tennis, Mozart in music—we tend to ascribe their success to "natural talent." The implication is that we could never be as good at something as they are because we just weren't born with "the right stuff."

Not so, according to a review of the evidence by Geoff Colvin in *Talent Is Overrated* (2008). It turns out that "natural talent" is a lot less important than people think. When researchers from around the world gathered to discuss "The Acquisition of Expert Performance," they concluded that what differentiated experts from the less accomplished in a wide array of fields was the amount of practice (Ericsson, Krampe, & Tesch-Romer, 1993). The more practice, the better. In other words, Mozart became Mozart by working furiously hard and, starting when he was three years old, by practicing more than anyone else. Gladwell (2008) argues that the Beatles became great only after playing up to eight hours a night, seven nights a week in Hamburg (p. 49). By the time of their first hit in 1964, they had already performed live some twelve hundred times.

But not just any practice will do. Anders Ericsson's research has shown that a special type of practice is needed—something he has termed "deliberate practice" (Ericsson, Krampe, & Tesch-Romer, 1993). Deliberate practice is repetition that focuses on technique as much as on results. It requires intense concentration, feedback on performance, and taking time for reflection: What contributed to a positive outcome and should be continued? What detracted from the desired outcome and should be reduced or avoided?

> What separates world-class performers from everybody else is the amount they practice.

Colvin (2006), writing in *Fortune,* summarized the findings this way: "The evidence, scientific as well as anecdotal, seems overwhelmingly in favor of deliberate practice as the source of great performance."

Daniel Coyle's study of "talent hotspots," *The Talent Code* (2009), came to a similar conclusion. Deliberate practice (which he terms "deep practice") is prerequisite to great performance in any field. "Deep practice is built on a paradox: struggling in certain targeted ways—operating at the edge of your ability, where you make mistakes—makes you smarter." It's similar to the way in which struggling against "desirable difficulties" in learning makes it richer, deeper, and more versatile (Brown, Roediger, & McDaniel, 2014).

So, while instruction, e-learning, and self-study can catalyze learning, there are no shortcuts to becoming highly proficient in any endeavor—it takes practice and lots of it. One to three months or more of daily practice is required before a new behavior becomes automatic (Lally, van Jaarsveld, Potts, & Wardle, 2010). It should come as no surprise, then, that so much of whether training "works"—that is, whether it improves performance—depends on whether or not people actively practice their new skills in the immediate post-training period. Thus, facilitating deliberate on-the-job practice is one of the most effective ways to drive transfer and increase the return on the training investment.

Transfer Deserves Greater Attention

From a process improvement point of view, improving learning transfer offers much greater opportunity for improving overall results than trying to improve learning per se. That's because enormous energy, creativity, and technology have been deployed to improve instruction, while learning transfer has been largely left to chance in most organizations (Figure I.8, page 23).

The consequence is that most learning providers are quite proficient at creating and delivering quality learning experiences, while techniques to improve transfer are much less well understood and

> In most organizations, learning transfer has been left to chance.

deployed. Although further improvements to learning strategies and technologies are certainly possible, they are likely to have much less impact on performance outcomes than improving transfer.

Weber (2014b), for example, reported a three times greater uptick in sales among consultants who participated in a series of structured and action-oriented coaching conversations after training, compared to those who attended the same program without the transfer support. Pfizer found that adding specific support for learning transfer increased the ROI for a leadership development program by more than 40 percent, compared to the same program without support (Trainor, 2004). Research studies summarized by Leimbach and Emde (2011) demonstrated that paying attention to learner readiness, design for transfer, and organizational alignment can increase transfer by as much as 70 percent.

By Way of Analogy

Imagine that you are the general manager of an automobile plant that is experiencing a high level of customer dissatisfaction because more than half of the cars you manufacture won't start once they reach the dealers, even though they worked fine when they were driven off the assembly line. You are receiving a lot of bad publicity and dealers are threatening to drop your products. Clearly, something is going seriously wrong between the production and the delivery. You have two choices:

- You can try to double plant production to generate enough cars that will actually run.

    −or−

- You can investigate what is going wrong in transit and take action to fix it, even though technically it is out of your hands.

Stated that way, choosing to increase production rather than address the real problem looks pretty stupid. And yet it is analogous to retraining employees or trying to improve instruction when the most common reasons that training fails to improve performance occur in the post-training period.

 Practical Application

- Re-direct some of the creativity, energy, expertise, and resources of the learning group to improving learning transfer.

What's the Problem?

As we discussed in the introduction, it is hardly a new observation that a significant percentage of corporate training ends up as "learning scrap." It's been discussed for fifty years. Why, then, is it still an issue? The learning transfer problem persists for three main reasons:

1. No one accepts responsibility for it.
2. Failure to take preemptive action.
3. Inadequate systems to manage the process.

No One Accepts Responsibility

Managers perceive training as the sole responsibility of the training department; they do not appreciate the essential role they have in ensuring its application. As Jim Trinka, chief learning officer, U.S. Department of Veterans Affairs, explained: "The typical manager believes that training or learning or whatever you want to call it, is important. But they think: 'Okay, that's really important. But obviously I'm too busy to do it myself, so I'm going to outsource that job to the training department. Now it's their job, not necessarily my job.'"

Business managers do not see learning transfer as their responsibility; neither do most learning professionals. As Rosemary Caffarella wrote in *Planning Programs for Adult Learners* (Caffarella, 2009), many training professionals "had never really thought about transfer of learning as being part of their planning responsibilities" (p. 22). Instead, they think: "My job is to be sure that program participants get the right content in the most effective way. I have no control over what happens afterward; that's the manager's job." The result is that learning transfer falls into a no-man's land in which no one has clear responsibility or accountability for its success.

In reality, the learning organization and line management co-own the success or failure of training. Unless they work together to actively drive learning transfer, it won't happen and the initiative will fail. The business and learning leaders will end up like people in a submerged boat,

> The learning organization and line management co-own the success or failure of training.

FIGURE D4.6.   WHEN TRAINING FAILS TO PRODUCE RESULTS, IT
DOESN'T MATTER WHOSE FAULT IT WAS; EVERYONE LOSES

arguing about whose end leaked the most (Figure D4.6). When the
learning-to-performance process fails, it doesn't matter where the breakdown occurred, everyone goes down with the ship.

That having been said, we believe that learning professionals need to
take the lead in solving the learning transfer problem because they have
the most to gain. Here is why: When performance fails to improve after a
learning initiative, the likely outcome is that the program will be reduced
or eliminated.

Everyone benefits when learning providers partner with line managers
to ensure that learning is transferred and applied. Because transfer is the
weakest link in the learning value chain for most organizations, it represents the single greatest opportunity for improvement. Indeed, we are
convinced that a truly meaningful gain in learning's contribution is impossible until the learning transfer challenge is met by a coordinated effort
between business managers and learning professionals.

Failure to Take Preemptive Action

That people tend to revert to old habits is old news, as is the observation that transfer is a key point of failure in the learning-to-performance process. Nevertheless, we—learning professionals and business leaders alike—have not done enough to prevent the breakdown before it happens.

We should borrow a concept from organizational safety and conduct a "pre-accident investigation" (Conklin, 2012). Instead of waiting for transfer to fail, and then conducting a post-mortem to try to figure out why, we should conduct a "pre-mortem."

Having a pre-mortem meeting, a meeting where you ask smart, experienced people what could go wrong before it does go wrong, provides a new set of data about a failure that has yet to happen. Knowing this new information allowed the researchers to avoid a whole series of problems. It was cheap, quick, simple, easy, and most importantly, 100 percent effective for the potential failures identified.

Conklin, 2012, p. xii.

The application of this concept to learning is to ask the sponsors and designers: "What could cause this initiative to fail to produce and sustain meaningful change in the way people do their work?" Then, armed with these insights, develop strategies and tactics to prevent the train wreck before it happens. Since the learning transfer step is the most likely point of failure, it is the area most in need of preemptive action.

Inadequate Systems to Manage

The third reason that the learning transfer problem persists has been a lack of systems and processes that could be applied effectively to large-scale corporate learning programs. That barrier is being reduced with the advent of systems designed specifically to support learning transfer and retention, such as ResultsEngine®, Qstream®, Cameo®, TransferLogix™, and others.

Such systems automate the process of reminding participants and causing them to reflect on their learning and its application.

Support systems are only part of the solution, however, and will fail unless they are deployed into a favorable environment (transfer climate). Numerous factors contribute to the favorability of the transfer climate. As such, it should come as no surprise that there is no single "magic bullet" that will solve the learning transfer problem. Because there are numerous contributing factors (Figure D4.7), it must be attacked on multiple fronts.

FIGURE D4.7.   CAUSE-AND-EFFECT DIAGRAM FOR MANY OF THE FACTORS THAT CAN CONTRIBUTE TO FAILURE OF LEARNING TRANSFER

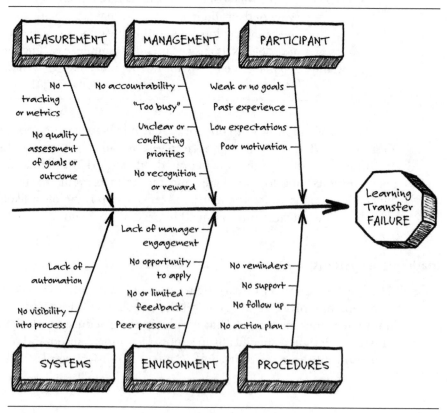

Practical Application

- Take responsibility for the transfer phase and plan for it as carefully as you plan the instruction.
- Educate business leaders about their shared responsibility for ensuring value from learning.
- Start by asking "What else needs to be in place?" during the initial discussion with business leaders (see page 65).

The Transfer Climate

The impact of the transfer climate was aptly illustrated in a study conducted by American Express (American Express, 2007). The original objective was to compare three different kinds of instruction: instructor-led, blended, and e-learning only. Three months later, managers who had attended the program were categorized as either "high-improvement leaders" or "low-improvement leaders" based on the productivity of their teams on measures such as improved cycle time, conversion rates, revenue impact, forecast accuracy, sales revenue, and customer satisfaction.

The differences were dramatic. The direct reports of "high improvement" leaders increased productivity by an average of 42 percent, while the productivity of the direct reports of "low improvement" leaders increased only 16 percent. The surprising finding was that the instructional medium was not the key differentiator; both high- and low-impact leaders were found in groups taught by any of the three approaches.

The key difference was the transfer climate. Researchers had included questions about the transfer climate in the post-program survey. They discovered that participants who achieved high improvement were:

> The transfer climate can make or break the success of any learning initiative.

- Four times more likely to have had a meeting with their manager to discuss how to apply the training;
- Almost twice as likely to perceive that their manager supported and endorsed the training; and

- More than twice as likely to expect to be recognized or rewarded for the training-related behavior change.

The study authors concluded:

- "The true impact of a training program will best be predicted by the work environment participants return to after the event."
- "A highly supportive transfer climate needs to be present in order for a solid and lasting transfer of the information back to the job."
- "These climate factors can quite literally make or break a company's training investments."
- "The importance of understanding and creating a high transfer climate should swiftly move to the forefront of any training initiative or strategy" (p.11).

Numerous other studies have come to a similar conclusion: the transfer climate to which an employee returns after training has a profound impact (see reviews by Burke & Hutchins, 2007; Saks & Belcourt, 2006; and Salas, Tannenbaum, Kraiger, & Smith-Jentsch, 2012). Writing in *Harvard Business Review*, Professor Herminia Ibarra of INSEAD noted that "the personal learning catalyzed by a top-notch program can be tremendous.... The problem, my research suggests, is what happens when a manager comes back to the day-to-day routine of the office" (Ibarra, 2004). If the culture doesn't support what the training teaches, it will have minimal or no impact (see Case in Point D4.1).

Case in Point D4.1
Culture Trumps Training

When Roxi Bahar Hewerston was director of administration at Cornell University, she learned a valuable lesson: culture trumps everything else. "What leaders say, and what training courses teach, doesn't matter much unless the cultural norms and the values that are espoused are truly embedded in the way people behave and interact every day. All the fine speeches, the lovely value statements, and the well-intended training will have little effect or could even have a negative effect if what is said and what is done do not match" Roxi told us.

"Leaders have responsibility for the culture, period," she said. "The leader's number one role is to create, model, and support a workplace environment in which the intended culture will thrive and the desired results can occur.

"The key is sustainability. There are three legs to the cultural stool: (1) creating and requiring the staff to participate in outstanding training, (2) creating clear expectations, clear metrics, and holding people accountable, and (3) implementing best practices, policies, and processes to support the new culture. When those three legs work well together, the culture shifts and the desired workplace results follow."

Changing an organization's culture is far more difficult than changing its structure or strategy. It takes time, but the payoff is huge. Roxi spent more than a decade building a collaborative culture with her colleagues, four unions, and a professional and support staff of nearly 2,000 people. Every staff member—union or non-union, salaried or hourly—was required to take part in leadership and staff development programs. Everyone was expected to be a role model.

It took a lot of persistence to shift the culture from a top-down, "my way or the high-way" culture into a collaborative, values-based one. But it paid off. Trust was high; fear was low. Creativity and innovation were rampant. Productivity skyrocketed. Customer service was outstanding, and the bottom line became much healthier.

A peer review of a similar university proved beyond a doubt that Cornell's leadership development investment was a slam-dunk in terms of return on investment. Because of its very unhealthy culture, the peer institution experienced dozens of employee complaints and regularly lost large and costly lawsuits. In the same ten-year period, Cornell faced only one lawsuit—which it won—and even in a heavily unionized environment had very little arbitration, all of which was decided in its favor.

The bottom line is summarized in the title of Roxi's book: *Lead Like It Matters ... Because It Does* (Hewertson, 2014).

But what constitutes the transfer climate and what determines whether it is a catalyst or an impediment to learning transfer? Holton, Bates, and Ruona (2000) developed a "Generalized Learning Transfer Systems Inventory" to help gauge the state of the transfer climate and whether it was likely to foster transfer of learning or impede it. The inventory has also proven useful as a diagnostic tool to guide learning transfer climate improvement efforts (Holton, 2003).

As its name implies, the Learning Transfer Systems Inventory recognizes the *systems* nature of the learning transfer environment, that is, transfer is affected by complex interactions among a large number of variables. Three main clusters of factors influence the probability of transfer: ability to use; motivation to use; and the catalysts and impediments in the work environment. All three influence transfer effectiveness directly as well as through their interactions (Figure D4.8).

FIGURE D4.8.   THREE MAIN CLUSTERS OF FACTORS THAT AFFECT LEARNING TRANSFER

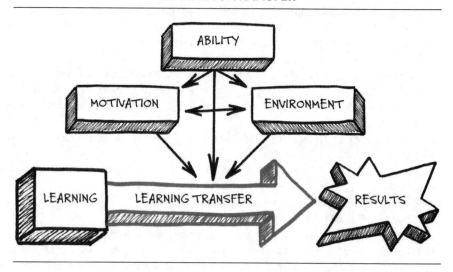

Ability

Four factors contribute to the *ability* of employees to apply new learning on the job (Figure D4.8):

- They must have the personal capacity (time, energy, and mental space) to make changes.
- Their work situation must afford them opportunities to apply the new skills and knowledge.
- They were taught *how*; the learning design and delivery focused on application rather than facts and theories.
- They must perceive that the content was relevant, valid, and applicable.

Motivation

Three factors largely determine whether employees are *motivated* to transfer and apply their learning:

- The extent to which employees believe that applying the new skills will improve their performance;
- The extent to which they believe that improved performance will be recognized and rewarded; and

- How much they value the potential rewards and recognition (see Vroom's Expectancy Model, pages 135 and 136).

Two additional factors also contribute to motivation. The first is the employee's personal confidence in his or her ability to adapt and improve ("self-efficacy"). Employees who have a strong internal belief in their ability to change and grow—what Dweck (2007) calls a growth mindset—are more motivated and more likely to try to apply new learning than those who feel they are victims of their environment, genome, and the like. Motivation is also influenced by the extent to which the learners were prepared to participate in the training to begin with.

Environment

The third cluster of factors that determines the transfer climate comprises the catalysts or impediments to transfer in the employee's immediate work *environment*. Environmental factors include the influence of the manager, the peer group, and the performance management and reward systems (Gilley & Hoekstra, 2003; Salas, Tannenbaum, Kraiger, & Smith-Jentsch, 2012). In the transfer systems inventory, managers' influence is further divided into:

- The amount of feedback and coaching they provide;
- The extent to which they are perceived to support and reinforce the use of learning; and
- Conversely, the extent to which they are perceived to be negative about the training and discourage its use.

Peer groups exert their influence through their general openness or resistance to change and the extent to which they support or discourage efforts to apply new skills and knowledge. Reward systems influence transfer through two mechanisms: (1) whether participants experience positive personal outcomes from applying the new skills and (2) that *not* using what was taught results in negative personal consequences (see Figure D4.9).

It is important to note that throughout the foregoing description, as in the discussion of relevance and utility in D3, we have used words like "belief" and "perception," because people act on their *perceptions* and *beliefs*, not necessarily on objective reality. If an employee *perceives* that his or her manager is negative about a new approach, then that employee is less likely to try to use it, even if, in reality, the manager is supportive but has been too distracted by other duties to make that clear.

FIGURE D4.9.   ALL SIXTEEN FACTORS OF THE LEARNING TRANSFER SYSTEM INVENTORY

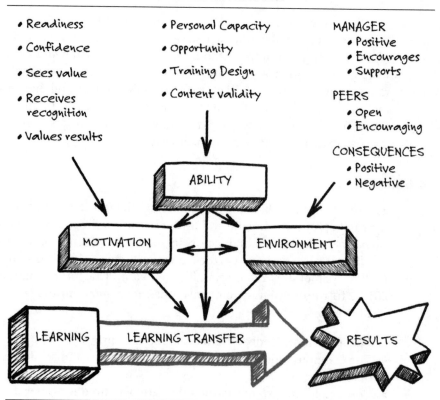

An important starting point, then, for increasing learning transfer is to make an assessment of the current transfer climate *as perceived by the employees*. The full Learning Transfer Systems Inventory contains ninety-nine items. Holton and Baldwin published a shorter "audit"

> People act on their perceptions and beliefs, not necessarily on objective reality.

version in *Improving Learning Transfer in Organizations* (Holton & Baldwin, 2003, pp. 73–76). We developed the self-assessment in Exhibit D4.1 based on the audit version to help organizations assess their transfer climate and identify their best opportunities for improvement.

Exhibit D4.1
Self-Assessment of Transfer Climate

For each of the items on the Transfer Climate Scorecard below, rate your post-program environment from *very unfavorable/unhealthy* (−3) to *very favorable/very healthy* (+3)

Factor	Description	Rating
Perceived Utility	Participants returning to work believe that they will be able to utilize their new skills and knowledge and that they will perform more effectively when they do.	
Opportunity	Individuals have opportunities to apply their new skills and knowledge on the job soon after training. They are provided with the resources they need to do so (time, tasks, assistance, materials, people, and so on).	
Expectations/ Rewards	Participants believe that they are expected to use their new skills and knowledge and that they will receive positive recognition for doing so. They also expect negative consequences for failing to use what they learned. The organization tracks progress and rewards improved performance.	
Feedback/ Coaching	When they attempt to use what they have learned, participants receive constructive input, assistance, and coaching from managers, colleagues, and others.	
Managerial Engagement	Managers actively support the use of new skills and knowledge. They discuss performance expectations both before and after training, help identify opportunities to apply new skills, set relevant goals, provide feedback, and help work through difficulties.	
Work Group Impact	Participants' co-workers encourage them to apply new skills and knowledge. They display patience with the difficulties of mastering new approaches. They are willing to accept new approaches and do not force conformity to existing norms.	
Personal Experience	Individuals experience positive outcomes from using what they have learned, for example: improved productivity; increased job satisfaction; additional respect; recognition, advancement, or reward. In addition, there are no negative consequences from attempting to use what they learned.	

In general, the more of the factors that are positive, and the more strongly positive they are, the greater the probability of transfer (Holton, 2003, p. 68). Not all of the factors have equal impact. Some, such as manager involvement, exert greater influence than others. The relative impact also varies among companies and the kind of learning.

Practical Application

- Understanding and positively influencing the work environment are critical to ensuring learning transfer and results.
- Use the Transfer Climate Scorecard or Transfer Systems Inventory to assess the health of the transfer climate in your organization.
- Target low-scoring areas for improvement.

The Special Role of Managers

Managers have a disproportionate impact on learning transfer and the transfer climate (Figure D4.10). They represent the most influential and most underutilized resource available to ensure that learning produces results. A recent review of almost one hundred research papers (Govaerts & Dochy, 2014) found broad support for the influence of managers on training transfer. Lancaster, Di Milia, and Cameron (2013) concluded that "what supervisors did prior to, during, and after course attendance was

FIGURE D4.10.   MANAGERS' PRIORITIES INFLUENCE WHETHER OR NOT TRAINING IS APPLIED

Copyright © Grantland Enterprises; *www.grantland.net*. Used by permission.

critical to training transfer." American Express (2007) went further: "an immediate leader can make or break the success of any training." Brinker-hoff put it succinctly: "When managers support training and learners, it works. When they do not, it does not" (2006, p. xii).

Nevertheless, persuading managers to actively and meaningfully sup-port learning transfer remains a challenge for most organizations. In their 1992 book, *Transfer of Training*, Broad and Newstrom concluded: "*Managers do not consistently and powerfully support the transfer of training in the work envi-ronment*. We believe that this represents a fundamental problem, and also a substantial opportunity for improvement" (1992, p. 53, emphasis in the original). That statement appears to be as true today as it was when it was published more than twenty years ago.

Why do managers exert so much influence on learning effectiveness? Because regardless of what employees may think of their immediate super-visor, they recognize that he or she holds the keys to salary increases, pro-

> Managers have a disproportionately great impact on learning transfer.

motions, and advancement. So they pay attention to the signals (inten-tional or unintentional) emanating from their manager. If she shows inter-est in something, they give it a higher priority than something she ignores or dismisses as unimportant. That applies to learning as well as to applying new skills on the job.

Managers are an integral and crucial part of the total system for help-ing employees convert learning into business results. That's why Agilent's CEO Bill Sullivan wanted to start cascading Agilent's new business-focused, applied-learning experience down from the top, starting with the com-pany's one hundred general managers: "Let's make sure the soil is fertile so that when people come out of the experience, they have a manager and a set of colleagues who are getting what they are talking about and we can have better transfer and application" (quoted in Prokopeak, 2009).

Range of Manager Engagement

Don Kirkpatrick (1998) proposed that managers' responses to training fall along a continuum (Figure D4.11). At the most destructive end of the range are the managers who actively *prevent* their subordinates from using what they have learned: "That may be what you were taught *there*, but that is not how we do it *here*." The most egregious example we have ever heard

FIGURE D4.11.   RANGE OF MANAGERS' REACTIONS TO THEIR SUBORDINATES' USE OF NEW SKILLS AND KNOWLEDGE

was told to us by an oil company executive in Canada. His company had sent him to a *year-long* executive education program at Harvard at substantial cost—not only in tuition, but also in his salary, travel, lodging, and so forth. The day he returned to work, his manager called him in to his office and said: "Welcome back. I don't want to hear any of that c**p you learned at Harvard."

That is an extreme example, of course, but in almost every company there are some managers who actively block the application of new learning. Such a complete disconnect between managers and training suggests a failure to define real business needs and garner management support up front.

Managers who *discourage* using new methods or approaches also squander resources and leave employees confused and frustrated: "If I am not supposed to use this stuff, why did you waste my time making me learn it?"

Kirkpatrick placed "neutral" or "indifferent" in the center of his scale as if it had no effect one way or the other. We disagree. Indifferent is negative. If employees attend an educational program and are excited about applying what they learned, but their boss says nothing about it one way or the other, most will interpret that to mean: "Don't waste your time."

> Indifference is negative.

"If you're a manager who really wants to demotivate your employees, destroy their work in front of their eyes. Or, if you want to be a little more subtle about it, just ignore them and their efforts" (Ariely, 2011, p. 76). Roxi Hewerston told us: "Indifference in the workplace is the most egregious form of devaluing people and their work; it's actually worse than criticism, which at least acknowledges the person is worthy of notice." Indifference is negative. When managers fail to show active interest in learning and its application, they kill intrinsic drive and waste opportunity.

On the positive side of the ledger are managers who *encourage* their direct reports to apply what they have learned. Such active encouragement is an important contributor to a positive transfer climate (Figure D4.9) and a key factor in whether or not the organization gets its money's worth from training and development. At a minimum, managers should be expected to encourage the use of new learning; ideally, they should *require* it as "the way we do business here." The latter is exceptionally powerful in effecting organizational change (see Case in Point D4.2).

Case in Point D4.2
Maximizing Value of Marketing Training

When Jorge Valls accepted the leadership of SmithKline Beecham Animal Health, he identified an urgent need to improve the quality of marketing. He contracted with the Impact Planning Group to conduct an intensive marketing workshop. He included all managers, not just the marketing department, to underscore his conviction that marketing is everyone's responsibility; every department contributes positively or negatively to the customer's perception of the firm and brand.

The training was excellent, but what made it *effective* was Valls's announcement at the conclusion of the training of a *non-negotiable requirement*: all future marketing plans were to be prepared in accordance with the principles that had just been taught. He *required* that the training be utilized, and he backed up what he said by his actions. All subsequent reviews were conducted in accordance with the agreed-on principles. He rejected out-of-hand any proposal that did not follow the guidelines; he would not even read it.

The result was that everyone began to use the new methods and tools. The quality of operational plans improved immediately, as did the quality of the discussions among managers, departments, and the leadership team, because everyone shared common concepts and vocabulary. Within months, the improved quality of planning and marketing were evident in both top-line and bottom-line growth, even in the absence of new products.

Had Valls only *encouraged* the use of the new methodology, or left it to individual discretion, some departments would have embraced the new approach while others clung to their old way of doing things. Improvement would have been slower and the results less impressive. By insisting that everyone use what they learned, Valls ensured that the company realized return on its learning investment.

Practical Application

- Recognize that immediate supervisors can "make or break" the success of any learning initiative; make securing their support an integral part of the plan.
- Do not settle for managerial indifference ("at least they are not negative"); it has a chilling impact on "Will I?" and on learning transfer.
- Show managers the evidence of the positive impact of their active engagement and the negative impact of indifference.

Why Managers Don't Coach More

For a long time, we puzzled over the question of why managers do not do more to encourage the application of learning by their direct reports. It is clearly in their best interest to do so. Their jobs become easier and their prospects for advancement improve when their employees become more effective and efficient. Moreover, their employees have already spent time learning. Why not make a small incremental investment to gain a significant return in enhanced performance?

The most common excuse that managers give for failing to follow up on training is that they "do not have the time." No manager in today's frenetic business climate has the time to do everything that he or she could do. So they must choose to make the time for some things and ignore others. So when managers say they "do not have the time" to follow up on training and coach their employees, what they are really saying is that it is not a priority for them.

> Managers have to be convinced that investing their time will be repaid.

Why isn't it a priority? We think there are two root causes:

1. They do not *see sufficient value* (payback) in doing so.
2. They are not *confident* of their abilities in this regard.

See Sufficient Value Faced with the dilemma of too much to do in too little time, the logical manager spends his or her time on those activities with the highest potential payback. Those that have minimal negative consequences are left undone.

If we want managers to actively reinforce learning on the job, then we have to convince them that the time they invest to coach their direct reports in the short run will be repaid by greater effectiveness in the long run. They need to be persuaded that they can increase the dividends that learning pays *to their department.* We should, at a minimum, share with managers the evidence about their impact. When Pfizer disseminated the results of an internal study that showed the value of managerial engagement, post-training coaching increased, because managers could see its value (Kontra, Trainor, & Wick, 2007).

Concomitantly, we need to educate senior managers about the waste that results when front-line managers fail to support on-the-job application of learning. Encourage senior leaders to make support for employee development part of annual reviews and assessments of managerial effectiveness. The best-managed companies hold their managers accountable for developing their direct reports and consider a proven ability to develop people prerequisite to further promotion.

Learning initiatives are more successful when there is active oversight and participation by the managers of participants' managers. In AstraZeneca's Breakthrough Coaching program, for example, the learning organization used an electronic learning transfer support system (ResultsEngine®) to help area sales managers identify which of their regional managers were doing a particularly good (or poor) job of coaching. Positive coaching efforts were recognized during regional discussions, which helped to reinforce the desired behaviors. The senior leadership's active support of manager involvement made it a higher priority and materially contributed to the program's success.

No Confidence Lack of confidence in their ability to coach effectively contributes to managers' belief that they "don't have time." No manager wants to be embarrassed by appearing uninformed or unskilled. Managers who are unsure about how best to coach to training in general, or who are unclear about what was covered in a specific learning program, can circumvent the problem by simply staying too busy to discuss the content or its application with their direct reports.

For managers to feel confident that they can provide meaningful post-course mentoring, they need to:

- Understand what was covered in the program;
- Feel that they have the requisite coaching skills; and
- Have a defined process to follow.

The ideal solution to ensure that managers know what is covered in the learning initiative is to have them attend that program either in advance of their direct reports or, preferably, at the same time. Unfortunately, that is often impractical. At a minimum, send the manager a short synopsis of the business needs the initiative is designed to address, the topics covered, some coaching tips, and the desired outcomes. Be sure communications are succinct and efficient. A brief introductory email with links to more in-depth information and suggestions is more likely to be read than a lengthy course description.

Geoff Rip, CEO of ChangeLever International, a learning transfer consulting firm, feels so strongly about the benefits of managerial support that he holds a special course for managers *in advance* of training their subordinates. The program for managers teaches coaching skills in general, as well as how to maximize the benefits of the upcoming training in particular.

At Centocor Inc., managers are brought together for a refresher session on maximizing the value of 360-degree feedback at the same time their direct reports are receiving the results of their feedback. One-on-one meetings between the attendees and their managers are scheduled immediately afterward while the material is top-of-mind for both parties.

Lisa Bell, manager of the North American Learning Center for Holcim, holds day-long "impact booster" sessions for managers of participants in the Building Leader Performance Program. "Initially, one of our biggest concerns was that managers would never give up their precious time to participate in the 'extra' steps we asked of them. And, now, lo and behold, they themselves have asked for more" (2008, p. 191). She feels strongly that these sessions were a key factor in the program's success.

> Provide easy-to-use forms, step-by-step processes, and examples.

Remember that a manager's impact on outcomes for her or his direct reports may actually be greatest *before* the learning opportunity. Encourage managers and their direct reports to meet prior to the program. Give them a simple and effective process to follow. Bill Amaxopoulos, leadership program manager for the Chubb Group of Insurance Companies, schedules pre-class teleconferences for both participants and their managers and structures them in a way that facilitates a discussion immediately thereafter (Wick, Pollock, & Jefferson, 2010, p. 241).

Also encourage participants and managers to meet immediately *after* a learning program to discuss key takeaways and their plans for application. For programs in which participants develop personal objectives or plans of action, collect them and send a copy to each person's manager or use an online learning transfer support system to do so. Provide managers with short, specific guidelines for post-training actions they can take to maximize the value of the investment (see page 208).

Finally, make sure that managers are aware of what their direct reports did (or did not) accomplish as a result of the training. This can be done in a number of ways, such as including the manager in a final session (in person or virtually) in which each participant reviews his or her goals, accomplishments, and "lessons learned" or by asking the manager to evaluate the change in performance. Cox Media Group, for example, asks the managers of participants to acknowledge observable performance improvements (Schwartz, 2014). Electronic learning transfer support systems can be programmed to automatically send each participant's manager a summary of the participant's accomplishments. Some of the spaced-learning reinforcement systems provide dashboards that allow managers to assess their team's performance (Lennox, 2014), as does Lever–Transfer of Learning (Weber, 2014a,b).

 ## Practical Application

- Work with senior leaders to make support for learning transfer a part of every manager's job—one that is monitored, recognized, and rewarded.
- Provide managers with the information and support they need to coach *before and after* each structured learning opportunity.

Essential Elements

The literature on learning transfer and our work over the past fifteen years has identified six essential elements of a transfer support process:

- A schedule of events
- Reminders
- Accountability

- Feedback and coaching
- Performance support
- Finish line

Schedule of Events The first prerequisite for a more effective approach to driving learning transfer is to have a clear schedule of events post-instruction. Having some definitive activities, such as assignments, reports, teleconferences, or other touch points, scheduled during Phase III (transfer) of learning, helps shift the paradigm away from "the end of class equals the end of learning." As discussed in D2, the schedule of post-course events should be part of the overall program design and should be included as an integral part of the program agenda (Figure D2.8, page 95).

Spacing post-course activities out over several weeks takes advantage of the powerful spacing effect (page 129), resulting in more durable and accessible knowledge and skills (Figure D4.12). Plan activities that will require the participants to recall and revisit what they learned. Something as simple as sending an application tip, a relevant article synopsis, or an example of successful application by a peer can help bring some aspect of the training back to mind.

FIGURE D4.12. WITHOUT REINFORCEMENT, MEMORY DECAYS EXPONENTIALLY

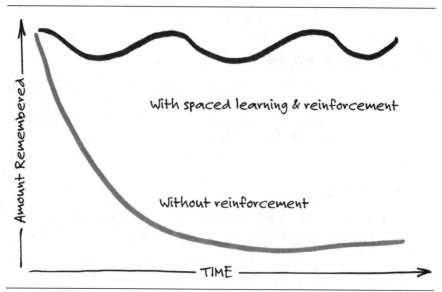

Assignments that require active engagement and thinking by the participant are more effective than simply pushing additional information to them. A series of studies conducted at the Harvard Medical School demonstrated the value of combining spaced learning with gamification. Students who were periodically sent questions to answer retained much more of the relevant information when tested months later (Kerfoot & Baker, 2012). More importantly, use of this approach resulted in sustainable behavior change in work habits (Kerfoot, 2013), the ultimate objective of corporate learning initiatives. Game elements—such as the use of a scoring system and leaderboards—increased motivation to participate. Regardless of whether they answered correctly or incorrectly, learners were provided explanatory feedback, which has been shown to promote learning better than corrective feedback only.

"Teach-backs" are a simple and effective tool to reinforce learning. Some companies require, as a pre-condition for attending a program or conference, that the attendees share a synopsis with their colleagues when they return. The benefits include broader dissemination of learning and—importantly—reinforcement for the person required to prepare and teach. McKinley Solutions combines several of these elements in a process they call "learning loops" to help sustain learning and ensure its transfer (see Case in Point D4.3).

Case in Point D4.3
Keeping Learning in the Loop

McKinley Solutions, a talent solutions provider based in Toronto, was asked to provide leadership development for the executive team of a large government agency. Consistent with McKinley's commitment to assessment-based training, the process started with 360-degree assessments from four perspectives—peer, self, boss, and direct reports. Three half-days were devoted to debriefing the results to ensure the team had time to truly explore and internalize them, and to understand themselves, their teams, and team dynamics.

Training on the content and theory was conducted only after that solid foundation had been established, once the team members knew what they needed to learn and why. To ensure that the learning didn't stop with the workshop—to keep it alive and make sure it was applied—McKinley introduced "learning loops," short follow-up assignments that leverage spaced learning and teach-backs to reinforce key concepts and—more importantly—include accountability for developing and implementing action plans.

Mark Thompson, president and chief engagement officer of McKinley Solutions, explained the process: "One of the things we focus on is the need to help employees connect with 'Why?' An example of a learning loop would be to ask participants to: (1) watch Simon Sinek's TED talk 'Start with Why'; (2) define their personal 'Why?'—Why do they get up in the morning to go to work?; (3) share it with a peer; (4) receive feedback from the peer; and (5) be prepared to share it at the next management meeting with the larger group.

"Another example would be to: (1) review the content of a particular topic in the course materials—for example, the avoidance tendency; (2) write three to five bullets of what it looks like in your department; (3) share the theory and your understanding of it with a direct report; and (4) come back with three things you are going to work on to reduce that tendency in your department.

"The beauty of the learning loop is that is drives learners back to content that they got in the session, makes them review the supporting documents, gets them to teach the theory—which is a powerful form of learning—and requires them to develop and share an action plan so that there is accountability.

"You reinforce the content with an activity that takes less than twenty minutes and have them put it in a format that allows a leadership team to hold each other accountable for implementation. We try to do between five and seven learning loops in a forty-five-day period, because we are working against the forgetting curve. The biggest drop-off, as you know, is in the first thirty to ninety days.

"What we are really jazzed about is that the client found so much value in the learning loop process that they have continued and extended it themselves. The CEO was determined to maintain the momentum that McKinley had started. So each month, he tasks a different member of his executive team to develop a learning loop assignment for the next management meeting, based on the content from the leadership program. The team then has two weeks to work on it, and they discuss it at their monthly management meeting. To set an example, he designed the first one himself.

"It is incredibly rewarding as a consultant to have provided a reinforcement process that the client embraced and ran with, because we know that the real value of leadership development is in the follow-through and application. The learning loop process is a simple, effective, and efficient way to ensure that the investment in learning leads to meaningful change and business value."

Requiring participants to submit periodic progress reports on their efforts to implement what they have learned is another powerful transfer strategy. It is analogous to the progress reports expected for other business initiatives. The learning transfer management system, *ResultsEngine*®, was developed to help automate this process. It also created an element of "co-opetition" by allowing participants to view one another's progress (Wick, Pollock, & Jefferson, 2010, p. 197) similar to leaderboards used in gamification. Requiring progress reports underscores the expectation that people will apply their new knowledge and that they will make progress toward the goals they set (or were assigned) from the program. Indeed, the typical practice of asking people to set goals but then failing to require any sort of progress report makes a mockery of the entire goal-setting and action-planning process.

Reconvening the group also can be a powerful stimulus to revisit and apply the initial learning, especially if the session begins with a report-out from participants of the progress they have made, the obstacles they have

> Reconvening the group can be a powerful stimulus to revisit and apply learning.

encountered, what they learned in working through them, and what they plan to do going forward. When a physical reconvene is not possible, a teleconference or web meeting can be used to good effect, as we do following 6Ds workshops.

Practical Application

- Plan and communicate a schedule of activities to reinforce learning and support its application. Reject any learning plan that does not include them.
- Aim for activities that require active engagement—recall, processing, or reflection.

Reminders A fundamental impediment to learning transfer is the "out-of-sight, out-of-mind" problem. Employees are constantly reminded of their other work obligations, but seldom of the need to apply what they have learned. For the great majority of training initiatives, participants never hear about learning again until they receive a solicitation to sign up for the next course.

The problem relates to what marketers call "share-of-mind." A consultant and colleague, Janet Rechtman, pointed out that "McDonald's doesn't tell you just once that they sell hamburgers." McDonald's is, without a

> McDonald's doesn't tell you just once that they sell hamburgers.

doubt, already one of the best-known and most-recognized brands in the world, and yet they continue to spend hundreds of millions of dollars on advertising annually (Hume, 2014). Why? Because they know that if they were to stop advertising, they would quickly lose share-of-mind to competitors whose message consumers encountered more often. So McDonald's invests enormous amounts of creative energy and resources to stay top-of-mind and maintain its market share.

In their classic book on marketing, *Positioning: The Battle for Your Mind*, Ries and Trout (2001) emphasize that the same message must be repeated many times to get through the clutter of competing ideas. In the welter of competing priorities that employees confront daily, the message about the importance of transfer and application will be lost if communication stops as soon as the course is over. Learning organizations need to take a lesson from McDonald's and keep reminding learners in order to secure a share of their mind and time for learning transfer and to trigger them to take action. In the absence of timely reminders, good intentions are easily forgotten (Figure D4.13).

FIGURE D4.13.   IN THE ABSENCE OF TIMELY REMINDERS, IT IS EASY TO FORGET GOOD INTENTIONS.

"I said I'd do it. There's no need to remind me every 6 months."

Copyright 2002 by Randy Glasbergen. *www.glasbergen.com*. Used with permission.

Some programs ask participants to write a letter about their goals for applying learning, which is then mailed to them a few weeks later. In our experience, this is too little and too late. Reminders and reinforcement activities must begin promptly because the forgetting curve is steepest early on. They then need to be continued long enough to help establish the new behavior as habit.

Post-course reminders can take any number of forms—mail, email, telephone calls, automated calendar items, or any combination thereof. The most important issue is that there *are reminders* so that the objective is not forgotten. As Will Thalhemier points out in the Afterword (page 287), our behavior is driven by environmental triggers much more than most of us realize. As a result, any reminder is of value. For example, Levinson and Greider (1998) developed a simple device they called the MotivAider®, which did nothing more than vibrate on a set schedule. Nevertheless, that simple, periodic reminder proved remarkably effective in helping people follow through on a wide variety of goals. Levinson and Greider defined the two key attributes of an effective reminder system as "(1) it must reliably get attention and (2) it must occur often enough to serve as a useful clue" (1998, p. 173).

Email is an obvious choice given its ubiquity and low cost. Rob Bartlett (2014), for example, described how—as a one-person training department—he was able to use email to

> The most important thing is that there *are* reminders.

create a low-cost, low-effort follow-up system. Surprisingly, despite the email overload we all experience, email reminders still work. In a study of over two thousand employees in five workplaces in Canada, Plotnikoff and colleagues (2005) tested the efficacy of email reminders for helping to change behavior related to exercise and nutrition. Compared to the control group, the employees who received weekly email reminders for twelve weeks showed improvements in both physical activity and healthy eating. A similar study at Kaiser Permanente, funded by the U.S. Centers for Disease Control, found that employees who received weekly email reminders with small, practical suggestions improved their lifestyle habits significantly more than those who did not receive such messages (Pallarito, 2009)—further evidence of the power of periodic reminders by email.

Practical Application

- Schedule a series of reminders after a learning initiative to maintain share of mind.
- Explore a variety of options, including the use of commercial systems developed specifically for this purpose.

Accountability In well-managed companies, systems of accountability are in place to ensure that business objectives are implemented, progress is monitored, and achievement is rewarded. Similar systems are needed to ensure that learning transfer is implemented, monitored, and rewarded.

Reminders alone improve transfer, but they are much more effective when they are backed by clear accountability for action. Participants exert more effort to apply their learning when they know they will be held accountable, rewarded for using their new learning and skills, and reprimanded if they fail to do so (Figure D4.9, page 168). A key factor in how participants answer the "Will I?" question is "Will anybody notice?"

Holding participants accountable for making effective use of company-sponsored learning is simply good business practice; in any well-run business, employees are responsible for making good use of their time and other company resources. Since train-

> Holding participants accountable is simply good business.

ing and development programs represent an investment, they are like taking out a loan. When you borrow money from a bank, you take on an obligation to repay it (with interest). There is a set schedule for repayment, and the bank does not hesitate to remind you if you fall behind. Should you fail to repay the investment, it becomes much more difficult to borrow money in the future.

We believe that when employees are given the opportunity to participate in learning programs, they should be informed that they are, in effect, entering into a contract and that they will be *held accountable* for making payments on the investment by using what they have learned (see Case in Point I.2, page 21). Those who are unwilling to do so (despite it being in their own best interests) should be considered poor candidates for further educational investments. They are probably also poor candidates for advancement, since learning agility—"the ability and willingness to learn from experience, and subsequently apply that learning to perform successfully under new or first-time conditions" (Korn Ferry, 2014)—is a key attribute of successful leaders.

Unfortunately, most learning management systems are not equal to the task. They were designed to record participation in learning events, not whether people actually apply any of it. Online learning transfer support systems have been developed to fulfill the need. Similar to performance management systems, they allow participants to create goals for learning application, record progress against them, and engage their managers and other coaches.

Feedback and Coaching Research on human expertise has stressed the importance of feedback and coaching. It is virtually impossible to improve any skill without some form of feedback. Imagine trying to learn archery wearing a blindfold. If you could not see where the arrows landed, and no one would tell you, you could take ten thousand shots and, in the absence of this essential feedback, never become any better. Feedback is essential to reinforce positive actions and correct ineffective or negative ones. In the absence of feedback, employees are unable to maximize their strengths or modify counterproductive or downright destructive behaviors.

For these reasons, finding ways to enhance feedback and coaching is an important aspect of improving the transfer climate. We will discuss ways to achieve this in greater detail in the chapter on D5: Deploy Performance Support. Suffice it to say at this point that learning organizations can accelerate mastery of new skills and behaviors by taking steps to make sure feedback providers and tools are available and used.

Performance Support Deploying performance support (D5) also contributes to ensuring transfer. Recall that motivation to transfer learning is influenced by the participant's confidence in her or his ability to do so successfully. Delivering instruction in ways that facilitate application (D3) helps build this confidence. Ongoing performance support enhances it.

How to deploy effective performance support is discussed in Chapter D5. The point here is that it is an essential element of the learning transfer process and synergistic with D4.

Finish Line In D2, Design the Complete Experience, we suggested that the fourth and final phase of learning should be an assessment of achievement—a summing up of what has been accomplished as a result of attending the training and applying it—a goal line to drive for. That's because most people, especially those who are attracted to business as a career, have a powerful, intrinsic drive to succeed. We argued that learning organizations cannot succeed unless they know the "conditions of satisfaction" in advance. The same is true for program participants. They need to know where the finish line is and how success is defined.

Having a definitive point at which achievement will be reviewed and recognized contributes to a positive transfer climate. For this reason, many progressive companies are redesign-ing their programs to include a transfer period of several weeks to several months followed by an assessment of achievement.

> People have a powerful, intrinsic drive to succeed.

The learning experience for front-line supervisors at HP, for example, includes participation in "pods" (collaboration groups) that meet five times over a ten-week period to help each other resolve their common leadership challenges. The program concludes with a web conference in which each of the pod groups is asked to share its learning, insights, actions taken, and results achieved for the past ten weeks (Goh, 2014).

At Honeywell, participants in the strategic marketing program are divided into project teams with a clearly defined reporting requirement. Rod Magee, former CLO, explained the process this way: "At the end of the program each team has to define deliverables and an action plan for the next ninety days. Rather than letting them go off and assuming they will do it, we keep them accountable by having scheduled teleconference updates. The teams know when they leave the program that at thirty, sixty, and ninety days they will have to report to management. At ninety days, each team has to report its success against its promised deliverables. On each of the calls, the team is joined and supported by the coach they had during the program."

The common thread in these approaches is that participants know in advance that there is a specific time and forum in which they will be required to account for what they have accomplished. The most effective forums include individuals of importance to the participants to create an appropriate "level of concern" (see page 129) and maximize the motiva-tional factors related to recognition and outcomes. Having clear expecta-tions and a known point in time at which they will be assessed helps drive learning transfer.

Practical Application

- Establish and communicate from the outset that the criteria for completing a learning cycle include learning transfer.

Summary

For at least fifty years, improving learning transfer has been recognized as key to converting more of learning into business outcomes. No matter how superb the instruction, e-learning modules, simulations, or other learning experiences, they are only costly learning scrap unless new knowledge and skills are transferred to and used on the job. In today's competitive environment, no company can afford to produce scrap in any business process—most especially not in learning. The cost of doing nothing to improve learning transfer is high indeed.

The root causes of learning scrap are numerous and originate both within and outside the learning organization. Therefore, the solution requires a thoroughgoing approach and cooperation between the learning organization and line management. Improving learning transfer (reducing learning scrap) begins with defining business goals, continues through instructional design and delivery, and, most importantly, includes systems and processes to support and drive deliberate application in the workplace.

Best-practice learning organizations drive learning transfer by actively managing the follow-through process. They use systems and procedures to ensure that participants put their learning to work by setting expectations, issuing reminders, ensuring accountability, and providing support. Companies that have implemented learning transfer support activities have experienced significantly higher levels of post-course effort, achievement, and return on investment (Leimbach & Maringka, 2014). The advent of effective and efficiently deployable transfer support systems represents a breakthrough in corporate education and a potent opportunity to increase its value.

Use the checklist in Exhibit D4.2 to review your transfer plan.

**Exhibit D4.2
Checklist for D4**

Use the checklist below to formulate a robust plan to ensure learning transfer and application to sustain the value of the learning experience.

	Element	**Criterion**
❑	Goals	Participants set, or are provided with, strong stretch goals that require learning transfer and application to achieve.
❑	Reminders	Learning is kept top of mind through periodic reminders about the program's content, the participant's personal goals and objectives, and the need to continue to practice new knowledge and skills.
❑	Accountability / Managers	Managers are reminded of the program's objectives and informed of their direct reports' personal goals for application.
❑	Accountability / Participants	Learners' objectives and progress are made public—at least to their managers and fellow participants—similar to business goals and progress.
❑	New Finish Line	A mechanism and predetermined reporting schedule are in place to underscore the need for action and reflection. These include a defined end point and method to assess achievement.
❑	Feedback	There is a mechanism in place to ensure that participants receive meaningful feedback on their efforts and progress.
❑	Recognition	Appropriate recognition is provided for those who make great progress and/or complete their objectives.

 # Recommendations

For Learning Leaders

- Answer the following questions for each of the key programs that your group delivers:
  - Is your organization actively engaged in driving learning transfer?

- Do you actively plan for the transfer phase as part of your instructional design?
- Do you know what the participants' learning transfer objectives are?
- Do you actively remind and support participants?
- Are managers actively involved in supporting learning transfer?
- Do you have systems in place to manage follow-through, transfer, and application?
- If you answered "no" to any of these questions, then develop a plan to address the issue, since you are ultimately judged by the business outcomes.
- Poll participants to find out to what extent they received support from their managers.
  - Share the results with senior management and explain how participants' managers can enhance or destroy the value of learning.
- Work with management to ensure that learning transfer occurs. It is a shared responsibility that requires a team effort.
  - Explain to managers, as Eldridge Cleaver put it: "Either you are part of the solution, or you are part of the problem."

For Line Leaders

- Reflect on your own experiences in learning and development programs.
  - Were you expected to follow through and generate a return on the company's investment?
  - Or was the last day of class treated as though it were the finish line?
- Interview employees in your organization who have recently attended programs or who have had direct reports attend programs.
  - Are developmental objectives taken seriously in your unit, or not?
  - Is there a culture of execution or a culture of indifference?
- Interview the managers of participants in recent programs.
  - Were they aware of the program's business objectives?
  - Did they know what their direct reports' personal objectives were?
  - Did they hold their direct reports accountable for using what they learned to create a return on the educational investment?
- If you discover that developmental objectives are afforded "second-class citizenship" and are frequently ignored by both participants and their managers, you are wasting time and money on training.

- Exert leadership to ensure that program participants are held accountable for following through and transferring their learning to the work of the firm in a way that improves their personal performance and the business's results.
- Work with the learning organization to address the problem.
- Hold your managers accountable for coaching to maximize learning's effectiveness.

DEPLOY PERFORMANCE SUPPORT

"Where improving worker performance is the primary goal—then the umbrella under which we work as learning professionals expands dramatically."

—DAVID KELLY

ONCE WE HAVE MADE THE MIND SHIFT from delivering training to delivering improved performance, then the importance of the Fifth Discipline—**Deploy Performance Support**—becomes apparent. Performance support extends, amplifies, ensures application, and in some cases, replaces other forms of learning. It helps participants answer "Yes" to the "Can I?" question.

In the preface to his book, *The First 90 Days: Critical Success Strategies for New Leaders at All Levels* (2003), Michael Watkins explains what piqued his interest in the topic. "I was struck by how few companies invested in helping their precious leadership assets succeed during transitions—arguably the most critical junctures in their careers. Why did companies leave their people to sink or swim? What would it be worth to companies if managers entering new positions could take charge faster?" (p. xii).

The same questions pertain to corporate learning initiatives. Why do most organizations leave people to sink or swim after training instead of investing to help them bridge the gap between the classroom and the workplace? What would it be worth to companies if employees consistently applied new learning to their work? Having already invested time, effort, and dollars in learning, why don't more companies make the modest incremental investment to ensure application?

Gottfredson and Mosher (2014) suggest the answer: "We seem to be unable to shake the formal-learning-event paradigm from our collective mindset...we fail to adequately design, build, and put in place the support infrastructure learners need to attain and maintain successful on-the-job performance." Research confirms our personal experience: support—especially during the first few crucial weeks of the transfer phase—significantly enhances the return on investments in learning by improving performance while simultaneously reducing the time to complete tasks (Nguyen & Klein, 2008).

New technologies and near-universal access to Internet resources have vastly expanded opportunities to provide performance support that reinforces, amplifies, and extends learning back to the workplace. Topics in this chapter include:

- The power of performance support
- What is performance support?
- How does it work?
- When is it most valuable?
- What makes for great support?
- Why support should be an integral part of the complete learning solution
- Checklist for D5
- Recommendations for learning and business leaders

Power of Performance Support

Surgical teams are arguably some of the most highly trained professionals on earth. It takes years of advanced education, training, and practice to become a surgeon, anesthesiologist, surgical nurse, or other member of the operating team. They are also highly experienced, performing hundreds of procedures a year. And yet, they make mistakes. When mistakes are made, people get hurt or die. Although such errors are relatively rare, the annual cost is millions of dollars; the emotional cost to patients and their families is incalculable. So there are powerful reasons to improve performance, but additional training isn't the answer.

The World Health Organization approached Atul Gawande, a surgeon at The Brigham and Women's Hospital, and asked him to lead a team to help reduce complications and deaths following surgery. He was skeptical, but nevertheless agreed to try and then rigorously test the results. The full story is told in his very readable account, *The Checklist Manifesto* (2008).

We mention it here as an example of the power of performance support. The solution Gawande and his team devised—a simple, nineteen-item, three-part (before, during, and after surgery) checklist reduced major complications by more than one-third and deaths by almost half. As Gawande wrote: "Checklists seem able to defend anyone, even the experienced, against failure in many more tasks than we realized" (p. 48).

If performance support can have that profound an impact on improving the performance of highly trained and experienced teams, think how much greater an impact it can have on relatively inexperienced workers or those new to a role. The message is clear: performance support should be an integral part of any learning and performance improvement initiative.

 Practical Application

- Recognize that the right support can enhance the performance of even highly trained and experienced individuals.
- Make it an integral part of any learning initiative.

Analogy to Customer and Product Support

Nowadays, companies invest substantial resources to provide customer support—from user's guides to online help, toll-free product support numbers, and live online chat with specialists—and they solicit customer feedback on the quality of that support. Why? Because they know that customer satisfaction depends on the "whole product" experience—which includes the quality of support as well as the features of the product itself (see Figure D5.1). It doesn't matter how good the product is; if customers can't figure out how to use it, or can't get a clear and timely answer if they encounter a problem, they will be dissatisfied.

Product support, therefore, is important because a satisfied customer is likely to purchase additional products or services and to recommend the brand to family and friends. A dissatisfied customer, on the other hand, will not only refuse to buy more products or services, but will voice his or her dissatisfaction to anyone who will listen.

The parallels to corporate learning are obvious. Participants' satisfaction with training and development depends on their *whole learning experience,* which includes whether they are able to use the learning in a way that helps them improve their performance and achieve their personal goals. Timely and useful support improves people's ability to use what they learned and therefore their satisfaction with the learning experience.

FIGURE D5.1.   CUSTOMER SATISFACTION DEPENDS ON THE WHOLE PRODUCT EXPERIENCE, WHICH INCLUDES AVAILABILITY AND QUALITY OF SUPPORT

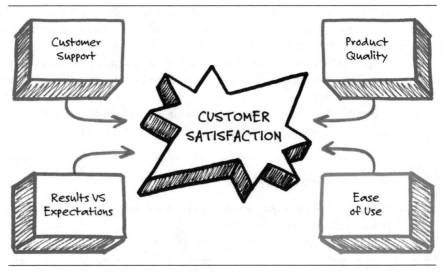

As with consumer products, a satisfied learner—and his or her manager—will be inclined to pursue more learning opportunities and recommend the program to others. Dissatisfied learners—in particular, dissatisfied managers who failed to see any improvement—are likely to voice their dissatisfaction widely and loudly. Such negative publicity undermines support for learning and makes it even more difficult for the organization to fulfill its mission in the future.

Bottom line: it is in everyone's best interest—the learners,' the company's, and the learning organization's—to provide effective support for performance, especially during the critical learning transfer phase. Improving performance support presents significant untapped potential for enhancing training effectiveness.

 Practical Application

- Monitor your learners' satisfaction with their ability to apply what they learned and the support they received.
- Provide support to your internal customers that is at least as good as the support your company provides to its external customers.

What Is Performance Support?

Performance support is anything that helps an employee do the right thing at the right time, every time. It can be as simple as a paper-based checklist, or as sophisticated as an electronic embedded performance-management system. Performance support includes everything from automated error-checking (think spell-checker), to a tool designed so it can be used in only the correct fashion. It includes materials, systems, and people— from co-workers to managers to experts.

The optimal kind of performance support depends on the nature of the task, where the workers will be, and what they will be doing at the time. The simplest and most cost-effective solution should be sought; avoid the temptation to over-engineer. If posting a simple paper list suffices, then do it.

Why It Works

Why can the right kind of performance support have such a profound impact? Because "there is a huge gap between mastering the content delivered in a learning event and being able to apply that content in an effective and productive way on the job" (Gottfredson & Mosher, 2011, p. 4). Performance support reduces reliance on notoriously fallible human memory. Human beings are much better at remembering the "gist" of things than at remembering the details. So while people are quite good at recalling in general how to perform a task, most have difficulty remembering all the steps in the correct order unless they perform them all the time (Figure D5.2). Providing a checklist, step-by-step procedure, or similar memory aid improves performance by ensuring that the task is done completely and in the correct sequence.

Second, even if the task is performed frequently—and therefore committed to memory—its performance can be compromised by environmental factors, sometimes with tragic consequences. Although veteran pilot Jacob Van Zanten had made hundreds of takeoffs and landings—so he knew the routines by heart—one day he was distracted by his need to take off quickly, before his allowable flight time expired. He neglected just one step: getting takeoff clearance before starting down the runway in Tenerife. His 747 slammed into another plane, killing 584 people (Brafman & Brafman, 2009). The higher the cost of an error, the more valuable performance support becomes.

FIGURE D5.2. PEOPLE HAVE TROUBLE REMEMBERING THE
DETAILS OF A PROCEDURE

Third, as we discussed in D3, working memory has a finite capacity. When people are trying to master a new skill, providing performance support reduces cognitive load, allowing them to concentrate all their short-term (working) memory on the actual performance.

> Designers should encourage learners to use working memory to process information, not to store it. For example, as learners first practice a new procedure, give them access to clear, written, summary steps for reference so that all working memory can be directed toward executing the procedure. The use of job aids, in the form of a written procedure table … can be especially powerful for this purpose.
>
> Clark, 1986, p. 19

For similar reasons, performance support is valuable for tasks that involve a large number of factors, steps, or considerations. Relieving employees from having to recall all the relevant factors and hold them in memory while simultaneously trying to process them allows them to focus their mental capacity on the task itself.

The advent of easily accessible video through tablet computers, smartphones, and similar devices has made it possible to move beyond providing guidance on *what* to do, and also illustrate *how* to do it. Applications include everything from how to locate or change a defective part to how to conduct an effective and appropriate job interview. Younger workers, especially, are conditioned to look first to such devices for guidance. Michelle Baker (2014) was reminded of this when she had a flat tire. While she stepped out to look at the tire, her thirteen-year-old was already on his phone, looking up the online user manual and tutorials on what to do next.

Last, it is hard to execute tasks in a new or unfamiliar way when some other way has already become habit. Performance usually dips temporarily when people try a new approach, whether that's changing their golf swing or the way they make presentations—even if the new approach ultimately produces superior results. Performance support helps sustain learning transfer by increasing the probability that employees will have success when first trying to apply new skills and knowledge. Those who experience early success are more likely to persist in their efforts to change (answer "Yes" to "Will I?") than those who fail in their first few attempts (Figure D5.3). "A huge body of research has shown that small wins have enormous power, an influence disproportionate to the accomplishments of the victories themselves" (Duhigg, 2012, p. 112).

FIGURE D5.3.   PERFORMANCE SUPPORT INCREASES THE PROBABILITY OF "EARLY WINS" AND OF SUSTAINED EFFORT TO APPLY NEW SKILLS AND KNOWLEDGE

When Is Performance Support Most Valuable?

The situations in which performance support is particularly valuable have been enumerated by Boyd (2005), Gottfredson and Mosher (2011), Rossett and Schafer (2006), and Willmore (2006). They include when:

- Trying to master a new procedure or skill;
- Performing an infrequently used procedure;
- Performing a complex task that includes many steps or factors;
- Procedures change frequently;
- The task is straightforward and there is no time or need for training; and/or
- An error would be very serious or costly.

In each instance, job aids and other forms of performance support remind (or instruct) participants how to apply learning, execute procedures, or approach a problem. They are an important adjunct to other forms of learning; what seemed clear during a classroom exercise is often a great deal less clear in the hurly-burly of day-to-day work. "If they could do it in class, that doesn't at all mean they're going to be able to do it out there on the job" (Rossett, personal communication, 2009).

Performance support can also reduce the need for training or, in some cases, eliminate it altogether. For example, no company wastes time training its employees how to fix a jammed photocopier because the instructions are built into the software and hardware—an example of embedded performance support. Similarly, given their high rates of employee turnover, fast-food restaurants minimize the need for training by simplifying tasks and prominently posting the essential steps at each workstation.

According to the U.S. Coast Guard:

- Job aids can be developed three to four times faster than developing training materials for the same tasks.
- Training how to use job aids is three to four times faster than training how to do the jobs and expecting that knowledge to be stored in human memory.
- Moreover, job aids can be revised much more quickly and less expensively than training materials (U.S. Coast Guard, 2009, p. 2).

Performance support is, itself, a powerful form of learning because it provides relevant information at the "teachable moment"—the exact time it is needed and wanted. For the first time in history, information is available almost everywhere all the time. You can find out exactly what you want to know, precisely when you want to know it—the ideal learning situation.

For example, we were having dinner with friends on the back porch at the farm. Somehow the conversation turned to the question of what cut of beef a "hanger steak" is. Dr. Orsini pulled out his smartphone and in a couple of minutes we had the answer: it is from the center part of the diaphragm. That bit of information has stuck with us because it answered a question we had at the time, in contrast to most training, which provides people answers to questions they haven't asked and didn't particularly want to know.

Range of Performance Support

The kinds of support that will improve performance, and the ways in which they can be delivered, are nearly infinite, limited only by our creativity and willingness to see support as an integral part of learning. The most common kinds of support include providing:

- Reminders
- Step-by-step guidance
- Flow charts and decision trees
- Templates
- Checklists
- Videos or illustrations
- Coaching
- Information access
- Expert help

That list is by no means exhaustive. Table D5.1 provides examples of many of the most common forms of performance support. Note that they include not only materials—such as paper- or computer-based forms, templates, etc.—but also human-based support, like coaching, mentoring, and expert help.

Practical Application

- There are many possible ways to deploy performance support. Think broadly and creatively.
- Look to the consumer products industry for effective and innovative ways to provide support.

TABLE D5.1. COMMON KINDS OF PERFORMANCE SUPPORT AND THEIR USES

Type	Especially Good for
Reminder	Making sure that time-dependent actions are not missed, such as attending a meeting, paying a bill, and so forth. Reminders are the simplest form of performance support and one of the most widely used. Nearly everyone nowadays depends on the reminders in their electronic calendars. The importance of reminders in learning transfer is discussed in D4 (page 181).
Critical Information	Providing key information at the time and place it is needed, such as embossing the maximum inflation pressure on the sidewall of a tire.
Embedded Design	Ensuring that machines, parts, or software are used correctly. The item or program is designed so that it can only be used in the proper manner, such as different fittings for different storage tanks to prevent putting in the wrong liquid or gas. Embedded design is especially important where errors could be costly or dangerous.
Checklist	Ensuring all the key items in a procedure are included or completed. Especially important when many actions are required or when omission could lead to serious adverse consequences.
Step-by-Step Procedure	Making sure that a procedure is followed in the correct sequence. Especially valuable for complicated or rarely performed procedures, when someone is learning a new procedure, and when the right steps in the wrong sequence will cause failure or harm. A cooking recipe is a common example.
Worksheet	Completing procedures that require calculations at various steps. A tax form is a good (albeit unpopular) example.
Flow Chart/If-Then Diagram	Guiding decision making or troubleshooting for well-defined problems that can be broken down into a series of discrete choices. Helps ensure logical, stepwise approach to problems.
Photo or Diagram	Showing where to locate a particular part or item.
"How-To" Video	Demonstrating exactly how to perform a specific procedure or sequence.
Script	Ensuring consistency, for example, to ensure that all customers receive the same marketing message or when describing the safety features on an airplane. Helpful for new employees learning company procedures.
Searchable Database	Providing rapid access to a large body of information. Online databases of products, models, and parts are good examples.
Peer or Expert Coach	Providing tips of the trade, qualitative assessment of performance, coaching guidance, and encouragement.
Help Desk/Access to Experts	Providing assistance with complex problems that simpler job aids and troubleshooting guides failed to solve.

Identify Opportunities for Support

In *The Field Guide to the 6Ds* (Pollock, Jefferson, & Wick, 2014), we offered the following suggestions for identifying when and where performance support will be most valuable:

- Talk to people who perform the tasks being taught. Ask them to think back to when they were first trying to perform them. Where did they struggle? What did they have trouble remembering? What would have helped them get up to speed more quickly?
- If the course has been previously offered, interview recent trainees. What did they find most difficult to apply and why? What would have made the application of new learning easier?
- Ask employees whether they have developed their own job aids such as sticky notes, spreadsheets, reminders, etc. Employees often develop simple but effective tools that they are willing to share. As Steve Rosenbaum taught us: If someone has developed an effective job aid, why don't we make it available to everyone?
- Interview managers of employees who perform the work. In their experience, where are employees new to the task most likely to have difficulty? Are there any critical points of failure that could be very costly to the company, an employee's career, or customer confidence? Target these for support.
- Tap the expertise of learning professionals. From the designers' experience and knowledge of human performance, where do they anticipate that people are likely to have trouble remembering "what to do" and "how to do" simultaneously? Check with trainers: Where do learners struggle the most in class during role plays and other forms of practice?

Characteristics of Great Performance Support

Effective performance support has the following characteristics:

- *Readily available at the time and place it is needed.* Since the goal is to facilitate on-the-job performance, the support has to be quickly and easily accessible at the same time and same place that the task, whatever it is, is performed. That determines the optimal format and delivery mechanism. A smartphone app, for example, won't be of any use in situations in which using a smartphone would be dangerous or prohibited. Online help for troubleshooting Internet connectivity problems is a bad idea. Embed the guidance as much as possible. Instructions attached to jumper cables will be used more often than those buried in the middle of the owner's manual.

- *Specific.* Good performance support is specific to the task. It is intended to be an aid to memory, rather than a compendium of everything that is known about the issue, object, or theory. "Good checklists ... are precise. They do not try to spell out everything—a checklist cannot fly a plane. Instead, they provide reminders of only the most critical and important steps...." (Gawande, 2008, p. 120).

- *Practical.* Performance support is designed to help people do the job correctly and efficiently. It needs to be designed and tested to be sure it can be executed by the intended audience with the time and materials they are likely to have on hand.

- *Clear.* Job aids and other forms of performance support have to be quickly and clearly understood by the target audience. For example, job aids in hotels with many non-native-speaking staff rely almost exclusively on illustrations.

- *Economical.* Performance support has to be economical in two senses of the word: low in cost and chary in its choice of words. It should provide only what is needed to accomplish the task: no more, no less. If it takes too long to find the information or glean its key points, it won't be used.

- *Effective.* The support you design—whatever it is—has to work under actual job conditions and should represent best practices. The only way to be sure the solution you have designed is effective is to test it. "The initial testing and piloting of the draft job aid always reveals unanticipated factors" (Willmore, 2006, p. 63). The best support is pilot-tested and revised before rollout, and then revised again as experience accumulates and suggestions for improvement are made.

- *Current.* Just as companies and individuals must learn and adapt to stay competitive, performance support systems also need to evolve and improve over time as conditions change and new best practices emerge. One of the advantages of computer-based systems is the relative ease with which they can be kept up-to-date.

Given these criteria, it is clear why program binders aren't job aids. They are designed to support instruction, rather than to provide performance support for transfer and application. Binders tend to be big and cumbersome; specific topics or suggestions for action can't be located easily. That may be why the participants we interviewed said that most of their program binders simply collect dust as soon as the instruction is over.

Training materials have to be re-tailored to the task if they are to be effective as performance support. "The more embedded, intuitive, and tailored the support is, the higher the probability that the performers will see value in it and will engage it again at another time" (Gottfredson & Mosher, 2011, p. 130).

 Practical Application

- Design support specific to the task. Use the same concepts and illustrations as in the training, but remember that a program binder is not a job aid.
- Rigorously test the performance support in the workplace to be sure that it is easily understood and that it works as expected.
- Ruthlessly eliminate unnecessary words, steps, and information, reducing the guidance to its essence.
- Survey participants about the impact and usefulness of the support; revise as necessary.

 ## Build It in

In our view, performance support should be part of every learning initiative. In the rare case in which it is deemed unnecessary, choosing not to offer support should be an active and reasoned decision, not merely an oversight. The best practice is to make performance support a required item on the checklist for approving learning designs. Support is most effective when it is conceived and executed as a truly integral part of learning, not just "tacked on" as an afterthought. A fully integrated approach has the following characteristics:

- It is designed into the learning experience.
- It is introduced and used during the training.
- It utilizes the same concepts, terms, and illustrations as the training itself.
- It truly represents best practices.

Introduce During Instruction

Common practice is still to introduce job aids at the end of instruction: "Oh, by the way, you may find this useful." That is a mistake. Job aids and other forms of performance support should be introduced and used

FIGURE D5.4.   INTRODUCE AND USE JOB AIDS DURING INSTRUCTION

throughout training to reinforce the message that their use on the job is encouraged and expected (Figure D5.4). Indeed, Terrence Donahue, corporate director, learning, for Emerson, feels that you should create the job aid first and then design the training to teach people how to use it effectively. Bob Mosher, chief learning evangelist at Apply Synergies, agrees. Moving content out of instruction and into the performance support system, he points out, reduces cognitive load and frees up class time for more practice (Mosher, 2014). The learning experience should be designed so that, over the course of instruction, the responsibility for finding answers and solutions shifts from the facilitator to the learners, with the goal of making them self-reliant by the end of class. That can only be accomplished when a robust performance support system is in place.

For certain skills, it may even make sense to introduce the job aid *before* training to give people a chance to become familiar with it (particularly if it is technology-based) and to allow them time to formulate questions about its use. One of our clients did this with a tablet-based job aid and found that it not only saved time in class that would have otherwise been devoted to introducing the job aid, but it also made the instruction much more effective.

Be Consistent

For maximum impact, performance support needs to be consistent with and reinforce the methods, approaches, and processes used during instruction. Employees can be confused when they are provided job aids that use different terminology for a concept or process they learned by another name. A welter of conflicting terms and concepts undermines the effectiveness of the support. To maximize utility, strive to ensure that all learning materials, including on-the-job guides, employ a consistent set of terms, concepts, and illustrations. Similarly, the processes described in performance support tools must match the ones taught in class and actually used on the job. Such consistency is obviously easier to accomplish if the instruction and support are created simultaneously and are seen as simply two different, but mutually reinforcing, forms of learning.

Ensure Best Practices

A third criterion for great performance support is that it truly presents "best practices." One approach is for learning professionals to research the best practices for a given task or skill and then build them into both the training and the performance support system. Another is to "crowdsource" best practices by inviting those who do the work to contribute.

An example is Aperian Global's GlobeSmart web tool, which provides information on how to most effectively communicate, manage employees, transfer technology, and improve relationships with customers and suppliers in countries around the world (Aperian Global, 2012). The system continues to get smarter by inviting executives who have experience working in particular cultures to contribute their ideas and insights. These are checked, edited, and added to the database, so the system continues to grow increasingly rich, deep, and specific. Companies can benefit by adapting the approach to build similar crowd-sourced systems of organization-specific knowledge for nuanced skills like managing, consulting, or selling.

Another example is Waggl®, a general purpose online "crowdsourcing" tool that companies can use to gather and disseminate best practices after a variety of learning and change initiatives. Individuals are asked to input their most effective actions and to rank the ideas of others in a pair-wise fashion. Those that win the most faceoffs bubble to the top and are shared among all the participants.

 Practical Application

- Introduce performance support during the instruction.
- Make sure it truly represents best practices and application.

New Technologies, New Possibilities

The capabilities afforded by new technologies and ubiquitous Internet access open up exciting possibilities for providing richer, more portable, more specific, and more personal just-in-time performance support. They are blurring the lines between learning and work. O'Driscoll presaged this convergence when he wrote:

> As the pace of technological change speeds up … the distinction between learning and work will disappear. A trend toward integrating training with on-the-job activities will be a result. This trend will extend itself to the point that training, as a distinct function, will no longer be the primary learning vehicle for many types of jobs. Workers will use on-the-job information systems instead.
>
> O'Driscoll, 1999

The challenge for learning professionals—as part of the paradigm shift from delivering training to delivering performance—is to think creatively about how to harness new technologies and possibilities to eliminate training when it is unnecessary, and to amplify it when it is.

Consider the revolution that occurred in getting directions from one place to another. Until a few years ago, you bought a map and worked out your own route. Alternatively, you asked someone local for directions and copied them down. That worked pretty well until you took a wrong turn, were forced to detour, or the roads had changed. Then trying to get back on the right highway could be a nightmare.

Now, as a result of GPS and map apps, you are given step-by-step instructions to your destination. If you deviate from the original plan, intentionally or unintentionally, the system rapidly recalculates what you need to do to get back on track.

Using the metaphor of personal development as a journey, we should aim for performance support tools that perform an analogous function. They should allow participants to specify their destination and then guide them in selecting the best routes, including alternatives and re-routing if they go off track.

The ability to use technology to *inform and guide planning and action* is especially well suited to situations in which:

- Performance depends on access to a very large body of information (knowing every road in the country, for example);
- The information or procedures change frequently (processing insurance claims or checking for drug interactions); or
- The information needs to be personalized (such as to meet your personal financial or developmental goals).

Help People Collaborate

Technology also facilitates social learning by helping people collaborate and harness more of the tacit knowledge of the organization. Or, as former Hewlett-Packard CEO Lou Platt allegedly quipped: "If only HP knew what HP knows, we would be three times more productive." Social networking tools can be used to supplement and extend planned instruction by helping a cohort of learners stay connected and assist each other as they work to implement new skills and knowledge (see also Learning Communities, below).

Two trends in organizations make fostering collaboration electronically both more feasible and more important. The first is the increasing number of "digital natives"—younger workers who have grown up with digital social media and who are used to communicating and collaborating that way. The second is the increasing number of people who work from their homes at least part of the time, making more traditional forms of connecting and collaborating more difficult. These trends assure that the role of digital social networking for both learning and learning transfer will continue to increase.

Social learning has always gone on in organizations, of course, but it was usually limited to the co-workers in your immediate vicinity or site. Digital networking technologies greatly expand the potential for continuous learning by removing the barriers of time and space (Gottfredson & Mosher, 2011). Workers can now reach out to others across facilities, countries, and even companies. Software developers commonly solicit assistance from one another and frequently receive solutions from people they have never met in companies they may never have heard of. People freely share solutions because they expect others to reciprocate and because everyone in the network learns from open exchanges.

Instructional designers should seek ways to harness the power of digital social networks to amplify other kinds of learning. It is not necessarily true, however, that "if you build it, they will come"; the network will survive and grow only if it provides real value to the participants.

▨ People

Although the discussion of D5 to this point has focused mainly on support materials and systems, some kinds of support can only be provided by fellow human beings. Colleagues, mentors, coaches, and others can provide uniquely human capabilities, such as empathy, wisdom, feedback, encouragement, collaborative problem solving, and motivation, in a way that no system, however sophisticated, can fully replace. "Whereas teaching and training are focused on telling and sharing content, real coaching is a genuine collaboration, which creates ownership for change" (Weber, 2014b).

Hence, devoting time, planning, and energy to creating human support systems is an important part of the practice of the Fifth Discipline and of designing the complete learning experience. Many different people can play a role in supporting learning transfer—from managers to the participant's friends or partners. Four—managers, instructors, peers, and coaches—have special impact and are discussed in detail below.

Managers

The critical role that managers play in facilitating learning transfer was emphasized in D4. The key point with respect to D5 is that managers also need performance support to excel in their roles. Just because someone has been promoted to manager does not mean that he knows how to coach or can do so effectively (Figure D5.5).

In an ideal world, managers would be given training on how to coach in general, as well as how to maximize the results of a specific learning initiative in particular. Unfortunately, this is often impossible or impractical. Given

> Provide easy-to-use forms, step-by-step processes, and examples.

that, many of our clients have discovered that they can increase both the frequency and the effectiveness of managerial support by providing managers with simple "how-to" guides on maximizing the benefits of learning for their direct reports.

Effective performance support to help managers fulfill their role in learning transfer is:

- *Concise.* Given how pressed managers are for time these days, the most important characteristic of coaching support for managers is brevity.

FIGURE D5.5.   MANAGERS NEED PERFORMANCE SUPPORT TO COACH EFFECTIVELY

"Keep up the good work, whatever it is, whoever you are."

© James Stevenson/The New Yorker Collection/*www.cartoonbank.com*. Used with permission.

Most will not take the time to read lengthy emails or multi-page documents. Strip the guide to its essentials.

- *Efficient.* For the same reason that the guidance must be concise, the process you recommend must be efficient. Recommend actions that produce the greatest impact for the smallest investment of time, for example, having a five-minute pre-training phone call.
- *Specific and Action-Oriented.* Be specific about what you want the managers to do and when. Don't simply exhort them to do more coaching. Provide a process for them to follow, including specific questions to ask or scripts to use to guide a discussion.
- *Layered.* Structure the support as a high-level outline with ready access to detailed examples or explanations for those who want them.

- *Accessible.* As with all performance support, be sure the guide is readily available at the time and place it is needed, with both print and online versions.

At the request of our clients, we developed a workbook detailing how to facilitate manager-participant interactions in support of learning called *Getting Your Money's Worth from Training and Development* (Jefferson, Pollock, & Wick, 2009). An example is given in Figure D5.6. We persuaded our publisher to print it as two books in one: one side for the manager and the flip side for the participant, to ensure that each can see what advice the other had received.

FIGURE D5.6.   A COMPLETED EXAMPLE OF A FORM TO FACILITATE PARTICIPANT-MANAGER DIALOGUE

Your Name: *Pat O'Brian*

Name of Program: *High-Impact Marketing*   Date of Program: *4/1/15*

	Most important deliverables of my business / organizational unit	Most important results for which I am personally responsible	What new or improved skills / knowledge would help me deliver better results	Topics covered in the training or development program	Therefore, what I want to get out of it (be able to do better or differently)
Your Input	- *revenue growth* - *sustained profitability*	- *effective marketing programs* - *strong branding* - *perceived value*	- *better segmenting and targeting* - *more effective project mgt*	- *positioning* - *segmentation / targeting* - *product life cycle management* - *selecting vendors*	- *improve the way I segment and target campaigns to increase impact*
Your Manager's Review	☐ Agreed as written ☐ See edits ☐ Let's discuss	☐ Agreed as written ☐ See edits ☐ Let's discuss	☐ Agreed as written ☐ See edits ☐ Let's discuss	☐ Agreed as written ☐ See edits ☐ Let's discuss	☐ Agreed as written ☐ See edits ☐ Let's discuss
	Comments:	Comments:	Comments:	Comments:	Comments:

From Jefferson, Pollock, and Wick, 2009, used with permission.

Most importantly, managers at all levels have to model the way, consistently acting in accord with the principles taught in the learning initiative. If they don't, then the initiative will fail to produce any meaningful change and may, in fact, be worse than doing nothing at all (Case in Point D5.1).

Case in Point D5.1
When the Video Doesn't Match the Audio

A biotechnology firm had sustained dramatic growth for a decade. Managers had been carried along by the momentum and rapidly promoted as the business grew, although with little formal management training and, because of the pace of growth, limited on-the-job experience and mentoring.

As a result, most middle managers led by the seat of their pants, mimicking the entrepreneurial style of the founder. Then the company encountered market turbulence and missed its forecast significantly. Its stock dropped precipitously. The senior leaders realized that the lack of professional management was a serious impediment to continued prosperity. So they worked with a vendor to design and deliver a five-day program to help managers increase the effectiveness of teamwork, foster innovation, improve efficiency, and create ownership for results through delegation.

The senior management team strongly endorsed the program and made stirring speeches about its importance for the future of the company. When it came time to attend, however, they were "too busy" to participate. They requested a special half-day "executive edition."

The result was entirely predictable. The senior managers never mastered the material and failed to incorporate the processes and terminology into their own leadership. For example, middle managers were taught to foster creative thinking by conducting brainstorming sessions in a particular way, but their own managers failed to do so. In fact, many actions by the company's senior leaders were directly contrary to what the middle managers had been taught.

Needless to say, the program failed to create the hoped-for change or to generate a return on investment. Indeed, the senior leadership's "do as I say, not as I do" attitude not only undermined the program's effectiveness, but engendered cynicism among middle managers about the sincerity of senior leaders and the value of training and development.

The lesson is clear: to impact performance, learning initiatives need management support in both word *and* deed.

Instructors and Facilitators

Another important source of support for learning transfer is the learning and development department itself. Participants often express the desire to have ongoing contact with faculty. When we surveyed participants three months after a program that included ongoing support from the instructor, participants rated access to the instructor during the learning transfer phase as being of significant value.

That makes sense, as Teresa Roche explained: "Facilitators are selected for their superior knowledge and teaching ability. During the program, participants come to value the facilitator's knowledge, opinions, and advice. Yet, historically, teaching ended when the class ended; communication was cut off. As a result, there was no support for learning transfer from the facilitators—the very people with the greatest insight into the material and whose opinion the learners value most" (Roche & Wick, 2005, p. 6). Because instructors are a trusted resource for participants, finding efficient ways to make them available to support learning transfer—and providing them the time and accountability to do so—will contribute to a healthy learning transfer environment.

To enable facilitators to provide ongoing performance support, however, requires a broader conceptualization of the facilitator's role and a reallocation of resources. Facilitators need to be given the time, responsibility, and accountability for sharing their expertise throughout all four phases of the learning process, rather than just in the classroom or virtual sessions. As with managers, facilitators need to model the way by exhibiting in their own work the values and behaviors they teach. (See Case in Point D5.2.)

Case in Point D5.2
Modeling the Way at the YMCA

The YMCA is the leading nonprofit in the United States committed to helping people and communities learn, grow, and thrive, with a presence in more than 10,000 communities. The Y understands that it needs inspired leadership at every level of the organization and that it must create the kind of work environment internally that reflects its values and aspirations for the communities it serves.

Jim Kauffman is the senior manager, Leadership and Volunteer Development, for the YMCA of the United States. He and his team create leadership programs and materials that they make available to support local organizations. They know, however, that for development programs to be effective, their principles must be applied in the everyday work of managers and become embedded in the culture.

"We are a cause-driven organization," Jim told us. "And that cause is building communities, strengthening and nourishing kids, and helping people give back and support their neighbors. We can't do that if our own staff are in a command-and-control environment. It will only happen if all our managers and supervisors understand that each person has a gift and that their job is to ask questions to help people bring out their best.

"It's incumbent upon us as instructors to model that behavior in the training we offer. We had to move away from 'I am the expert, I am in command, and I am going to tell you what you *should* do.' Our courses are now far more about the learner. Instead of being up there lecturing, we are asking powerful questions: 'What did you see in that exercise?' 'How are you going to take this back?' 'What is the gift in what you just learned for your life?'

"When we were training our camp counselors for the summer, we said, 'If you do what you are trained to do here, the kids in your group will have a desire to do well in school and eat healthier.' And they look at us and say, 'But I thought I was here to teach them swimming.' And we tell them, 'You are, but your impact goes far beyond that. If you approach your job right, your kids are going to want to do better in school, they are going to get excited about some career, and they'll have more confidence in themselves and more desire to excel.'

"Then there is this look of, 'Wow, I can have that much impact?' And they think 'This is exactly why I am here!'

"And that is what we are encouraging all local Y's to do. Quit talking about the number of activities, the number of kids, the dollars, how many partners, and start talking about the outcomes—the changes you have made for individuals and the community. Help people understand how their work contributes to those outcomes, understand their values, assess their own performance, and make the changes that they want to make to achieve the vision."

Such a redefinition of the facilitator's role supports Broad and Newstrom's contention that learning professionals should evolve from "strictly trainers/presenters to *facilitators of behavioral change on the job*" (1992, p. 113) and the Robinsons' (2008) concept of workplace learning professionals as "performance consultants." Roche and Wick (2005) put it this way: "Facilitators must move from the 'sage on the stage' to the 'guide by the side,' from facilitator of learning to facilitator of performance" (p. 13).

Bob Sachs, vice president of learning and development at Kaiser Permanente, agreed: "It's not just about how many programs we have. We are continuing to work on the

> Move from the "sage on the stage" to the "guide by the side."

idea that doing a lot of programs is less important than doing fewer programs with greater impact. In order to do that, you need to change the role of the instructors so that they are not just responsible for the classroom delivery, but they are actually following a cohort of people into the follow-through stage. That means that you're going to have instructors who do fewer programs, but with more impact."

Recognizing that facilitators' time is valuable and limited, use technology to make the process efficient as well as effective, such as electronic transfer support systems that allow facilitators to interact with the group asynchronously and efficiently and provide them with a dashboard that shows how the group is doing.

Peers: Learning Communities

A third potent but underutilized resource for ongoing support is the other participants in a learning program. While using peer coaches or "learning buddies" is often limited to on-boarding or basic-skills training, it has value across the spectrum, even in the senior-most executive education programs. For example, when Linda Sharkey was director of leadership development at General Electric, she noted the value of peer-to-peer coaching in GE's renowned leadership development programs: "When the leadership teams share their developmental needs with each other and use the coaching model, they often find three things: (1) they have similar issues, (2) they get great improvement suggestions from each other, and (3) they get support from each other to improve" (2003, p. 198). Both members of the learning pair benefit because helping someone think through an issue or challenge is, itself, a great learning experience.

Learning initiatives should take advantage of the collective knowledge and experience of the group by encouraging shared learning throughout the entire learning process. Etienne Wenger, who studies communities of practice, explained why they are so powerful: "There is something about hearing the words of someone who is a peer that makes the relevance of the knowledge that you get very immediate. So for me that is the fundamental value proposition in a peer-to-peer network" (quoted in Dulworth & Forcillo, 2005, p. 111).

Gary Jusela, who has led learning organizations at Boeing, Cisco Systems, and Home Depot, said: "What I love is bringing people back together and having them reflect on their

> Participants' actions don't always match their good intentions!

experiences in small groups and then also share some of that collectively in the larger room. What people discover is that they are not so alone, or they are not so weird. Everybody struggles with these things and they can learn from each other and get some tips about how to overcome some of the most perplexing struggles."

Learning and development can help build and sustain the learning community by reconvening groups, either in person or virtually. We reconvene participants on a web conference two months after a 6Ds workshop and ask them to share their experiences, successes or failures, and lessons learned. This establishes a finish line for the program beyond the workshop itself, and the participants benefit by continuing to learn from one another. Kirwan (2009) recommends that the learning organization set up the learning communities before participants leave the course, rather than leaving networking to chance, noting that "participants' actions don't always match their good intentions!" (p. 60).

Critical Mass How co-workers react to an employee's efforts to apply new learning is a key contributor to the learning transfer environment (Figure D4.9). When a cohort of employees—especially if they are an intact team—is given the same learning opportunity simultaneously, it creates critical mass. The mutual support generated by a common experience creates an environment in which learners can provide mutual support and reinforce each other's use of the new language, concepts, and behaviors (Kirwan, 2009, p. 82). It positively impacts the answer to the "Will I?" question. We find, for example, that learning teams are more successful at implementing *The Six Disciplines* if all the team members have attended a 6Ds workshop simultaneously.

Targeting specific departments, business units, or working groups and training a significant percent of the employees in them quickly has a greater chance of success than the "shotgun" approach of one here, one there. When only a small number of individuals in a group are trained at one time, the freshly minted "evangelists" for the new approach are under tremendous pressure to conform to the old way of doing things when they return to work. "If you are looking for a substantial uplift in company performance, a lot of people need to be learning similar things, all at the same time" (Bordonaro, 2005, p. 162). When Hewlett-Packard set out to transform the effectiveness of internal communications through its

> A lot of people need to be learning similar things, all at the same time.

Dynamic Leadership program, they trained thousands of employees in just a few months to get to critical mass; the effort was repaid many times over in improved proficiency (Burnett & Connolly, 2003).

Designated Coaches

Designated coaches are another potential source of active support. More experienced employees, for example, can help less experienced employees "learn the ropes" about how the job is done in real time with real issues. But getting the most from such pairings requires forethought and preparation of both the coach and the coachee (see Case in Point D5.3).

Case in Point D5.3
Don't Leave Support to Chance

"Go and work with Joe and watch how he does it." Job shadowing—pairing less experienced workers with more experienced ones—*can be* a valuable learning experience and an important part of bringing new employees up to speed.

"Can be, but usually isn't," according to Steve Rosenbaum, president of Learning Paths International. That's because most companies fail to think through how to make the experience an integral and complementary part of the learning path to proficiency. They leave it to chance and individual initiative, which means that everyone's experience is different and frequently suboptimal.

Moreover, pairing is usually scheduled when it is convenient. "Mary has some time this afternoon, so why don't you work with her?" But when Mary has time may be two weeks later than when the new employee really needed the skill.

"To maximize the value of job shadowing," Rosenbaum told us, "you've got to plan it carefully and schedule it when it will add the most value, not just when it is convenient. You have to give the experienced workers explicit guidelines for the interaction—the purpose, what to cover, and how to debrief it—otherwise you'll end up with the blind leading the blind."

Rosenbaum helps his clients define how shadowing fits into the overall path to proficiency. They rigorously define what a new employee needs to take away from each interaction. Then they prepare detailed guidelines that include directions on:

- What to make sure the newer employee observes during the session
- What questions to ask to be sure he/she has absorbed and internalized the key teaching points

"Since we have started helping our clients be more formal about their approach to informal learning, they have been able to get employees to a higher level of proficiency much faster than when they just put learning pairs together and hoped for the best. It saves time for both the mentor and the trainee, and that translates into real dollar value for the organization."

Mentors can help employees master their craft in the same way that professional coaches help musicians, actors, athletes, and others master their arts. When Daniel Coyle (2009) studied "talent hotspots" around the world—places that produced a disproportionate number of outstanding performers—he always found "master coaches"—men and women who had a talent and love for helping others achieve their personal best.

Emma Weber, founder of Lever–Transfer of Learning, believes that using trained coaches and a defined process has significant advantages over relying on managers, because managers frequently lack the skill, confidence, and know-how to maximize learning transfer (Weber, 2014b). Her approach, called Turning Learning into Action®, uses trained coaches who engage participants in a series of structured ACTION conversations over a twelve-week period (Weber, 2014a). The results are impressive, with substantial gains in coached groups versus those with no special follow-up efforts.

Professional coaches can be invaluable in helping participants maximize the value of formal training, 360-degree feedback, and on-the-job learning experiences. Having a coach is in itself an incentive to follow through, practice, and reflect. According to Mary Jane Knudson, vice president of human resources at Fidelity Investments, "Nearly every major corporation—and progressive smaller ones as well—identify executive coaching as one of their critical executive and leadership development activities" (2005, p. 40).

Using executive-level coaches is cost-prohibitive for most learning and development programs, however, and not always necessary. Goldsmith, Morgan, and Effron (2013) compared the results of development programs in five different companies. Some used paid external coaches, others used internal coaches. Both internal and external coaches added value. They concluded that "Coaching can be a great complement to training" and "Leaders can clearly benefit from coaching, but it does not have to be done by external coaches." Some programs we have worked with have used recent program graduates as mentors, a process that enriches and deepens the knowledge of both teacher and student.

Geoff Rip, research director for the Institute of Learning Practitioners in Australia, recommends a process he calls "proficiency coaching" because it can be delivered by a variety of people including other participants, past participants, facilitators, or managers (Rip, 2014). The process includes four phases:

- *Phase 1: Preparation.* To raise perceived relevance and importance of the training.
- *Phase 2: Course/Workshop (Warm-Up).* Any combination of live workshops, e-learning modules, virtual sessions, and experiential learning.
- *Phase 3: Proficiency Development (Workouts).* At least three proficiency coaching sessions.
- *Phase 4: Proficiency Story.* Participants have completed the training only when they have submitted a proficiency (achievement) story.

Learning transfer support and virtual coaching technologies enable exciting new forms of coaching that foster interaction and, at the same time, reduce the time commitment for the providers. For one thing, the time wasted playing telephone tag is eliminated. Second, when coaching is part of a transfer support system, coaches can review the participants' objectives, most recent activities, successes, issues, and insights before the interchange. This is not only more efficient and accurate than an oral retelling, but it allows the coach more time to reflect and formulate the most helpful advice or questions—rather than having to respond off the cuff in real time.

A particularly interesting and innovative use of technology is the Allego system, which allows sales representatives to record a brief segment of their sales pitch and send it to their managers for review. The manager can review the video clip when he or she has time and stop the recording at any point to provide feedback about strengths and opportunities for improvement. The system was used by Vertex Pharmaceuticals to prepare representatives for an upcoming launch (Short & Plunkett-Gomez, 2014). The results were extraordinary: it was possible to qualify 100 percent of the sales force within twenty-four hours of approval at a fraction of the time and cost of previously used approaches. Perhaps most importantly, many of the recordings were labeled "take 10," "take 16," or even "take 35." In other words, a substantial and unexpected benefit was that the representatives were doing a great deal of self-coaching—recording, watching, and re-recording until they felt they had achieved a level of performance worthy of sharing with their managers.

Feedback Sustains Learning Transfer

Feedback is important to support learning transfer as well as to sustain employee commitment and enthusiasm in general. Ken Blanchard has complained that the only way most employees know that they are doing a good job is when "no one's yelled at me lately" (Blanchard, 2004). Simple acknowledgement of participants' efforts to transfer and apply their learning, especially from their managers, is a powerful incentive to continue those efforts.

Ongoing feedback is especially important in trying to change habits (Duhigg, 2012). Anyone who has driven a car with continuous feedback on fuel consumption, or worn one of the new generation of digital pedometers, like a Fitbit®, knows first-hand how powerful feedback can be in influencing behavior. Direct evidence for how feedback impacts learning transfer is illustrated by work we did with an international technology company. We reviewed the records from the learning transfer support system for more than 5,000 employees who had participated in a company-wide skills program. We compared the behavior of those who requested *and received* feedback with that of those who requested feedback but received none.

> Simple acknowledgement of effort is a powerful incentive.

The difference was dramatic. The group that received feedback in response to their requests completed, on average, twice as many subsequent progress updates as those who asked for feedback but received none (Figure D5.7).

This makes sense and supports the findings by Ariely and by Amabile and Kramer that we discussed in D3 (page 101). If employees ask their managers for assistance with learning transfer and the manager provides it, that sends a clear signal that what they are doing is important to their manager and worth their time. Conversely, if they ask for feedback and the request is ignored, that sends an equally clear signal (intentional or unintentional) that their manager does not value the effort and that they should spend their time on other things.

The conclusion is that learning professionals who want to see more of their efforts generate real business results need to pay attention to—and find ways to facilitate—the amount and quality of post-course coaching and feedback.

FIGURE D5.7.   PARTICIPANTS WHO RECEIVED FEEDBACK
COMPLETED TWICE AS MANY PROGRESS UPDATES AS THOSE WHO
DID NOT

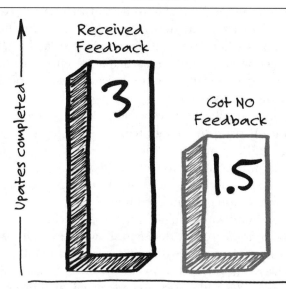

 Practical Application

- There are times when effective performance support can only come from a person.
- Use peers and past participants as coaches; they can be very effective sources of performance support.

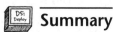 **Summary**

The Fifth Discipline that characterizes breakthrough training and development programs is that they deploy active, ongoing performance support after the traditional "course" is over. Support increases the learner's probability of success, extends the learning period, enhances motivation, and accelerates learning transfer, leading to improved performance.

The best corporate learning programs provide performance support of the same caliber as the customer support provided by the best consumer-brands companies. They understand that high-quality, just-in-time performance support enhances learning transfer and the value of learning initiatives.

Highly effective programs provide appropriate job aids, smartphone apps, online help, access to experts, and other forms of support to help employees apply learning and achieve success. They prepare and engage managers to provide support throughout the process, supplemented by learning and coaching professionals as needed. They facilitate collaborative learning through social networking and software.

Companies that effectively manage the complete learning experience by investing a portion of their resources on performance support enjoy a greater return on their learning investments than companies that limit their thinking and investment to courses and classrooms (the event mentality). The checklist in Exhibit D5.1 can help you develop a robust plan for post-course performance support.

Exhibit D5.1
Checklist for D5

Use the checklist below to ensure that you have a robust plan to provide the post-course coaching and performance support necessary to maximize the value of the learning experience.

	Element	Criterion
❑	Integration	Performance support is an integral part of the design; difficulties or memory lapses that trainees might encounter are anticipated and addressed.
❑	Integration	Job aids and other forms of support are introduced and used in the learning process, not left until the end.
❑	Tools	Learners are provided with job aids, online materials, reference works, and so forth to reinforce course principles and support application.
❑	Collaboration	Continuing peer-to-peer learning and sharing after the formal instruction period is encouraged and facilitated.
❑	Feedback	Mechanisms are put in place to ensure that learners receive feedback on their performance to help them establish new habits.
❑	Coaching	Learners are provided easy and efficient ways to engage their managers, subject experts, instructors, peers, or other advisors during the transfer and application process.
❑	Supervisor Support	Managers are encouraged to provide coaching and are provided with simple, efficient, and explicit coaching guides to maximize their probability of success.
❑	Continuous Improvement	Former participants are polled to discover what additional support would have helped them; aids they have developed for themselves are solicited and incorporated in future programs.

Recommendations

For Learning Leaders

- Require a discussion of performance support as part of any learning plan.
  - Almost every program will benefit from some kind of support.
  - Include all three kinds of support: materials, systems, and people.
  - If the decision is made not to provide support, it should be an active decision, not an oversight.
- Focus on performance rather than training.
  - If a job aid or other performance support tool will be sufficient, use it.
- Interview a sample of participants three months or so after a learning initiative to find out whether they received the support they needed.
  - If they have developed their own performance support tools, consider adapting and distributing them to all participants.
- Pilot test job aids and other kinds of performance support. Use the feedback to revise and continuously improve.
- Remember to provide performance support to managers and coaches to maximize their effectiveness.

For Line Leaders

- Review the plans of learning initiatives at your company and make sure that they include adequate systems and resources for performance support.
  - Help the learning team focus on performance rather than training by rejecting any proposal that does not include performance support.
  - Challenge the learning team to be more creative and innovative in their use of performance support.
- At the same time, review your own actions and those of your team.
  - Do you hold your managers accountable for providing performance support to maximize return on learning investments?
  - Do you recognize and reward managers who do a superior job of developing their direct reports?
  - Do performance reviews and the performance management system reward the right behaviors?
  - If not, put your own house in order. Otherwise, employees will sense the disconnect between your words and your actions.

DOCUMENT RESULTS

"You, your leaders, and your investors are interested in learning only insofar as it improves performance and gets business results."

—MICHAEL DULWORTH AND FRANK BORDONARO

A T THE END OF THE DAY, the questions that must be addressed about any learning initiative are:

- Did it work?
- Was it worth it?
- If it did work, how can it be made even more effective?
- If it did not work, or did not produce enough value to justify the investment, why not, and what are we going to do about it?

The practice of the Sixth Discipline—**Document Results**—is essential to inform decisions about future action, which means: Should the learning initiative be continued, expanded, revised, or abandoned? Relevant and credible evidence of learning's impact is needed to answer those questions. An assessment of the factors that contributed to success or failure is prerequisite to repeatability and improvement.

The most effective learning organizations document the results of learning initiatives in ways that inform investment decisions and support continuous improvement. The challenges are what, when, and how to measure outcomes and then how to report the results so that they lead to informed and effective action.

In this chapter, we discuss:

- Why document results?
- Guiding principles for effective evaluations
- What to measure
- When to measure
- A six-step process
- Managing learning's brand
- A checklist for D6
- Recommendations for learning and business leaders

Why Document Results?

Documenting the results of learning initiatives is necessary to *prove* training's value and *improve* future initiatives. Proving that the initiative was worthwhile is essential because leaders have a fiduciary obligation to use an organization's assets responsibly—that is, in ways that maximize its ability to fulfill its mission and achieve its goals. Doing so requires making decisions about asset allocations:

- How much of the available resources (time, money, facilities, and personnel) should be dedicated to marketing, how much to sales, research, manufacturing, infrastructure, and so forth?
- What distribution best balances short-term realities with long-term opportunities?
- What mix of investments will create the greatest long-term value for shareholders, employees, and customers?

Getting the resource allocation right—or wrong—has profound implications for the future of the organization and its employees.

There is no escaping the necessity of making such choices. Even in the best of times, there are always more good ideas for spending time and money than there is time and money to spend. When the economy slows, resource allocation decisions become even more difficult and critical. Learning professionals need to provide business leaders with relevant and reliable data about the value being created by training so that they can make informed decisions about resource allocation.

Thus, the first and foremost purpose of evaluation is to provide *sound evidence* to support *informed decisions* that are in the *best interest* of the organization. Every evaluation should include clear recommendations for

> Business leaders need relevant and reliable data to make wise decisions.

action based on the results. In our view, an evaluation isn't effective if it isn't sound, if it isn't actionable, if it fails to influence, or if it leads to erroneous and detrimental decisions.

Learning Competes for Resources

Learning and development initiatives consume time and money. Therefore, like it or not, learning competes with other departments, needs, and investment opportunities for corporate resources. Business leaders have to make hard choices among, for example, funding a promising new product idea that could fuel future growth, hiring more sales representatives to improve the top line immediately, investing in technology to reduce costs, or providing a training program to improve managerial effectiveness.

All of these proposals have merit, but it is rarely possible to fund all the meritorious initiatives in a given year. Even if funds are available, there may not be enough time or personnel to execute them. So choices have to be made; leaders must balance the strate-

> Learning competes with other departments, needs, and opportunities.

gic importance, relative contribution, and probability of success of all these disparate opportunities, winnowing them into those that will be funded, scaled back, or rejected (Figure D6.1). Business leaders also know that they will have to defend their choices; whatever they decide, their allocation will be second-guessed by more-senior leaders and, ultimately, shareholders. If they choose to fund training instead of an advertising campaign, for example, they had better have a good reason, especially if sales fall short of target.

Some learning and talent development professionals find the idea of competing for resources in this way offensive. In Idalene Kesner's *Harvard Business Review* Case "Leadership Development: Perk or Priority?" the learning director complains: "I hate it when people make those kinds of

**FIGURE D6.1.   MANAGEMENT MUST DECIDE WHICH INITIATIVES
TO FUND AND WHICH TO REDUCE, ELIMINATE, OR POSTPONE**

comparisons. First, we are talking about people in my case. That's different
from calculating the payback from a machine" (2003, p. 31). We agree that
demonstrating the value of learning *is* different from calculating the payback of a machine. Indeed, we think that trying to apply the same methodology uncritically to both is a mistake. But there is no exemption from
having to prove *worth*. Learning initiatives consume resources that could
be put to use elsewhere; there had better be a compelling business case for
the value they are expected to generate.

Leaders want better evidence of
the value of learning than most training departments provide today. "In
keeping with a trend toward increased
accountability in all organizational
activities, CEOs want information that

> Leaders want better
> evidence than most training
> departments provide today.

the organization is gaining value for its investments in performance
improvement interventions" (Rothwell, Lindholm, & Wallick, 2003, p.
218). Fortune 500 CEOs said that the most important data they want is
evidence of business impact (Phillips & Phillips, 2009), yet this is the outcome least often measured and reported (American Society for Training
and Development, 2011).

Although management in some organizations is still satisfied with smile sheets and numbers of "butts in seats," it is a mistake to wait until management demands that you document results. "If you wait until the CEO asks for an ROI study to … demonstrate how your training group adds value to your company, it is too late—the CEO has already decided to greatly reduce your budget or to eliminate the training group altogether … " (Tobin, 2009).

A well-established track record of adding value is the best defense for the learning and development budget in times of economic restraint (see Case in Point D6.1). Start documenting results now to establish unassailable evidence of learning's contribution before its value is called into question.

Case in Point D6.1
Making the Case

When Ross Tartell was director team leader of the LEAD (Leadership, Education, and Development) group at Pfizer's Learning Center, he knew that the group needed to document its contribution to business success. He used his background in research to develop a partnership that brought together instructional design experts and the Metrics and Strategic Assessment group. This integrated partnership created and implemented a metrics strategy tied to issues facing the business and core objectives supporting Pfizer's business strategy. The studies and natural field experiments, implemented over several years, demonstrated both the tangible and intangible impact of learning programs developed and delivered by the LEAD group in support of individual and organizational performance.

When changes in the pharmaceutical market and its portfolio forced significant retrenchment at Pfizer, the LEAD group—like virtually every other function—was scaled back, but not nearly as much as learning functions that did not have a clear track record of documented value.

"There is no time like the present to start building your brand and demonstrating your value," said Tartell, now adjunct associate professor at Teachers College, Columbia University. "That gives you time to build the perception of your function's contribution and demonstrate its value to the business. Ultimately, when the organization needs to weather tough times, you have a foundation of strength, and will be seen as a key contributor to the future."

 Practical Application

- Start documenting learning's value before you are asked to do so.
- Remember that you are always competing for time and resources; make sure there is a convincing business case for investing in training.

Continuous Improvement

In today's highly competitive, rapidly changing global economy, no organization can afford to stand still. If you are not improving while your competitors are, then you are falling behind. To stay competitive, every function in every company needs to perform better this year than last year, and better next year than this year. Evaluating results is at the heart of process improvement: "The purpose of measuring any business process is to obtain *actionable information for improvement*" (Bersin, 2008, p. 13). "We see evaluation as the principal tool that learning leaders can use to accomplish this mission: building and strengthening learning capability so that organizations reap continuously better results from their learning investments" (Brinkerhoff & Apking, 2001, p. 165).

Continuous improvement tools and practices were initially developed in manufacturing, where they have resulted in extraordinary increases in quality and, simultaneously, reductions in cost. The methods have subsequently been applied to other business processes with similar success; Jack Welch ascribed a significant portion of GE's success to its aggressive six sigma improvement program (Welch & Welch, 2005). Approaching learning as a process includes applying the techniques of process improvement to training and development. Workplace learning professionals ought to be role models for a never-ending cycle of planning, doing, checking, and adjusting their approach.

> Evaluation is the principal tool to strengthen capability.

 Practical Application

- Learn to apply the core practices of continuous improvement to learning initiatives.
- Expect to be asked how you have improved the learning-to-performance process and be prepared to provide evidence.

Model for Improvement Langley and colleagues (2009, p. 24) proposed three fundamental questions as the basis for process improvement:

- What are we trying to accomplish?
- How will we know that a change is an improvement?
- What change can we make that will result in improvement?

The first question, "What are we trying to accomplish?" is critical. You cannot evaluate or improve a process until you know what it was supposed to produce. While that seems patently obvious, one of the most common evaluation errors reported by Frechtling (2007) is "not having shared definitions for what it means to achieve success" (p. 12). Making learning more efficient and effective starts by defining what, precisely, the business hopes to achieve as a result (D1).

The second question, "How will we know?" is at the heart of D6. The only way to know whether the current approach is effective, and whether any changes have been positive, negative, or superfluous, is to assess the outcomes.

The third question, "What are our options?" reflects a fundamental premise of continuous improvement: no matter how good a current process is, there is always something that can be done to make it better. In the context of corporate learning, that challenges learning professionals to continually look for ways to make good programs even better.

PDCA Cycle The Plan–Do–Check–Act (PDCA) cycle was popularized by the late Dr. W. Edwards Deming, one of the most important early contributors to the process improvement and total quality movements. The PDCA cycle, combined with the three fundamental questions above, constitute the Model for Improvement (Figure D6.2). The four elements of the PDCA cycle are:

1. **Plan**—design an initiative or change to an existing process
2. **Do**—implement the plan
3. **Check**—measure the results against the objectives
4. **Act**—utilize the insights gained to initiate the next cycle

The PDCA cycle (also referred to as the PDSA, or plan-do-study-act cycle), is a simple but powerful tool that can be applied to any process, including learning. Six sigma quality initiatives use the related DMAIC cycle (Define, Measure, Analyze, Improve, and Control) (Islam, 2006). The importance of the check (measure) step should be obvious. Unless you assess the results and compare them to the intended outcomes, you have no idea whether the changes you made—such as switching to e-learning, adding a simulation, or introducing game mechanics—improved the outcome, had no effect, or actually made it worse. "You can improve performance without measurement, for example, by gut feel, by experience,

FIGURE D6.2.   THE MODEL FOR IMPROVEMENT

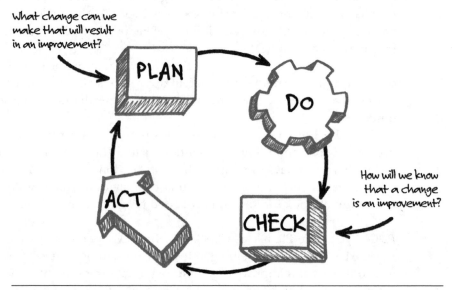

After Langley, Moen, Nolan, Nolan, Norman, and Provost, 2009.

by recognizing patterns, and so on, but you cannot do so reliably or in a repeatable way … " (Gaffney, 2007).

In the second edition of *The Six Disciplines*, we made the analogy to hitting a target:

Process improvement can be likened to hitting targets with artillery. The first few shells are "ranging shots." After each, a comparison is made between the target and where the shell actually landed. The results are used to adjust the aim before the next shot is taken. With each cycle of aim, fire, measure, and assess, the accuracy improves. Eventually, every shot is squarely on target, but the cycle of checking and adjusting must continue to make sure they stay on target as conditions change.

Now imagine the results of a gunnery crew that has been given the finest artillery piece, plenty of ammunition, and strong management support, but which is so busy shooting that they never bother to find out where their shots land. They carefully track the number of shots, cost per shot, shots per hour, and so forth, but they have no feedback on whether the shots are on target or a mile wide. With each shot, they alter the controls in the direction they think will help, but since they have no reliable information on whether or not it improves the outcome, they only occasionally hit a target. When they do, the shot cannot be repeated because they don't know which factors made it successful. In the absence of trustworthy outcome data, they are unable to improve their performance.

Wick, Pollock, and Jefferson, 2010, p. 261

Sadly, many corporate educators are like the gunnery crew we described. They know what the targets are, they have resources, and they are able to make adjustments, but they either fail to evaluate the relevant results—or worse—they rely on misleading "measures of convenience" (like immediate reactions) that have little or nothing to do with hitting the target. Will Thalheimer argues that the lack of reliable measurement has stunted our development as a profession: "The fact is that we receive very little valid feedback about how we are doing as learning-and-performance professionals. Our impoverished feedback loops leave us in the dark. We simply don't receive good-enough feedback to improve our performance" (Thalheimer, 2008).

United Parcel Service recognizes the importance of assessing whether or not learning initiatives hit their targets: "We have to be able to create learning and development programs that drive strategy execution, and, even after we have developed programs that do that, we have to measure the business impact" (Ann Schwartz, quoted in Margolis, 2010).

Achieving continuous improvement requires evaluating the *complete* learning experience, not just the effectiveness of instruction. It must take into consideration *all* of the factors that influence the answers to both the "Can I?" and "Will I?" questions. For example:

> You can improve performance without measurement, but you cannot do so reliably.

- Were the right people trained?
- Were they adequately prepared?
- Did their managers actively support application?

- Were they given the tools, time, and support they needed to apply their learning?
- Did the learning occur at the right time?

   Breakdowns can occur anywhere in the learning-to-results process. Evaluation should seek to identify the weakest links so that they can be addressed. One of the strengths of the Success Case Method (Brinkerhoff, 2003) is that it intentionally seeks to identify impediments as well as to document success (Figure D6.13).

 Practical Application

- Ask three questions about every learning initiative: "What are we trying to accomplish?" "How will we know whether the change is an improvement?" and "What are our options?"
- Apply the PDCA cycle to each new learning initiative or significant change, with special emphasis on the check step.

 ## Guiding Principles

H.L. Mencken (1917) famously remarked: "For every complex problem there is an answer that is clear, simple, and *wrong*." Given the range of organizational goals and the variety of learning initiatives taken to achieve them, using the same evaluation technique for every learning initiative will undoubtedly prove to be "clear, simple, and *wrong*." As Ridge (2013) noted: "There are no set formulas for program evaluation, evaluation instruments, or outcomes. There are so many variables that make most programs unique and, as such, they cannot be evaluated in the same way any other program was evaluated" (p. 29).
   On the other hand, it is possible to define a small set of universal principles that can be used to guide the design and execution of an evaluation of any initiative. To both *prove* and *improve* the effectiveness of learning, an evaluation must satisfy four criteria. It must be:

- Relevant
- Credible
- Compelling
- Efficient

FIGURE D6.3.   AN EVALUATION MUST CLEAR FOUR HURDLES TO BE SUCCESSFUL

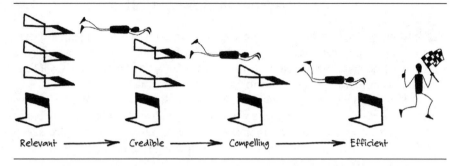

Relevant ⟶ Credible ⟶ Compelling ⟶ Efficient

Your evaluation strategy must clear all four hurdles (Figure D6.3) if it is to support informed decisions. For example, it doesn't matter how relevant the data are or how efficiently they are collected if they are not believed by the target audience.

Relevant The first characteristic of an effective evaluation is that the measures are *relevant*—that is, they have a direct and unambiguous relationship to the business goals (D1) and the logic model of the initiative. In the evaluation literature, this is known as *face validity* (Russ-Eft & Preskill, 2009, p. 219). That measures need to be relevant to the business purpose seems so obvious that we are almost embarrassed to mention it, were it not for the frequency with which this principle is violated.

The most common violation of the relevance principle in program evaluation is to present positive Level 1 reaction scores as if they were evidence that the program was effective. Reaction data are a relevant outcome measure only when the

> What is measured ought to reflect the program's objectives.

objective is to get people to come back for more, such as to an entertainment event like a movie, theme park, or football game. Corporate learning initiatives are not funded for their entertainment value; they are initiated to solve performance issues, seize business opportunities, improve service, enhance efficiency, or in some other way enhance the productivity of the enterprise. Measuring whether people liked it, or perceived it to be valuable, does not address management's burning question: Did it or did it not achieve its business purpose? (See Case in Point D6.2.)

Case in Point D6.2
A Real Wake-Up Call

When Chris Goins was executive director, Sales Training and Management Development for Wyeth, he got a real wake-up call about the importance of documenting results. Chris's boss called him into the office one day and said, "Chris, what would you say if I were to tell you that I am thinking of outsourcing your whole department?"

At first Chris did not know what to say. Then he started to stammer, trying to come up with all the reasons that outsourcing would be a bad idea: "People really like our training." "We have a lot of good people, a lot of good talent." "Look how many courses we ran." And so forth. The more he tried to explain why training shouldn't be outsourced, the more he realized he didn't really have any compelling evidence.

His boss let him twist in the wind for a while before he said, "Chris, relax. I am not really thinking of outsourcing you guys. But I have vendors in here all the time pitching me on why I should. And they come with facts and data to support their proposals.

"Remember that I might not always be in this chair, and your next boss might have a different point of view. So next time you had better be prepared with a better answer than you just gave. If I were you, I'd make sure that I had data to support a much stronger business case for training than 'they really like us.'"

Reaction Scores Largely Irrelevant Despite their nearly universal use, reaction scores (Kirkpatrick Level 1) have essentially no correlation to either behavior change or business impact. Dixon (1990), for example, found no significant correlation between post-course test scores and participants' perceptions of the program's relevance, their estimation of amount learned, enjoyment, or instructor's skill. Alliger and colleagues (1997) analyzed thirty-four previous studies and found very poor correlation between reaction data, objective measures of learning, and on-the-job learning transfer. Ruona and colleagues (2002) studied the relationship between learner reactions and learning transfer. They concluded: "The results of this study continue to raise questions about the role and value of reaction measures" (p. 218). That should not come as a surprise given the myriad factors that impact learning transfer (see page 162).

Among eight possible measures of training effectiveness, CEOs ranked Level 1 reactions dead last in terms of the data they want to see (Phillips & Phillips, 2009). Why, then, do training providers persist in gathering, analyzing, and reporting reaction data? First, because it *seems* like they should

> CEOs ranked end-of-course evaluations dead last.

matter. It seems logical that people will have learned more from an experience they rated highly. That assumption is not only wrong, but potentially dangerous, because maximizing reaction scores can actually sub-optimize learning (Case in Point D6.3).

Granted, very low or negative reaction scores can highlight a problem. As one CLO told us, "If people hate the pilot, I'm not going to roll it out." But the opposite is not true; that people loved the pilot does not necessarily mean that it should be rolled out. Relying solely on reactions tends to favor entertainment over substance.

Case in Point D6.3
Better Reaction Scores May Not Be Better

A European technology company was having serious concerns about one of its instructors. The instructor consistently received poor ratings on an end-of-course questionnaire that asked, "How do you feel about the trainer?" and "Do you think he or she was effective?" So they asked Neil Rackham, best-selling author of *SPIN Selling,* for his advice. When he looked into the issue from the perspective of *effectiveness* rather than reaction, the results were startling.

When the instructors were instead ranked by learning gains for students, the poorly rated trainer was actually among the best on staff. "In the end," said Rackham, "Level 1 smile sheets had given management the exact wrong impression" (quoted by Boehle, 2006).

Rackham's story was corroborated by the work of Roger Chevalier at Century 21 Real Estate. Chevalier and his team tracked graduates of each course based on *business results* (number of listings, sales, and commissions generated post-training). He found that a trainer who was rated in the bottom third of all trainers by his students on Level 1 satisfaction surveys was found to be one of the most effective in terms of how his students *performed* during the first three months after they graduated. According to Chevalier: "There turned out to be very little correlation between Level 1 evaluations and how well people actually did when they reached the field" (quoted by Boehle, 2006).

Why the discrepancy? Because the very things that make an instructor *effective* (requiring role play, challenging participants to think, giving candid feedback) do not necessarily make him or her popular.

Conversely, instructors and instructional designers can do things to boost reaction ratings like including superfluous humor, letting people out early, going easy on assessments, and including fun, but pointless, games, etc.) that are actually counterproductive to learning and application. Paying trainers or vendors a bonus for high reaction scores can actually lead to less-effective learning (Wick, Pollock, & Jefferson, 2010, p. 269).

The point is that "what you measure is what you get." Achieving the highest possible reaction ratings does not equate to delivering the highest possible value from training.

Probably the main reason that Level 1 reaction data are so common is that they are easy and inexpensive to collect—what Steve Lindia of Enterprise Organizational Development and Analytics for Bank of America calls "measures of convenience" (see Case in Point D6.4). Automated systems have made Level 1 assessments even easier and more ubiquitous. Most organizations feel "Level 1 reactions are all we can get and they are better than nothing." As Case in Point D6.3 illustrates, however, they may not necessarily be better than nothing. In any event, we can and should do better.

What Is Relevant? If reactions aren't a relevant outcome measure of corporate learning initiatives, what is? A relevant measure is one that directly relates to the business objective and that *the sponsor agrees is relevant.* The latter is important, given the subjective nature of worth (see page 251). That is why a discussion of the sponsor's criteria of success needs to be part of D1. The decision about which results to document should always be made in collaboration with the business sponsors. Learning professionals should not presume that they know what the customer wants or values.

The Coherence Principle of instructional design requires alignment between learning objectives and learning assessments (Washburn, 2010). The Coherence Principle applies equally to evaluations of learning initiatives as a whole. There should be complete agreement between the business goals and what is measured; D1 and D6 should be bookends for any learning initiative (Figure D6.4).

Depending on the goals of the program, relevant results can include observations, opinions, business metrics, examples, or estimates or a combination thereof (Table D6.1). For example, if the desired outcome is

FIGURE D6.4. THE PRACTICE OF D1 AND D6 ARE THE BOOKENDS THAT SUPPORT THE ENTIRE LEARNING INITIATIVE

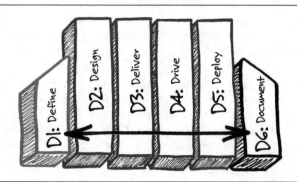

TABLE D6.1. KINDS OF EVIDENCE AND DATA COLLECTION METHODS

Kind of Data	Examples	Collection Methods
Business Metrics	Sales Production figures Quality index Lost days Turnover	Extract from business systems
Observations	Use of proper procedure Telephone etiquette Sales technique Coaching technique Self-assessment	Survey of observers Direct observation (overt or covert) Recordings Demonstrations/role play Simulations
Estimates	Time saved Number of times used Financial benefit	Surveys Interviews
Opinions	Quality of service Ratings Leadership efficacy Quality of presentation Amount of improvement Value of program	Surveys Internet reviews Rating services Interviews Focus groups Learning transfer support systems
Incidents	Citations Lawsuits Unfavorable reviews	Regulatory agency Legal department Internet
Examples	Success stories Critical incidents Achievements	Surveys Interviews Learning transfer support systems
Work Products	Business plans Computer code Writing	Audit Expert analysis Rating against rubric

to improve customer satisfaction, then you need, in some way, to measure changes in customer satisfaction, such as their opinion of the quality of the service they received. If the goal is to increase compliance with SOPs, then you need to measure compliance, and so forth. It is not always necessary or desirable to attempt to translate results into financial return or to calculate

ROI; it depends on whether the sponsors value such analyses (see Case in Point D6.6, page 251). A study at the Ashridge Business School, for example, found that learning professionals overestimate business leaders' interest in financial ROI as a measure of learning effectiveness (Charlton & Osterweil, 2005).

The relevant parameters to measure and appropriate data collection methods to use differ for different initiatives, but the principle is the same: you need to agree on the definition of success (for example, what does better customer service mean?) and then find (or develop) methods to measure it as reliably, accurately, and as efficiently as possible.

Bottom Line Relevance is the *sine qua non* of an effective evaluation. If the sponsor does not consider your metrics relevant to answering the question "Did it work?" then it does not matter how much data you have or how impressive the results: the evaluation is a failure.

 ## Practical Application

- Execute D1 well; relevance depends on it.
- Use common sense. Would a reasonable person agree that the measures you propose are directly relevant to answering the question "Did it work?"
- Check with your stakeholders to be sure that *they* agree that the proposed measures are relevant to what they want to see in terms of proof.

Case in Point D6.4
Connecting the Pipes

When Stephen Lindia was head of talent assessment at a financial services company, the CLO nicknamed him "The Plumber" because of his insistence on connecting up the talent metrics pipes, that is, making sure that the measures used in one part of HR—for example, learning—connected up with measures used elsewhere—like the competence model in performance management or employee measures on organizational assessments and culture surveys. He always wanted to know, "How does this fit into the larger talent development / employee lifecycle scheme?" He says he still finds it amazing when HR functions don't talk to each other and align their efforts and measures.

Steve, now executive, Enterprise Organizational Development and Analytics for Bank of America, shared with us some of his insights from fifteen years of assessing talent development efforts.

"You have to take a step back," he said, "and think about the behaviors you are really trying to change and measure them over time to be sure whatever experience you are providing is having an impact. You have to think about 'What are the key performance indicators? How do they impact business and client/customer outcomes?' You can't just rely on 'measures of convenience'—easily obtainable data like reaction scores, or the results of employee engagement surveys that are not directly linked to the content or objectives of the program or to specific organizational initiatives.

"You also have to think about what constitutes a valid comparison. It's tempting to compare the results from people in a program to 'everybody else,' but the people in the program aren't comparable to 'everybody else,' and doing so will almost surely obscure the real impact. You need to compare the results of people who participated in an initiative to people who are like them—same level, years of experience, geography, and so forth—to find out if it is really making a difference.

"When I think about evaluation, I think about 'What problem are we trying to solve here?' Once you can articulate the desired behavior changes in clear, simple terms, evaluation becomes a whole lot easier.

"We also need to provide information in a way that allows managers to take action. The most rewarding experience I have had was when I was reviewing the results of an assessment of new managers as part of our larger succession-planning process. I looked at the managers who scored in the bottom 10 percent of their cohort and I took the time to alert their managers to the fact that they had direct reports who were struggling. I pointed out the areas that needed attention and I suggested specific training they could recommend for their direct report.

"I actually had several senior managers call me and thank me for bringing it to their attention. They had seen the results, of course, but so much data goes across their desks that they needed help pulling out the critical points for action. It was important that they support their struggling young managers early in their careers. I was able to facilitate that by translating the data into useful information. I think that is where we can make a much greater contribution."

Credible The second criterion for an effective evaluation is that the data, analysis, and conclusions be considered *credible*—that is, trustworthy or believable—by the intended audience. Even if your measures are relevant and the results are impressive, the evaluation will fail to fulfill its purpose of guiding informed decisions if the decision-makers question the validity of the data, analysis, or conclusions.

You probably have a pretty good sense from your own experience of what credibility means. Every day you are bombarded with messages from people who want to sell you something, want you to vote for them, or otherwise want you to take some course of action that they recommend.

Some you believe, some you are skeptical about, and some you reject out of hand. The criteria that you use are probably similar to those your stakeholders will use in evaluating *your* recommendations.

Although you may not be aware of it, one of the key factors you use in assessing credibility is how well the results match what you already believe. People more readily accept data that support a point of view they already hold than information that challenges a preconceived notion (Kahneman, 2013). What that means for learning professionals is that those who are already skeptical about the value of training will be much more critical of your results than those who already support it. That probably explains Bersin's observation that the more the business is convinced you are aligned to their needs, the less data they demand (Bersin, 2008).

Remember that all evaluation is political, since money, power, reputation, and authority are always at stake (Patton, 2008). If the merit of the initiative was hotly debated at the proposal stage, you can be certain that the results will be more closely scrutinized and that the credibility of the evaluation is sure to be challenged.

Additional factors that contribute to the assessment of credibility include the amount of data, the reasonableness of the results, perceived bias, understandability, and the reputation of the evaluator.

> All evaluation is political.

Amount of Data   In general, the more subjects who can be included in a study, the higher its credibility. A recommendation based on the study of one hundred participants will be more credible that one based on half a dozen. There are two reasons: (1) the larger the size of the groups being compared, the more likely they are to be truly comparable and (2) the larger the group size, the more confident you can be that any differences can be attributed to the training as opposed to mere chance.

There is a point of diminishing return, however, at which the cost of gathering additional data outweighs its contribution to understanding and credibility. Rob Brinkerhoff suggested that we apply the legal standard: "beyond a reasonable doubt" (Brinkerhoff, 2006, p. 9). In other words, it is not necessary to prove the case for training's effectiveness beyond *any* doubt, but only to the level of rigor necessary to give management confidence in its decisions. Absolute proof is neither necessary nor attainable.

Reasonableness   A second factor that affects credibility is whether the results seem reasonable. In the vernacular, this is known as the "sniff test," or as the expression goes, "if it seems too good to be true, it probably is." That leads to an interesting paradox: the better your results, the less likely they are to be believed. Credibility is a special challenge for ROI studies, which often report returns that are many times higher than the business itself enjoys, and which are therefore considered suspect by business managers.

Likewise, if everything you report is always an outstanding success, your credibility will suffer. Not everything in business works, especially not the first time. You'll build credibility by reporting the failures and shortcomings as well as the successes.

Bias Credibility is undermined if the audience perceives bias in the way that the data were collected, analyzed, or reported. Take care, or obtain expert advice, in the selection of subjects and data to avoid common sources of bias such as:

- *Selection bias*—including only those likely to produce a positive response. For example, asking only those who did well to rate the initiative, or training only "high-potential" candidates and then comparing them to untrained, but more typical, employees.
- *Questionnaire or interviewer bias*—setting up data collection forms or processes that "lead the witness" by making it easier to answer in the affirmative.
- *Response bias*—always a concern with surveys, especially if the response rate is low. When only a small number of people surveyed respond, it raises the concern that they may not represent the group as a whole.
- *Reporter bias*—if employees think that their identities might somehow become known and that negative responses could result in reprisals (even if this is not true), they tend to "sugar coat" their responses or select "politically correct" answers. There is, for example, evidence that participants rate programs more highly when the facilitator is present, apparently for fear of hurting his or her feelings.

If the program is a political "hot potato," consider using independent raters or evaluators to enhance its credibility.

Intelligible Credibility also depends on understandability. In particular, no one likes to feel he or she is being "snowed." If people do not understand the way the evaluation was conducted or the terms used in the report, they will tend to discredit it. Avoid overly complex designs or arcane analytical techniques unless absolutely necessary, and employ terms and concepts familiar to business leaders; eschew learning jargon and avoid the technical terms of your art.

Reputation Last, whether or not the results will be believed depends on your personal credibility and that of the learning organization of which you are a part. As the Kouzes-Posner First Law of Leadership puts it: "If you don't believe the messenger, you won't believe the message" (Kouzes & Posner, 2008, p. 38). Other things being equal, a report from a source known to be trustworthy in the past will be considered more credible than the same report from an unknown or previously unreliable source.

Gaining a reputation for credibility takes time. Maintaining it requires vigilance: "Credibility is one of the hardest attributes to earn. And it is the most fragile of human qualities. It is earned minute by minute, hour by hour, month by month, and year by year. But it can be lost in very short order ... " (Kouzes & Posner, 1990, p. 24). To earn a place at the table, a voice in strategic discussions, and the resources needed to achieve its mission, the learning function must consistently deliver credible evidence of its impact.

> If you don't believe the messenger, you won't believe the message.

Practical Application

- Confirm with stakeholders that they consider your approach adequately rigorous, understandable, and unbiased.
- Work hard to build and maintain a reputation for credibility through forthrightness in reporting results—good and bad.

Compelling The third attribute of an effective evaluation is that it makes a *compelling* (persuasive) case for a particular course of action—for example, to continue, expand, revise, or discontinue a learning initiative. Even if your evaluation fulfils the first two criteria (relevance and believability), it could still fail if it is not sufficiently compelling.

So what makes a compelling case? At a minimum, it is unambiguous, memorable, impactful, and concise.

Unambiguous In our view, every evaluation should include unambiguous recommendations for action. If it is your program, you are the expert. You owe it to management to be clear about what you think the data say with respect to future actions. This is the concept of "completed staff work" developed by the military during World War II to ensure rapid and effective decisions. The late Francis Boyer, chief executive officer of Smith, Kline & French, summarized the concept this way in a memo to his operating committee: "Your job is to study, write, restudy, and rewrite until you have evolved a single proposed action—the best one of all you have considered."

Whether or not your recommendations are ultimately accepted, you will gain respect as a strategic thinker and person of action by being specific about what you think should be done based on the evidence at hand. Put your recommendations right up front in the executive summary. State them clearly and boldly and show how the results support them. Don't bury them at the end of the report; few will read that far. And don't undersell them by using "weasel words" like "it might be advisable to consider." Have an opinion; that's what you are paid for.

Memorable Managers, even more than the rest of us, are constantly bombarded by hundreds of (often conflicting) messages. Most are promptly forgotten; only a few stick. You need to make sure your message stands out so that it is remembered above all the background noise.

In their best-selling book, *Made to Stick*, Chip and Dan Heath (2008) set out to answer the question: "Why do some messages stick, while others die?" After reviewing a host of "sticky" messages—from urban legends to Aesop's fables—they concluded that memorable messages have six attributes (p. 16); they are

- Simple
- Unexpected
- Concrete
- Credible
- Emotional
- In story form

Those attributes are in sharp contrast to typical corporate presentations and reports, which tend to be complex, predictable, abstract, boring, and "just the facts, ma'am." Sullivan put it bluntly: "Most reports from development are too long, too dull, and just plain uninteresting" (Sullivan, 2005, p. 282).

> Most reports from development are too long, too dull, and just plain uninteresting.

To create a compelling evaluation:

1. *Simplify.* Make sure there is a simple, clear, and unambiguous recommendation that follows from the analysis.
2. *Surprise.* Find an unexpected element or angle, if there is one, or present the information in an unexpected way. Use the latter approach with caution; there is a fine line between presenting information in an interesting and unexpected manner and being perceived as "gimmicky" or too clever to be taken seriously.
3. *Use stories to make the results concrete, emotionally interesting, and memorable.* Even if you have solid quantitative data, include a few select stories to make them more memorable (see Case in Point D6.5).

Case in Point D6.5
Too Many Numbers; Not Enough Stories

We made the mistake of being too formal and too scientific in one of our early consulting engagements. We had been asked to help a company assess the impact of a major training/change-management initiative. To help gauge the impact, we asked participants to supply examples of the results—if any—that they had achieved by utilizing what they had been taught.

We collected hundreds of rich, detailed, specific, and concrete examples of ways in which the training had helped accelerate processes, eliminate waste, delight customers, and so forth. With the help of the finance department, we assigned credible dollar values to these and compared the results to the costs of the program. The ROI was impressive.

We prepared what we thought was a powerful set of charts, tables, and slides. *But we failed to include the stories.*

The presentation was eventually made to the board of directors of this Fortune 50 company. The board was positively impressed. But it is unlikely that any of them remembered a single graph or statistic the following day. Had we included a few of the remarkable stories of success, however, those stories would probably still be being told now, years later. Such is the power of stories.

The take-home message is that, while stories alone are not a substitute for quantitative analysis, they are the leavening that transforms an eminently forgettable presentation into a memorable one.

There is a tendency in business to dismiss stories as fluff, anecdote, and not serious enough to be included in reports or presentations to management (Denning, 2011). That is a serious mistake. It flies in the face of what is known about what makes things memorable. The identification, collection, validation, and use of stories "worthy of the telling" is the core of the Success Case Method for documenting results and "telling training's story" in a memorable and compelling way (Brinkerhoff, 2003, p. 19). Daniel Pink observed in *A Whole New Mind* (2006) that "Stories are easier to remember—because in many ways, they are *how* we remember" (p. 101).

Regardless of what other data collection and analytical methods you use, look for opportunities to include illustrative stories when reporting results. It will make the message more memorable. If there is an emotional element to the story, so much the better.

Impactful Impact is a matter of both substance and style. Substance is prerequisite; you have to show that the consequences of pursuing (or failing to pursue) your recommended course of action will have significant impact on those making the decision.

Style is about how you convey the message. That means communicating results in the language that your audience uses and highlighting the things they care about most. Don't undersell your findings. It is a tragedy to have great results and then to fail to communicate them in a manner that has impact.

> It is a tragedy to fail to effectively communicate great results.

Concise Finally, a compelling evaluation is short and to the point. People are more likely to be swayed by a short, sharp analysis than by a long and convoluted one. Be sure your chain of reasoning is easy to follow and include only as much detail as is necessary to make the case. Put everything else in the appendix or back-up slides.

 Practical Application

- Be sure your report is unambiguous, memorable, impactful, and concise.
- Use stories to bring the results to life.
- Evaluation is only as useful as it is actionable. Include specific recommendations based on the findings.

Efficient Efficiency is important in any business processes, but it must always be considered last. The efficiency of the evaluation only matters if the first three principles are satisfied. In other words, measuring the wrong thing is never efficient—no matter how cheaply or quickly it can be done. As Drucker put it: "There is nothing as useless as doing efficiently that which should not be done at all."

Efficiency matters because evaluation itself consumes time and resources. The cardinal rule is to never invest more in an evaluation than the value of the information it generates (Phillips, Phillips, & Aaron,

> There is nothing as useless as doing efficiently that which should not be done at all.

2013, p. 26). Evaluation should be done only to the level of rigor necessary to support the relevant business decision and satisfy the target audience. The goal is to produce relevant, credible, and compelling information at the lowest possible cost.

Efficiency is also important because results are time sensitive. "Part of the success of any evaluation effort is the timeliness of the evaluation's findings.... Sometimes these [time constraints] are related to the budgeting cycle, a deadline for a request for funding, a production and delivery launch date, or a 'need to know' before taking other actions. When evaluations miss these deadlines, their findings may be of limited use" (Russ-Eft & Preskill, 2009, p. 29).

Efficiency can be gained by using data that are already being collected as part of normal business operations, individual assessments, or as part of driving learning transfer. If additional aspects of performance have to be assessed, look for ways to automate data collection. For large programs, use a random sub-sample of the whole population; trying to include every participant drives up cost but, beyond a certain point, adds no additional insight. Find expert help if you are not familiar with the nuances and potential pitfalls of population sampling.

Surveys The advent of simple, inexpensive online survey tools has greatly increased the efficiency with which information can be collected from a large number of people. Unfortunately, these tools have also contributed to a decline in validity and credibility because surveys are often misused, poorly constructed, or badly administered.

For example, asking people to rate how much they think they learned, is *not* the same as actually measuring the amount of learning that took place (Level 2 assessment); it should not be represented as such (although at least one vendor does so). Similarly, asking people how valuable they *expect* the training will prove to be is not the same as evaluating how valuable the actual outcomes are.

How the survey is constructed—
the wording of the questions, number
of questions, choice of rating scales,
and so forth—profoundly affects its
validity, reliability, and completion
rate (Babbie, 2012). Phillips, Phillips,

> How a survey is constructed affects its validity and reliability.

and Aaron (2013) have provided a useful primer on survey design, administration, and analysis. If you are not yourself well-versed in sociologic
research methods, ask for assistance from your marketing research department or other experts in data collection and analysis.

Toward Standardization

The Center for Talent Reporting (CTR) is a non-profit, industry-led organization created to "improve and standardize the measurement, reporting,
and management of human capital to deliver significant business value"
(Center for Talent Reporting, 2014). The Center's goal is to develop a set
of commonly accepted definitions and principles for talent management
similar to the Generally Accepted Accounting Principles (GAAP) used to
provide standardized reporting and analysis of financial data. The rationale is that "the L&D profession would benefit tremendously from a set of
guiding principles and from standardizing the definition, calculation, use,
and reporting of volume and ratio measures" (Barnett & Vance, 2012).

To that end, the Center has developed standard definitions and reports
for six key HR processes, including learning and development initiatives.
The Center provides detailed guidance, sample reports, and templates
without charge through its website: *www.centerfortalentreporting.org*. The
core talent development reporting principles are very much in line with
the principles of D6, in particular the need to run learning efforts in a
more business-like fashion by:

- Identifying key company goals;
- Aligning learning to these goals and establishing the expected impact
  of these initiatives on business outcomes;
- Identifying, reporting, and managing the most important effectiveness
  and efficiency measures; and
- Managing key initiatives through the year to deliver planned results
  (Center for Talent Reporting, 2013).

While the logic of the approach is unassailable, and was effective
in managing Caterpillar University (Vance, 2010), it remains to be seen

whether it will become the generally accepted standard. Some early adopters have found great value in the approach—especially the emphasis on aligning learning with business needs—while others consider the approach overkill (Kuehner-Hebert, 2014).

The proposed measures of efficacy, in particular, are problematical. They are based on surveys completed at the end of the course. The authors assert that "although the respondent has not had time yet to apply the learning, he/she can provide intent to apply, and likely impact and value. Answers to these questions tend to be excellent indicators or predictors of actual Level 3 to 5 results" (Barnett & Vance, 2012, p. 31). We are not aware of well-designed studies that support that assertion, and we question whether participants' intent to apply and projections of "likely impact and value" will be accepted by management as credible measures of efficacy, especially for key or strategic programs.

Summary of Guiding Principles

No single approach can be used to evaluate the wide range of goals, types, and varieties of learning initiatives. Four principles, however, can be applied universally to guide evaluation. They are summarized in Table D6.2.

TABLE D6.2. ATTRIBUTES OF AN EFFECTIVE EVALUATION

Relevant	To the course objectives (desired business outcomes) To the customer
Credible	Sufficient data points Unbiased Reasonable Intelligible From a credible source
Compelling	Unambiguous Memorable Impactful Concise
Efficient	Fulfills the first three criteria Uses no more time and money than the decision is worth

The Evaluation Challenge

Despite dozens of books on the subject and innumerable seminars on how to measure learning's impact, evaluation remains a source of frustration for most learning organizations. More than one-third are dissatisfied with their evaluation efforts (ASTD Research, 2009). In a study by the Wharton School of Business, learning executives ranked "how to measure and communicate value" as their top challenge (Betoff, 2007).

We believe there are three main culprits:

- Worrying about *how* to measure before clearly defining *what* to measure;
- Confusing process metrics with business results; and
- Insisting on a do-it-yourself approach.

What to Measure

In our 6Ds Workshops, we like to ask people: "Which is the best measurement instrument?"

- A graduated cylinder
- A tape measure
- An electronic scale

The answer, of course, depends on whether you need to measure a length of a rope, the volume of a liquid, or the weight of an elephant. As obvious as that is when presented in this way, it is surprising how many discussions about evaluation among learning professionals deteriorate into a debate about the relative merits of Brinkerhoff's Success Case Method, Phillips's ROI, or Kirkpatrick's New World Model, without first specifying *what* has to be measured.

Indeed, the most common mistake we see learning organizations make is confusing *what* with *how*. As soon as the topic of evaluation comes up, they say, "But we don't know how to measure it!" before they even define what "it" is. In our experience, we have found that once you can clearly state *what* you'd like to measure, you can usually find someone to help you or some method that you can adapt. But until you are clear about what needs to be measured, any discussion of *how* to measure the results is putting the cart before the horse.

> Don't worry about *how* until you are clear about *what*.

FIGURE D6.5.   THE LOGIC MAP OF A LEARNING INITIATIVE MAKES EVIDENT THE OUTCOMES THAT MUST BE MEASURED AND THE KEY OUTPUT VARIABLES

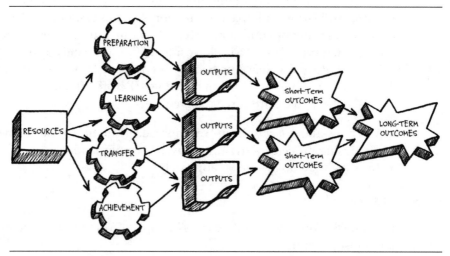

What needs to be measured is dictated by the logic model for the initiative (Figure D6.5), which lays out the:

- Expected outcomes and
- Assumed relationships between activities, outputs, and outcomes.

Expected Outcomes The importance of knowing the expected outcomes is obvious: you cannot meaningfully evaluate whether an initiative was successful unless you have first answered the "What are we trying to accomplish?" question. The outcomes you were trying to achieve are, ultimately, what you need to measure.

Essential Outputs You will also want to measure a number of the key outputs (process metrics) that the logic model shows as vital to achieving the desired outcomes. For example, if completing an e-learning module is considered essential preparation for a hands-on learning experience, then it may be important to track the number of participants who actually completed it in order to understand whether this part of the process is working. Keep in mind, however, that *outputs*—the number of people trained, amount learned, modules completed, and so forth—are not the same as *outcomes*—the changes in behavior and results the business was seeking (see below).

FIGURE D6.6.   VALUE IS BOTH SUBJECTIVE AND SITUATIONAL

What the Stakeholders Value   Finally, *what* to measure depends on what the stakeholders value. Evaluation, as its name implies, is an assessment of *value* or worth. But worth is not a universally agreed-on metric like a kilogram or a joule. The same object has different values to different people—or even to the same person at different times. For example, the *measure* of a 10-meter-long rope is constant, but its *value* is situational: high value if you need to rappel eight meters, worthless if you need to descend twenty. Likewise, if you are a wine connoisseur, you may be willing to pay top dollar (indicating your sense of its value) for a vintage Bordeaux. But the same wine would have zero value to a colleague who does not drink alcohol, regardless of how highly the *Wine Spectator* rated it (Figure D6.6).

> The same object or quantity has different values to different people.

The point is, you need to discuss with your stakeholders how *they* define value before you can decide what you need to measure. One senior management team may insist on a financial ROI analysis, while another may find no value in such an approach (see Case in Point D6.6).

Case in Point D6.6
Ask First

A large company in the automotive industry spent over $100,000 to evaluate the ROI of a high-priority learning initiative. The results were impressive, suggesting a many-fold return. The training department was elated ... that is, until they presented the results to the management team. The chief financial officer took one look at the analysis and said, "This is not how I define ROI at all. These results are worthless."

The point of the story is not whether the specific methodology they used was right or wrong *in the abstract*. The point is that it was not the right approach *in their situation*. Before embarking on the study, the training professionals should have asked the management team whether they would consider the proposed evaluation relevant, credible, and compelling.

The voice of the customer will always make itself heard; it is just a question of when. Far better to ask the stakeholders *before* you commit the time, funds, and effort to conduct a study, than *afterward*, when it is too late.

Practical Application

- Always identify *what* needs to be measured before spending any time worrying about *how*.
- Be certain you measure what your stakeholders actually define as value, not just what you *assume* they value.
- Include key factors in the transfer climate as part of the evaluation.

Outputs Versus Outcomes

Einstein famously remarked that not everything that can be counted counts. What that means in relation to program evaluation is that just because you can put a number on something doesn't mean that it answers the question of whether or not the learning initiative was worthwhile.

There are two broad categories of things that the training department can measure: outputs (process metrics) and outcomes (Table D6.3). Process metrics—things like the number of people trained, the cost, and their reactions—are important for managing the learning function and for identifying opportunities for improvement. They are not, however, the *outcomes* that are *of interest to the business* (Figure D6.7) and they should not be represented as such.

Output measures alone are not sufficient because it is impossible to assess the *worth* of activities without also knowing whether those activities contributed to a successful outcome (one that fulfilled the business need).

> Document the outcomes that are of interest to the business.

For example, suppose that employees completed twice as many e-learning modules this year as last year (a 100 percent increase in output). That is a good thing *if, but only if,* completing the e-learning modules contributed

TABLE D6.3. EXAMPLES OF INTERNAL LEARNING PROCESS METRICS (OUPUTS) VERSUS BUSINESS OUTCOMES

Outputs	Outcomes
number of participants	documented increases in positive behaviors
courses taught	increased productivity
e-learning programs developed	higher quality/fewer errors
number of courses completed	improved customer satisfaction
hours of instruction	greater employee engagement
costs per program, participant, or hour	reduced accidents and downtime
post-test scores	shorter time to productivity
satisfaction ratings	more effective presentations
business alignment	lower costs of production
assessments completed	increased sales effectiveness
number of coaching interactions	faster time to market

FIGURE D6.7. MEASURES OF OUTPUTS, SUCH AS REACTION AND KNOWLEDGE GAINED, ARE NOT OUTCOMES OF INTEREST TO THE BUSINESS

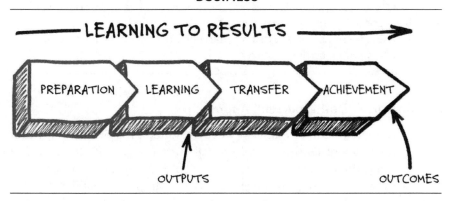

to better performance. If, on the other hand, there was no demonstrable outcome (change in performance) as a result of the e-learning, then twice as much time was wasted this year as last. That is no cause for celebration. As Van Adelsberg and Trolley (1999) observed: "If you are spending just $1 on training but getting no business value in return, then you are over-spending" (p. 75).

Likewise, an end-of-course knowledge test may be important to meet a regulatory requirement or to ensure that the material can at least be recalled, but learning as such—Level 2 measurement—is not the business objective; it is simply a milestone on the logic map to improved perfor-mance. Perhaps for this reason, the U.S. Army Center for Lessons Learned doesn't even consider that something has been learned *unless it results in a change in behavior* (Darling & Parry, 2001). Even if participants are able to answer yes to the "Can I?" question, "knowledge of what needs to be done frequently fails to result in action or behavior consistent with that knowledge" (Pfeffer & Sutton, 2000, p. 4).

It does not matter how much you spend, or how busy you are, or even how much people learned. What matters is that the training you provide produces a worthy result (value in excess of cost). Proving that requires assessing the outcomes defined in D1, not just the activity and outputs.

 Practical Application

- Measure both the outcomes and the process's outputs, but do not confuse them.
- Report outcome measures as results.
- Use process measures to manage the learning function, gauge efficiency, and iden-tify opportunities for improvement.

Insisting on a "Do-It-Yourself" Approach

A final impediment to the effective evaluation of learning initiatives is the tendency of learning professionals to try to "go it alone" and do every-thing themselves. Evaluation is a professional skill. There are numerous full-length books on the subject (for example, Russ-Eft & Preskill, 2009), university courses on evaluation, and even a certification process for eval-uators (George Washington University, 2014). It is unreasonable to expect every learning professional to be expert in evaluation as well as in adult learning, instructional design, facilitation, and a host of other skills.

Unless you or someone in your department has specific expertise in evaluation, get help. "If you don't have the training or experience to do valid measurements, involve others in your organization who are trained in measurement and statistics. You can usually find them in the quality department" (Rosenbaum, 2014). Not only will engaging subject-matter experts produce superior evaluations, but you will deepen your own understanding and expertise by working alongside them.

Practical Application

- Don't feel you have to be an expert in everything; seek evaluation guidance from market research or process improvement experts.
- Start simple, and learn by doing.

 ## A Six-Step Process of Evaluation

There are six steps in the practice of D6: Document Results (Figure D6.8):

1. Confirm the outcomes that really matter.
2. Create a project plan.
3. Collect and analyze the data.
4. Report the findings.
5. Sell the sizzle.
6. Implement improvements.

 ### 1. Confirm the Outcomes That Matter

Deciding *what* to measure is the single most important decision in the process of evaluating learning initiatives. Ideally, the definition of success should have been part of the D1 discussion with the sponsor. If you used

FIGURE D6.8. A SIX-STEP PROCESS FOR EVALUATING RESULTS

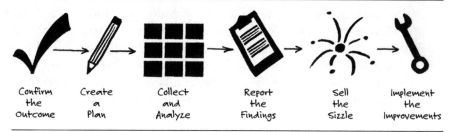

Confirm the Outcome → Create a Plan → Collect and Analyze → Report the Findings → Sell the Sizzle → Implement the Improvements

FIGURE D6.9. OUTCOMES PLANNING WHEEL

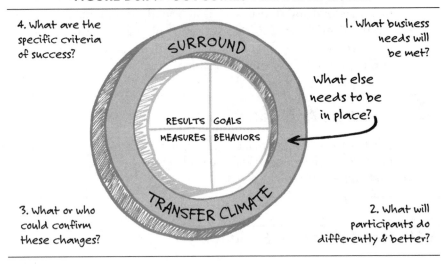

4. What are the specific criteria of success?

1. What business needs will be met?

What else needs to be in place?

RESULTS | GOALS

MEASURES | BEHAVIORS

SURROUND

TRANSFER CLIMATE

3. What or who could confirm these changes?

2. What will participants do differently & better?

the Outcomes Planning Wheel (Figure D6.9), then in D6 deciding what to measure consists simply of reviewing your summary of the discussion and, if the program has evolved, reconfirming criteria for success. If the outcome criteria have not already been specified, then use logic modeling (Frechtling, 2007; Parskey, 2014; Ridge, 2013), the GAPS! methodology (Robinson & Robinson, 2008), a six sigma tool like quality functional deployment (QFD) (Islam, 2006), or some other method to identify the most important outcomes. The key to success is to not start collecting data until you know how the sponsors define success and thus what you need to measure.

Of course, for any intervention, many things could be measured. The challenge is to reduce the universe of things that *could* be measured to the "critical few" that *will* be measured.

> More is not necessarily better.

More is not necessarily better. The more parameters you track, the more it costs (in time as well as money), the more you have to explain, and the more likely that you will encounter something that you cannot explain. For those reasons, we disagree with the suggestion that you need to assess all four Kirkpatrick levels sequentially. While building a "chain of evidence" makes sense in theory, it is costly, cumbersome, and unnecessary. That is why the New World Kirkpatrick Model puts much less emphasis on Levels 1 and 2 and focuses on measuring the "return on expectations"—Levels 3 and 4. If you can demonstrate that relevant outcomes were achieved, you don't need to also prove that participants learned something; it's obvious that they did.

On the other hand, you do not want to "put all your eggs into one basket" by measuring only one parameter. Unexpected problems with data collection or analysis can occur in the course of any study, so be sure to have some complementary or alternative measures in place. Use the flow chart in Figure D6.10 to help you.

You also need to decide what output measures—beyond the number of people trained and so forth—you will need to assess in order to gauge efficiency and identify opportunities for improvement. Review the

FIGURE D6.10. FLOW CHART TO HELP SELECT WHAT TO MEASURE

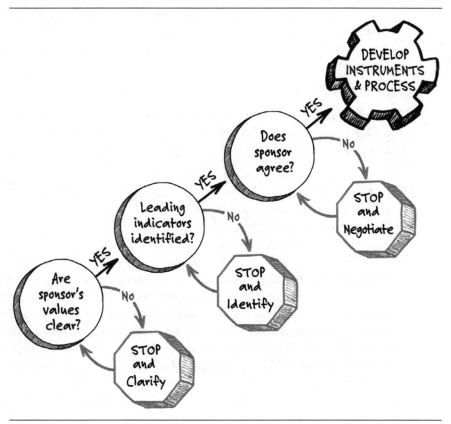

logic model or value chain for key dependencies that will impact the outcomes.

One approach that we have used with success is to write up the executive summary of the evaluation *before conducting it.* Share the draft with the sponsors to confirm that such an analysis will address the outcomes that matter most to them. We leave the results section blank, of course, but we describe the methodology, the kinds of data collected and how, and the sort of conclusions we expect to be able to draw. Seeing it written out in summary form helps the sponsors decide whether it will meet their needs.

Practical Application

- Select a small number of outcome metrics that will answer the question: "Is the initiative working?"
- Select a small number of outputs (process metrics) that will answer the question: "What parts of the process can be further improved?"

---

2. Create a Project Plan

Once you have selected the critical few measures to evaluate, it is time to roll up your sleeves and create the detailed evaluation project plan. That includes:

A. Deciding *when* to collect the data
B. Choosing comparators
C. Selecting data-collection techniques
D. Planning the analysis
E. Creating a project timeline

A. Decide When to Collect Data Deciding *when* to collect the data is almost as important as deciding *what* to collect. Since D6 is about documenting business-relevant outcomes, that means that relevant results can only be collected *after* participants have had enough time to transfer their new knowledge and skills to their jobs and apply them long enough for the results to be evident. For some types of training—such as customer service or manufacturing-machine operation—demonstrable improvement might be manifest within days. For others—such as strategic selling, management, or leadership training—it might be weeks or months before the desired outcomes can be documented.

Time is of the essence. The sooner the impact can be assessed, the more useful the data are for deciding whether to expand, continue, revise, or discontinue the initiative. For programs that require a long time before

> Deciding when is almost as important as deciding what.

results are manifest, look for leading indicators. The concept of leading indicators stems from Kaplan and Norton's groundbreaking work on the "Balanced Scorecard" (Kaplan & Norton, 1992). The idea is that forward-looking indicators—such as customer satisfaction scores and the number of new products in the pipeline—are better predictors of a company's future performance than financial statements, which reflect only past performance.

The "leading indicators" of training success are changes in behavior (Figure D6.11), since people must do their jobs in new and better ways if they are to improve their performance. While Gilbert (1978) was quick to point out that the real goal is *accomplishment,* not behavior per se, changes in behavior necessarily precede changes in performance. In many cases, demonstrating a meaningful change in behavior is all the evidence of effectiveness that management requires, since—as illustrated in the logic model—they have already accepted the correlation between specific behaviors and business outcomes.

FIGURE D6.11.   CHANGES IN BEHAVIOR PRECEDE CHANGES IN RESULTS

LEADING INDICATORS:

Successful training & development → More effective or efficient actions & behaviors → Improved business results

David Brennan, CEO of AstraZeneca, explained it this way:

"Obviously, people want to quantify business results. I think that, while that is an important measure, the kinds of things that are much more measurable are the quality of the behavioral outcomes of the programs.

"If we believe that coaching is an important part of the performance management process, and we put coaching programs in place, then what we want to measure is the quality of the coaching—not as perceived by the coaches, but by the people being coached.

"If we say that demonstrating behaviors about the team's passion for winning is important to us, then what we have to do is ping the environment to see whether or not those behaviors are being demonstrated by people and that they are being reinforced by management. There are other, harder measures you can put in place … but in terms of the operating environment of the organization, evaluation needs to be much more focused on the behavioral outcomes that you're driving for."

Logic models usually differenti-ate between short-term, and long-term outcomes (Frechtling, 2007). Behavior changes are shorter-term outcomes. Besides their earlier avail-ability, the other advantage of using

> Evaluation needs to focus more on behavioral outcomes.

changes in behavior as indicators of effectiveness is that they are less affected by factors other than learning and performance support.

It can be very difficult to isolate the effect of training on broad business metrics like sales, retention, or brand reputation. So, while the ideal mea-sure of a program designed to boost sales would seem at first blush to be sales performance, the problem is that sales revenues are influenced by a host of factors in addition to training, such as advertising effectiveness, sea-sonality, competitors' actions, manufacturing issues, and so forth. If sales increase, then every department will try to claim the credit. If they don't, it is training's fault.

Evaluating changes in behavior provides more direct evidence of the contribution of learning. Suppose that the goal of an initiative was to boost sales by teaching sales representatives to ask more probing questions before launching into their sales pitch. An early outcome measure of success, then, would be an increase in the number and quality of the questions that representatives ask in real-life discussions with customers. Documenting a significant increase in the desired behavior would be a more credible indicator of the impact of training and performance support than the sales results, because so many other factors influence the latter.

 ## Practical Application

- Evaluate as soon as results are expected to be evident to find out whether the initiative is working.
- If the sponsor agrees, use behaviors as outcome measures because they are available sooner and are less affected by extraneous factors.

B. Choose Comparators Claiming that a learning initiative improved performance begs the question: "Compared to what?" Is the claim that people's performance was better after training than before? Or is the claim that those who were trained performed better than those who weren't? One way or another, evaluation always implies some form of comparison.

So part of designing (or contracting for) a program evaluation is to decide what comparisons will be made to demonstrate effectiveness. The decision is important because, any time you make comparisons, you may be challenged to show that they are legitimate.

Comparisons can be historical or contemporaneous. A typical historical comparison would be to measure each person's performance before and again after training. Another approach is to ask people to compare someone's current performance to his or her past performance. This is the approach used by Goldsmith and Morgan (2004) to demonstrate the importance of follow-up.

> Evaluation always implies some form of comparison.

Because each person serves as his or her own "control," an historical comparison avoids many potential sources of bias that can arise when comparing two different groups of people. It has high face validity: if the great majority of employees perform better after training, that is a pretty compelling argument that the learning added value.

The approach is not perfect, however. People's performance tends to improve with experience anyway, so that some or all of the improvement in the second observation might simply reflect the benefit of greater experience, rather than the learning initiative as such. Likewise, approaches that ask people to compare someone's present performance to his or her past performance rely on demonstrably fallible human memory. Last, improvement over time may be the result of changes in the environment that have nothing to do with learning. Nevertheless, before-after comparisons are generally a good choice because they are well understood and accepted by business leaders.

Contemporaneous case-control evaluations obviate many of the concerns about historical comparisons. A case-control approach is the classic experimental laboratory study in which the performance of an experimental group (in this case, people who received training) is compared to a similar control (untrained) group. Ideally, subjects would be assigned at random to one group or the other to avoid any systematic differences (bias). However, such rigor is rarely practical in corporate training programs and probably unnecessary for practical purposes, so long as an effort is made to be sure the two groups are similarly comprised.

Consult a textbook on evaluation (for example, Russ-Eft & Preskill, 2009) or on experimental design (Ryan, 2007) for a more thorough discussion. The key point is that for an evaluation to be credible, any comparisons must be perceived as legitimate. When bias cannot be completely eliminated, acknowledge it and its potential impact on the conclusions.

Much has been written about the importance of isolating the effect of training. Our perspective is similar to that of Brinkerhoff (2006). We feel that trying to calculate the percent of improvement that can be ascribed to the training is an exercise in futility. In the first place, the effects of training can never be disassociated from the transfer climate. When training succeeds, it is the result of training *and* support for transfer; when it fails, it is usually a breakdown in the transfer process. The two are inseparable. "When we evaluate programs or interventions, we are in effect evaluating the impact of performance systems . . . ." (Binder, 2010).

Hence, we do not recommend trying to isolate the impact of training by having participants estimate the percent that was due to the learning. The reliability of such estimates has never been rigorously demonstrated; using them potentially undermines the credibility and usefulness of the whole exercise.

Such considerations are not merely academic. The purpose of evaluation is to support informed decision making. The choice of the wrong metrics or wrong comparators can lead to erroneous conclusions

> The purpose of evaluation is to support informed decision making.

and, therefore, detrimental decisions. An evaluation that overestimates the true value of a program would lead to a wasteful decision to continue it. Conversely, a poorly designed evaluation that underestimates the true value of an effective program could contribute to a tragic decision to scale back or eliminate it.

Practical Application

- Decide to what you will compare the results from the learning initiative.
- Don't try to calculate a percent of learning's contribution; it is not particularly relevant, credible, or useful.

C. Select Data-Collection Techniques How will you collect the data on the groups and metrics you've selected? As always, "The devil is in the details." *What* you have chosen to measure determines the evaluation's relevance; *how* you measure affects its credibility. Thus, you need to be sure that the client agrees not only with *what* you propose to evaluate, but also *how* you propose to gather the information.

For example, the sponsor might agree that a certain change in behavior constitutes success for a particular initiative. But there are a number of different ways that a behavior can be documented. Will self-reports ("I am doing much more of that") suffice? Is a supervisor's confirmation required? Or is it necessary to have a third party observe and count or score the behaviors?

Similarly, it may be that the sponsor wants to see a financial analysis of the impact. How rigorous does that analysis need to be? Will estimates from the participants themselves suffice, or must the analysis come from the finance department? The "correct" answers to these questions are situational; they depend on what is feasible with the resources available *and* what is acceptable to the target audience.

There are five basic kinds of data you can collect: business metrics, observations, estimates, opinions, and examples. Once you are clear about

TABLE D6.4. KINDS OF EVIDENCE AND DATA-COLLECTION METHODS

Kind of Data	Examples	Collection Methods
Business Metrics	Product sales Employee retention First time quality Reportable accidents Repeat purchases	Extract from business information systems
Observations	Customer interaction Response to inquiry Sales technique Employee interactions Task performance	Direct observation (overt or covert) Demonstrations/role play Simulation
Estimates	Frequency of use Time saved Financial benefit	Surveys Interviews
Opinions	Quality of support Leadership Net promoter score Teamwork Quality of work product	Surveys Interviews Focus groups Expert review
Examples	Achievement stories Critical incidents Work products	Surveys Interviews Review of submitted plans, reports, etc.

to which category the outcomes you want to measure belong, then the ways in which to collect them follow, since there are a limited number of methods for each (Table D6.4).

Business Metrics Business metrics are data that the company routinely collects as part of its ongoing operations. These include everything from sales (items and dollars) to number of errors or cost of scrap, manufacturing costs, lead times, out of stocks, shrink, forecast accuracy, and so on. If an existing business metric meets the criteria of a relevant outcome for the program—and is one that won't be completely obfuscated by other factors—by all means use it. Business metrics have the advantage of being immediately credible and relevant to the business. Since they are already being collected, there is no additional cost to gather them.

FIGURE D6.12. THE MOST RELEVANT AND RELIABLE MEASURES OF BEHAVIOR ARE DIRECT OBSERVATIONS

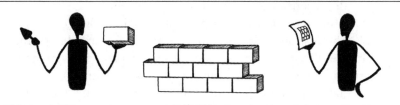

If you plan to use business metrics as an outcome measure, just be sure that you can gain access to them at the level of detail you need (individual participant). You'll need that degree of specificity in order to make before-after or trained-to-untrained comparisons. Meet with IT, or finance, or whoever owns the data, and explain what you need, for which employees, and covering what period. Use pseudonyms or coded numbers for participants if privacy is an issue.

Observations For training programs in which the outcome of interest is a change in on-the-job behavior and actions, the most relevant and credible data are direct observations (Figure D6.12). These range from self-observations on the low end of reliability to performance checklists completed by trained observers on the high end, such as the use of "mystery shoppers" to rate customer service (Donohoe, Beech, Bell-Wright, Kirkpatrick, & Kirkpatrick, 2014). A mid-level of rigor will usually suffice, such as asking a customer "Were you greeted when you came into the store?" or "Did the salesperson adequately address your questions or concerns?" Other examples would include asking managers, peers, or direct reports about specific behaviors. A variety of formats can be used, including counts, rating scales, or requests for specific examples.

For observational data to be valid, evaluators need to have had the opportunity to personally observe the behavior, they have to clearly understand what you are asking, and the timing must be such that they can remember accurately. Reliability can be increased by providing raters with rubrics that spell out what to look for and how to rate it (Goodrich, 1997).

Estimates Estimates are widely used in business for planning purposes: "How long do you think it will take?" "What is your sales projection for next quarter?" Estimates are sometimes co-opted for use in evaluation, such as: "How many times did you use something you learned from the program?" "How much do you think it was worth?"

Because they are estimates, however, they necessarily are less reliable than business metrics or direct observations. For estimates to be credible, the respondents need to have sufficient knowledge and expertise to provide a reasonable estimate. A claims processor can probably reliably estimate how long it takes her to process a claim. On the other hand, her estimate of how much money the claims processing training program saved the company is likely to be wildly inaccurate.

If you decide to use estimates as one of the outcome measures in your evaluation, be sure your client agrees, and then design a questionnaire or interview guide that asks people to provide estimates that are appropriate to their perspective and expertise.

Opinions Opinions, or perceptions, would seem to have the lowest credibility of all. Yet there are times when opinions are both the most credible and most critical outcomes to measure. Remember that people make decisions based on their *perceptions,* not on objective reality. Hence, customers' opinions are leading indicators of their willingness to use your services again or recommend your firm to others. Opinion data are usually collected by survey or interviews, typically through some sort of rating scale.

You could, for example, ask people to rate how likely they are to recommend a product or service on a score of 0 to 10. Indeed, the developers of the Net Promoter Score® (NPS), which is based on responses to that question, claim that it is the single

> Sometimes opinions are the most important and most credible outcomes.

most important predictor of a company's future growth (Reichheld, 2003). Sylvain Newton, of GE's Crotonville Leadership Center, used the NPS to gauge how well a leadership development initiative was meeting stakeholders' needs as well as to drive continuous improvement (Newton, 2014).

Expert Opinion A special subcategory of opinion measures is "expert opinion"—assessment of an outcome by someone "skilled in the art." Expert opinion can be an appropriate measure for initiatives that seek to improve a "work product," such as presentations, computer code, or strategic plans. Only people skilled in the art of presentations, software, and strategic planning are in a position to adequately judge whether the quality of the output was improved by the learning initiative. When the desired outcome is an improved work product, then the measurement strategy is to find a person (or, if possible, an objective rating system) able to render an informed opinion on the quality of the output.

Examples A fifth category that, to some extent, cuts across the others is case examples—narratives in story form about what participants accomplished as a result of a learning or developmental opportunity. There is growing recognition in business of the power of stories to illuminate, educate, motivate, and create lasting impressions (Denning, 2011).

Stories are at the heart of the Success Case Method developed by Rob Brinkerhoff (Figure D6.13). The process is straightforward. At an appropriate time after training (depending on its nature and objectives), the participants are polled. They are asked whether they have used specific aspects of the program and to rate their success from "none" to "clear success with measurable outcomes" (Brinkerhoff, 2003, p. 102). A sample of those who claim they have had real success is interviewed to gather the details, confirm the claims, and, if appropriate, document or estimate the financial impact.

A sample of those who report no success is also interviewed to understand why they were unable to achieve successful outcomes. The impediments they identify are targets for continuous improvement. Comparing the value created by the percent of successful participants to the percent

FIGURE D6.13. BRINKERHOFF'S SUCCESS CASE METHOD

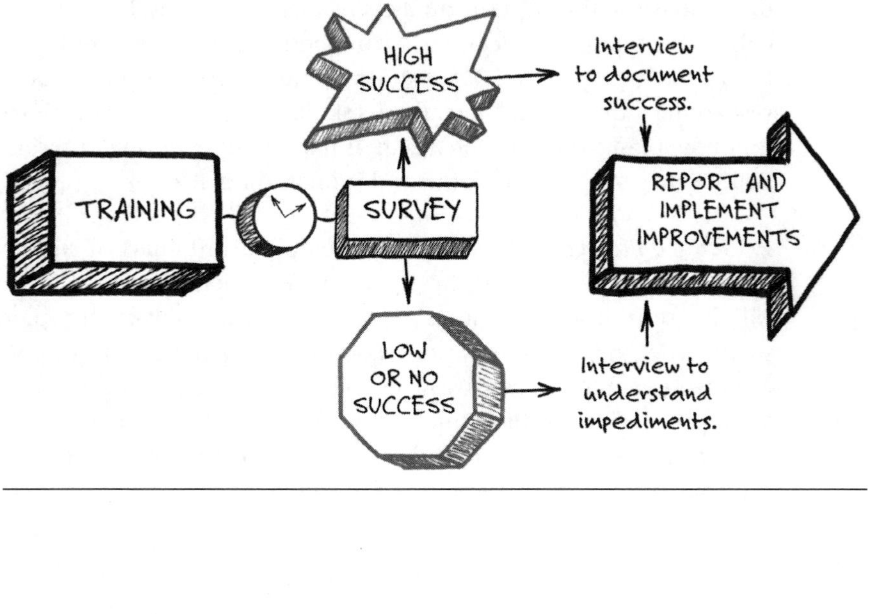

who reported no success helps management appreciate the true cost of learning scrap and how much potential value is being "left on the table."

Success stories are both memorable and compelling. A critical caveat when using this approach, however, is to be sure to always independently confirm the cases that you plan to use as exemplars. If the participant

> Success case stories are memorable and compelling.

reports that she used the training to land an important new account, check the sales records or contact the client. If another claims he saved a key employee who was about to quit, check with the employee. Why? Because it is human nature to overstate accomplishments and nothing will destroy your credibility more quickly than to present an example of learning's success that later turns out to be greatly exaggerated.

 Practical Application

- Select the data collection method that best matches the expected outcomes and is most likely to produce relevant, credible, and compelling data.
- Use routinely tracked business metrics when possible for their credibility and cost savings.
- Include compelling and memorable examples in story form.

D. Plan the Analysis An important aspect of designing an effective evaluation is to think through the analysis *in advance.* That is, how will the data be collated, encoded if necessary, "crunched," and summarized? What statistics (if any) will you use? Consult with your company's statisticians, market researchers, or external consultants skilled in evaluation before you implement the plan to be sure the design is likely to have enough power to detect a difference and yield reliable and unbiased results.

E. Create a Project Timeline Finally, create a Gantt chart or similar project timeline that includes all the key activities (when surveys and reminders will be sent, follow-up interviews scheduled, analysis completed, and so forth). There are numerous commercial software programs, such as Microsoft Project, to assist you. If you are new to evaluation, or are using an approach for the first time, it would be smart to have an expert review your plan. There may be ways to streamline the process or strengthen the analysis.

Practical Application

- Think through how you plan to analyze the results BEFORE you start collecting them.
- Seek expert help to ensure the data *can* be analyzed.

3. Collect and Analyze the Data

Once the evaluation plan has been reviewed and agreed on, it is time to execute. Someone has to be assigned the responsibility for managing the project and implementing the plan, because even a relatively simple design—for example, gathering opinions from internal customers—has a fair number of moving parts.

If no dedicated resource for project management is available, you'll have to manage the project yourself or contract it out. In either case, don't underestimate the importance of doing it right; poor execution is a more common cause of failure in business than poor planning (Bossidy, Charan, & Burck, 2002).

Gather the Data If you are using a newly developed questionnaire or data-collection system, pilot it first to be sure the questions are understandable and the answers are being correctly recorded (Phillips, Phillips, & Aaron, 2013). If you are using interviews, take precautions to ensure consistency and impartiality, as discussed in texts on qualitative research like Babbie (2012). Other than that, gathering the data is mainly a matter of periodically monitoring the incoming information to be sure that response rates are adequate and that the systems are working.

Analyze the Data Once the data have been collected, the most exciting phase begins: analyzing the results to see to what extent the program delivered on its promise. The process involves comparing one set of results (for example, post-training) to another (for example, pre-training or untrained). If the data are quantitative (counts, rating scales, dollars, etc.), then the analysis will require some level of statistical analysis to confirm that any differences are not just random variation. If the results are qualitative, then they will need to be analyzed for themes and examples. It is also important to analyze the key process outputs to identify opportunities for improvement. For example: Were managers actively engaged? Was the learning perceived as relevant? Was the performance support utilized?

Keep in mind that there is always the possibility that the evaluation will show that the program produced no demonstrable benefit or that the benefit was too small to justify its cost. The time to decide what to do with nega-

> There is always the possibility that the evaluation will show no demonstrable benefit.

tive findings is *before* the evaluation is begun. Prior to putting the plan into action, answer the question: "Suppose the evaluation is not favorable, what will we do?" Once the data have been collected, they cannot be "buried" or ignored. You have both a moral and management responsibility to report negative as well as positive findings and to make a recommendation consistent with the data: fix the program or kill it if it is truly "a dog" (see page 71).

Negative results are still valuable. The possibility that the outcome won't be favorable should not deter learning organizations from asking hard questions. As Kevin Wilde, CLO of General Mills, explained to us: "Some studies did not pan out, some did. But unless I am asking, I do not know exactly where the value is. By doing this kind of work, I am interacting with the CEO in a very business-like way that he expects out of all the other business leaders—getting results, producing insights. Some things work out, some things do not. You have to have the courage to ask and figure it out" (Wilde, 2006).

Practical Application

- Consider how you will analyze the data before initiating the evaluation.
- Think through, in advance, how you will handle negative findings or evidence of no effect.

4. Report the Findings to Management

Once you have the results—good, bad, or indifferent—you need to report them in a manner that leads to informed decision making. Communicating the results should serve two purposes. The first is to report to management; the second is to build the learning brand (what we refer to in the next section as "selling the sizzle").

Sponsors want to know what value they received in return for the time and resources invested in the learning initiative. They need relevant,

FIGURE D6.14. MANAGEMENT HAS FOUR CHOICES BASED ON THE RESULTS OF THE EVALUATION

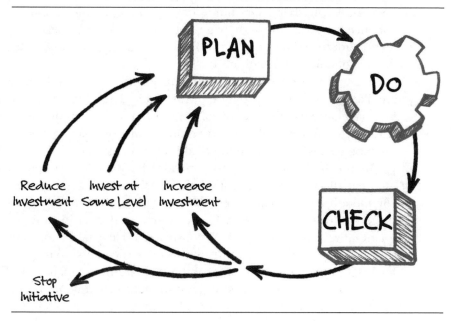

credible, and compelling evidence to help them decide on an appropriate course of action (Figure D6.14). Of course, no matter how good your results are, management will want to know how you plan to do even better in the future. You never can rest on your laurels for long in business.

The report to management should be a concise, fact-filled, no-nonsense analysis with recommendations. It should be written in language familiar to business leaders and should eschew learning jargon (such as "Level 3," etc.). Sullivan (2005) put it plainly: "History has proven that managers will not learn your language or shift to your focus, so it is you who must adapt" (p. 283).

A similar caveat applies to the use of statistics. Most analyses will require some level of statistical analysis to show that the results are due to more than chance. Knowledge of and faith in statistics varies widely among business leaders, however. Don't try to dazzle them with complex analyses. Whatever you do, be sure *you* can confidently discuss any analysis you present. Nothing undermines your credibility like being unable to explain something that you, yourself, are presenting.

Finally, get to the point quickly. Business leaders tend to be "drivers"; they have neither the time nor patience to wade through pages of text or dozens of slides trying to find the actionable information. If they

> Never present anything that you cannot confidently explain.

cannot find the meat of the matter in the first paragraph or two, they are likely to set the report aside or discard it. Therefore, always make the first page an executive summary. It is all that many senior managers will read. State the key findings and recommendations clearly, concisely, and unambiguously; don't keep the reader in suspense.

In the body of the report, provide the data that support the recommendations in the executive summary, including the design of the complete learning experience, the evaluation methodology, data tables, success stories, and analyses. Business managers deal in numbers. Show quantitative information in well-constructed, clear tables and graphs. Be sure to acknowledge the contribution of participants' managers and be forthright about any limitations of the evaluation or conclusions. Explain your "lessons learned" and your plans to make subsequent programs even more effective. Remember to include illustrative examples in story form (see page 244).

Although a formal written report to senior leadership is necessary, it isn't sufficient. To make sure that your message is heard among all the competing noise, it must be reinforced. If possible, ask to give a short presentation of the results in person. Get to the point quickly; use only as much time and as many slides as absolutely necessary; deliver the message succinctly; and finish in less than the allotted time.

 ## Practical Application

- Report the findings to management clearly and concisely.
- Summarize the results and recommendations for actions in a one-page executive summary.

 ### 5. Sell the Sizzle

An evaluation that documents superb results is of little value if no one knows about it. Effectively disseminating and marketing the results is vital to building learning's brand. The concept of a "brand" for learning may seem odd, but a whitepaper from Corporate University Xchange put it well:

Everything has a brand, and the learning organization is no exception. This is because brand is made up of opinions, and it is impossible to prevent people from having opinions.

Dresner and Lehman, 2009

The opinion that leaders have of learning's "brand" shapes their willingness to commit money, time, and effort to learning initiatives. Because of this, it is important for you to know what learning's brand is in your organization and to actively manage it. You have to "sell the sizzle," and promote the value of learning; "you can't be subtle or naïve if you want managers to pay attention to your metrics" (Sullivan, 2005, p. 282).

Professionals, in general, believe that the value of their work should speak for itself. They have been acculturated to think of marketing as beneath their dignity. That is a very naïve point of view. According to Chris Quinn, president of Imprint Learning Solutions, "A brand is something that exists in the mind of the customer that summarizes a product's attributes, benefits, and value. Brands matter. And because brands matter, they have to be managed. Strategic marketing is an integrated set of targeted activities and communications that positively influences the perception of value" (Quinn, 2009).

> Everything has a brand, and the learning organization is no exception.

As Sue Todd pointed out, "Your learning organization has a brand, whether you choose to manage it or not" (Todd, 2009). Failing to strategically market the benefits that learning has delivered leads to a learning brand that is undervalued. The president and group chief human resources officer for Reliance Industries, Prabir Jha, explained it to us this way: "If you don't blow your own horn, someone else will use it as a spittoon."

Mars applied its marketing expertise to create a brand for Mars University. Both the learning organization and the company as a whole benefited: "With a sharper focus we were able to clarify what we stood for and

> A brand exists in the mind of the customer.

what we would and would not do. We turned our strategy into a talk-able story format that would grab people's attention and engage the hearts and minds of all associates, no matter what their roles in the business are. This would help to get us NOTICED" (Grigorova & Moffett, 2014).

"Branding is much more than a logo, a witty tag line, or a beautiful design, however" (Anand, 2012). Brand perception depends on the sum total of all a person's interactions with the product or service. Building a high-quality learning brand requires ensuring that every output—every course, all the materials, each support tool, and every report—be of high quality. Like credibility, it takes time and effort to build a brand and vigilance to maintain it. A single bad experience, superficial evaluation, or poorly written report can seriously damage a brand.

Creating a positive brand reputation also requires staying on message. Advertisers understand that, no matter how compelling the product, it takes repetition to build a brand and create share of mind. Companies that are good at marketing repeat the same core message over and over in a variety of media (magazines, television, direct mail, and so forth) and in a variety of ways. Effective CEOs use a similar approach: they emphasize a few core themes over and over until everyone in the company gets the message.

Learning providers need to do the same to be sure that "the message gets through." Communicate the value of learning and development initiatives multiple times in different settings and formats.

 Practical Application

- Decide what you want your learning brand to be (what you want to be known for); then actively build that reputation.
- Communicate the results of training broadly, effectively, and repeatedly.

 ## 6. Implement Improvements

The last—and critical—step of the process is to implement the improvements identified in the course of the evaluation. No matter how spectacular the results were, no matter how compelling the success stories, no matter how efficient the learning transfer, there is always room for improvement. The continual search for and implementation of improvements is what differentiates truly outstanding organizations from the merely good. The Japanese practice of *kaizen* (small, incremental, continuous improvements) over time adds up to a substantial competitive advantage (Imai, 1986; Liker, 2004).

The most effective learning organizations have a process that ensures that both the output and outcome metrics for every program are reviewed periodically and that a specific plan of action is developed for improvement.

Use the following questions to help you develop a continuous improvement action plan:

1. *Is this a trend or are these isolated, individual comments?* You will never be able to meet the needs or preferences of every individual learner. Concentrate your efforts on those issues that were identified in the analysis of process metrics or that were raised by a significant number of participants. Be sure to consider the *complete* learning experience.

2. *Is it worth fixing?* Not everything that can be improved should be improved. Look for the areas that have the greatest potential to have *business impact.*

3. *What's the root cause?* Look below the surface. If participants feel that what they learned was of low utility, what's behind that? Is it really the content? Could it be that these were the wrong participants, or perhaps the right participants at the wrong time? Identify the real problem before you start devising solutions.

4. *What options do we have?* Don't feel you have to "reinvent the wheel." Read the literature and talk to other learning professionals who have tackled similar issues.

5. *Which shall we tackle first?* Pick one or two areas to tackle first. Look for "low-hanging fruit"—opportunities that are relatively easy or inexpensive to fix, but which have significant payback potential.

6. *Decide how you will know.* Include the check step of the PDCA cycle as part of the plan. Decide what you will measure to know whether you have, indeed, improved the situation, made it worse, or had no impact.

7. *Repeat.* Repeat the cycle for each initiative to build, step-by-step, a competitive advantage for your organization.

Finally, take a proactive approach to continuous development. Step back from the day-to-day execution periodically and give the learning team time, permission, and space to reflect. Challenge what you are doing currently and scan the environment for new opportunities or developments that could be disruptive (see Case in Point D6.7). Curiosity, integrity, intellectual honesty, and openness to change are hallmarks of a true professional.

Case in Point D6.7
Integrity

We asked Teresa Roche, long-time CLO at Agilent Technologies, who was named a "Learning Luminary" by the L&OD Roundtable in Asia, what her advice would be for learning professionals who are truly committed to making a difference. She talked about the importance of integrity at the organizational level all the way down to the individual level. She explained it this way:

"Agilent is giving my team and me resources to play a critical role in the development of our workforce. And so I feel compelled, morally and ethically, to ensure that we use these wonderful gifts well. This includes people's precious time—both the participants and the leaders who co-lead with us. When people commit their time to a learning experience, I owe it to each individual to make sure that the experience provides them the opportunity to build capability that allows them to achieve their goals and aspirations. And I owe it to the company to make sure we use those resources well. I feel that's really important. It is good for me to be able to say that 95 percent of all our new hires all around the world receive their orientation experience within sixty days, but that's just an operational metric. What the CEO should be holding us accountable for is whether we accelerated the new hires' time to performance. If you are in integrity—if you really care about what you are trying to do—then you need to go down the home stretch."

Teresa also stressed the need for learning professionals and organizations to make time to think proactively about their craft and how the changing environment impacts what we do: "One of the greatest things that we have done for years is to take the time to say: 'What do we know? And what are some of the ways that what we know is changing? And out of those changes, is there anything that we need to do differently?' And we do that in community. Because one thing that I have truly learned is that development happens in community. It is in the space between people. We give some time for individual reflection, but the dialogue is in a collegial atmosphere.

"Executive control—our task orientation—is one part of our brain. But if we never take the time to reflect, to contemplate, to make meaning, by using the other parts of our brain, then we are doing a disservice to ourselves and to the world. The challenge for any of us who are creating educational opportunities is to make sure that in the course of any experience, there is time free of technology for reflection. That's paramount; our brain needs it. Otherwise, I don't know how we make meaning, see the patterns, gain insights. I think the best developers of talent create the environment for people to craft their own insights."

Practical Application

- Create competitive advantage by converting insights from the evaluation into action.
- Make changes in those areas that have the highest potential for payback on the effort required.
- Take time to reflect and scan the environment for threats and opportunities.

Summary

The last of the Six Disciplines—to Document Results—is essential to demonstrate the value created by all the effort and investment that have gone before and to identify opportunities to create even greater value in the future. Rigorous assessment of outcomes establishes learning's credibility and demonstrates its value. It is prerequisite to optimizing the learning portfolio.

Evaluations are most effective when they are included as part of the program planning from the very beginning (D1). The measures and analyses must be seen as relevant, credible, and compelling by the target audience. The time and resources invested in evaluation should be commensurate with the importance of the decision it is intended to inform.

Design the evaluation based on stakeholders' needs and definition of value, the nature of the program, and the intended business outcomes, rather than some theoretical ideal. Focus on outcomes of interest to the business, rather than measures of activity or achievement of learning objectives. Assess key process metrics and outputs to identify opportunities for improvement.

Report process failures and suboptimal results as well as successes. Include examples to make the conclusions more memorable and compelling. Keep the final report concise and to the point. Spell out the key conclusions and recommendations in the executive summary.

Finally, market the results. Communicate them broadly through a variety of media to build and maintain a positive brand for learning. Use the checklist in Exhibit D6.1 to evaluate your approach to evaluation.

Exhibit D6.1
Checklist for D6

Use the checklist below to help ensure that you have a robust plan to document results, prove the value of the learning experience, and improve subsequent iterations.

Aspect	Criterion
❑ Agreement	The way in which the program will be evaluated has been discussed with the program's sponsor(s) and agreed to in advance.
❑ Guiding Principles	The plan fulfills the guiding principles of relevant, credible, compelling, and efficient.
❑ Leading Indicators	The earliest (leading) indicators that the program is working have been identified. A plan is in place to use these as in-process checks during the rollout.
❑ Data Sources	The sources of the data that will be used in the evaluation have been identified; their availability has been confirmed.
❑ Data Collection	A plan is in place to gather needed data that are not already collected routinely.
❑ Comparators	Consideration has been given to what the post-learning results will be compared with to make the claim of "better," "improved," and so forth.
❑ Credibility	Assistance from the finance department has been secured if the sponsor has defined financial analysis or the return on investment as a criterion for success.
❑ Improvement	The evaluation plan actively seeks out information to identify opportunities for improvement of subsequent initiatives.
❑ Review	The evaluation plan has been reviewed by someone "skilled in the art" for validity and reliability.
❑ Presentation Plan	How the data will be reported and presented has been considered.
❑ Marketing	The key audiences for the results have been identified and there is a communication plan for each.
❑ Continuous Improvement	There is a mechanism in place to ensure that the data are reviewed for improvement opportunities, that plans of action are created, and that they are put into place.

 # Recommendations

For Learning Leaders

- Review the evidence you currently have to illustrate learning and development outcomes.
  - Can you make a compelling case for economic value added (worthy performance)?
  - Can you convincingly show why reducing the investment in learning would hurt the company's long-term performance?
  - If not, begin at once to rectify the situation.
- Ensure that the plans for evaluation and the definition of success are part of the plan for any learning initiative *from the outset.*
- Ensure that every evaluation plan and finding you report is:
  - Relevant,
  - Credible,
  - Compelling, and when those are satisfied,
  - Efficient.
- Be proactive. Begin to measure outcomes before you are asked. If you wait until you are required to do an ROI study, it may be too late.
- Report the results—good, bad, or indifferent—clearly and succinctly.
  - Always include recommendations for action.
  - Summarize the findings in a one-page executive summary.
- Market the value.
  - It does not matter how great your results are if no one knows about them.

For Line Leaders

- Review the information you currently receive regarding the outcomes of learning and development initiatives.
  - Are you satisfied?
  - Do you find them relevant, credible, and compelling?
  - Do they measure business-relevant outcomes, or just activity?
  - Are they as rigorous as the criteria you use to assess other investments of similar magnitude?
  - If not, meet with your heads of learning and explain what you need in order to make informed decisions about training investments.

- Require that the plan for every learning and development initiative includes a section that discusses how it will be evaluated that is commensurate with the magnitude of the investment.
- Provide learning leaders with access to internal experts on evaluation or external consultants as necessary.
- Save budget presentations—particularly the section on promised benefits. In the following year, require an evaluation of whether or not these were achieved before approving any new budget request.

CODA

"In the end we retain from our studies only that which we practically apply."

—JOHANN WOLFGANG VON GOETHE

THROUGHOUT THIS BOOK, we have emphasized four key themes:

- Learning and development initiatives are strategic investments that an organization makes in its human capital. They are as important to a company's future as the investments it makes in research, new product development, sales, marketing, acquisitions, and so forth.
- Training and development initiatives can generate significant returns and competitive advantage *provided* they are planned, delivered, and managed in a comprehensive and systematic way.
- Six disciplines differentiate highly effective initiatives from less-effective ones and support a cycle of continuous improvement (Figure C.1).
- Learning adds value only when it is transferred and applied to work.

The last point applies equally to the time and effort you have invested reading this book. For that investment to pay a dividend, you need to put what you have learned to work. But don't try to do everything at once. "The journey of a thousand miles begins with a single step" (Lao Tzu, 6th Century BCE). We have provided suggestions for steps you can take at the end of each chapter.

Case in Point C.1
From a Fellow Traveler

Steve is the learning and development manager for an international technology company. His principal responsibility is to make sure that learning and coaching programs are transformed into business results. He has worked across the spectrum of learning and development, including designing, developing, delivering, and evaluating the impact of a wide range of approaches, from mobile learning, to accelerated learning and informal and social learning, as well as traditional classroom-based learning. Steve is still in the process of adapting the 6Ds process to his organization and shared his "lessons learned so far" with us.

"Every organization is unique," he said. "You will have to tailor the implementation of the 6Ds to your organization's culture, style, and structure. The most significant and obvious observation is the need for a project plan template that serves as the readiness planner, holds the project together, and keeps all stakeholders accountable for their commitments."

His other suggestions to augment the implementation of the 6Ds include:

D1: Define Business Outcomes

- Summarize the business problem in a one-pager.
- Present the business problem using visual aids to reinforce understanding.
- Make sure that the problems as perceived by the front-line managers are in line with the way they are viewed by the more senior leaders.
- Ignore engaging with front-line managers at your peril! The business leaders may have a clear vision of what they want, but it is the front-line managers who must execute and manage ("I could write a book on this one!").
- Assess the transfer climate *before* the design phase.
- Evaluate the ability of the organization to support the learning program and learning transfer with tools such as LMS, call monitoring, and so forth. Without this, the question of feasibility must be asked.

D2: Design the Complete Experience

- Integrate the front-line managers into the design process to increase ownership.
- Ensure you have a feedback process that keeps stakeholders in the loop (for example, communicating the results of preparation surveys, manager meetings, etc.).

- Sell the sizzle to the right stakeholders. Getting the wrong champion can negatively impact a project.
- Plan workshops on the skills that managers need to support the process.

D3: Deliver for Application

- Communicate the outcomes of the training needs analysis with the participants.
- Focus on application of skills, as opposed to knowledge gaps.
- Utilize a series of events spread out over time, instead of just one; most of our initiatives span a period of months.

D4: Drive Learning Transfer

- Provide a support structure/technology for managers to manage action plans.
- Merge separate L&D programs into an ongoing quality process.
- Establish a bi-weekly "executive summary" review and invite stakeholders to attend and present updates on actions they are responsible for implementing. Creating a PowerPoint template will help structure their contributions.

D5: Deploy Learning Support

- Leverage existing tools and technologies to support application.

D6: Document Results

- Establish a pre-training baseline to allow for post-training comparison.

"Our journey is still a work in progress. We have documented evidence to show that our initiatives have had the desired impact on behaviors and metrics. We have been told by the leadership that our approach has added credibility to the Learning and Development group as a business partner. A number of our outside business partners have implemented our strategy aggressively and report that it is the most important development in successfully driving performance."

Pick one or two things that you are passionate about and start there. The most important discipline to tackle first, and details of how you go about it, will be peculiar to your organization (see Case in Point C.1). Experiment and learn as you go. Be prepared to encounter

FIGURE C.1.   THE SIX DISCIPLINES SUPPORT A CYCLE OF
CONTINUOUS IMPROVEMENT

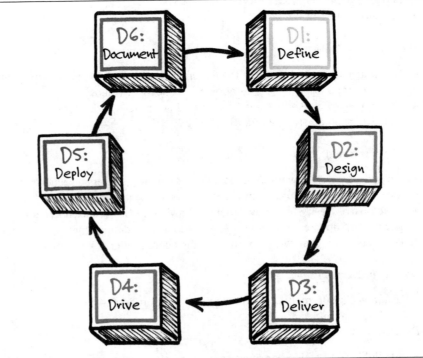

some resistance; it's proof that the changes you are making are substantive. Celebrate small wins and practice continuous improvement. Most importantly, keep learning and enjoy the journey!

The Journey So Far

Since the publication of *The Six Disciplines of Breakthrough Learning*, we have been delighted to learn how its principles have helped organizations around the world make their learning initiatives even more effective. Forty-three case examples of application and impact are included in *The Field Guide to the 6Ds* (Pollock, Jefferson, & Wick, 2014).

Case in Point C.2 illustrates how much can be achieved by going back to basics—starting with the business challenge and then using the 6Ds to develop a process solution—rather than creating yet another learning event that won't be much more effective than just "sending them the bagels."

We are proud that the 6Ds has contributed to success stories like this one and those in the *Field Guide*, but we know that the real credit belongs to the forward-looking learning leaders who were willing to champion change rather than be satisfied with the status quo. We salute them, and you.

Case in Point C.2
Revolutionizing Results at Securian

Securian Financial Group is one of America's largest providers of financial security for individuals and businesses in the form of insurance, retirement plans, and investments. When Chris Jenkins took over leadership of the learning function, he faced daunting challenges: the four-year retention rate for advisors was well below the industry norm and it took more than a year to get a new advisor "client ready." Together, these two issues were costing Securian's member agencies hundreds of thousands of dollars.

Chris and his colleagues persuaded management that to achieve meaningfully different results, they had to significantly change the way they approached training. They rigorously applied *The Six Disciplines*, with special emphasis on learning transfer (Phase III of the learning-to-performance process).

What they were able to accomplish was extraordinary:

- The time to client readiness for new advisors was reduced from eighteen months to ninety days.
- Advisors trained under the new system outperformed those trained in the old way by 100 percent.
- First-year retention rates increased by more than 50 percent.
- Program costs for the member firms were cut by 68 percent.

It did not happen overnight, however. Jenkins told us: "Do not underestimate the effort required to achieve a cultural shift from old methods of training—meaning a talking head downloading information—to learning that actually changes behaviors and delivers results." Surprisingly, much of the resistance came from management, even from managers who faced some of the greatest challenges with retention. "Prepare for 'we have always done it that way ... they expect it,'" advised Jenkins.

To find a champion for change, Jenkins and his colleagues identified a firm that had some of the greatest financial challenges and persuaded the manager that if he wanted a different result, he had to try something new. Because he was in the most pain and had the most to gain, he was willing to cooperate, and over time became a stalwart champion.

The new approach had three key elements:

- A complete learning experience that began with a (scripted) discussion about the process and expectations *during the hiring process* and continued through a rigorous certification process ten weeks later.
- The accountability for coaching and support resided in the local office where the advisor worked. The central learning team did the "heavy lifting" by providing turnkey processes, scripts, and so forth—even rehearsing with the managers—but local leadership had the responsibility to make sure that learning was practiced and applied.
- There was a well-defined, rigorous assessment—the Checkpoints to Mastery—at which new advisors had to show that they could discuss, explain, and demonstrate during a live interview/examination with senior managers after ten weeks of training and on-the-job coaching.

According to Jenkins, "*The Six Disciplines* gave us a framework to approach training in a new and more effective way. The proof is in the results Securian member firms were able to achieve. As a result of this experience, I've come to the conclusion that, unless there is a commitment to the whole process, you shouldn't do the program. Just send people the bagels; it will be a lot cheaper and just about as effective."

The Road Ahead

We've been working on the 6Ds for more than a decade now, and the journey is far from over. We continue to learn from our colleagues and clients, refine the approach, and find new applications.

We invite you to build on the concepts we have presented here and to share your insights, accomplishments, and—yes—failures, so that we all get smarter and are able to make an even greater contribution to the success of our organizations and co-workers.

We look forward to hearing from you.

AFTERWORD

Will Thalheimer, Ph.D., President
Work-Learning Research, Inc.

What a journey! In reading this new edition of the now-classic text, *The Six Disciplines of Breakthrough Learning*, I imagine us, as readers, having been guided through a challenging, transformational journey. Like a combination of Boot Camp, Outward Bound, Consciousness Raising, and a Harvard Business School Executive Retreat; we've been given all the tools and insights we need to transform our workplace learning practices.

Roy Pollock, Andy Jefferson, and Cal Wick have provided a proven conceptual structure—the 6Ds—as a foundation. We've been shown how the 6Ds approach works in real organizations. We've been given practical tools that have been refined and updated. We've been privy to one of the best compilations of industry wisdom ever assembled in one book. We've been read the riot act, heard the gospel truth, and made to wonder why so many of us are failing on the fundamentals. This book lays it out for us, if only we have the guts and perseverance to do the right thing.

My afterword is intended to be part campfire, part sermon, and part call to action.

I've been a learning consultant for the better part of two decades. My work has focused on compiling research from the world's preeminent scientific journals on learning, memory, and instruction—and then using the wisdom I've gained in my consulting work. Pollock, Jefferson, and Wick come at workplace learning from a different place—and yet, their work is complementary to the scientific research—and indispensable in its own right. Research and practice must work together for our profession to capitalize on the significant investments we make.

Our field—the workplace learning field—is in the middle of a transformation. It's a slow transformation, so we may not even recognize it as it happens, but the fundamentals are changing because of four distinct vectors.

First, the science of learning has begun to coalesce around a few fundamental learning factors. From my *Decisive Dozen*, to Ruth Clark's compendium of books, to the recently published book *Make It Stick: The Science of Successful Learning*, the research base is strong enough to suggest fundamentals that must be followed. These include realistic practice set in real work contexts, learning events spaced over time, and supporting learners in developing appropriate mental models. Where traditional training tends to focus on content delivery, research-aligned training teaches fewer concepts, but enables the most important concepts to be understood, remembered, and readied for real-world application.

The second force of change is the focus on performance—as opposed to learning delivery. This meme has been bubbling up for at least three decades, but it's begun to hit a tipping point. More and more organizations are learning how to make this happen. More learning departments care about performance. Pollock, Jefferson, and Wick are among the strongest advocates in this vector, as should be obvious from reading this book.

The third force is technology, particularly digital technology that intimately connects with learners/performers in ways that go well beyond standard e-learning. The technologies that matter are those that help us reach learners when they're ready and when relevant contextual cues are visible and actionable. Performance support tools are part of this, but only a part. Mechanisms like subscription learning (short nuggets of interactions threaded over time), integrated gamification (game elements utilized without gaminess), and performance coaching tools will give rise to a learning ecosystem that feels more intimate than what we've experienced in the past.

The fourth force really derives from the same well of wisdom as the first force—from psychological science. I call this fourth force "triggering," although researchers use more formidable terminology. Triggering is based on the reality that humans are more reactive than they are proactive. In fact, our working memories are almost always under the influence, if not control, of the environmental cues we encounter. Here are some examples: When we eat our food on smaller plates, we eat less. The small plates trigger us to think we're getting more food. When we drive, narrower roads make us drive more slowly. When we shop, subtle upselling triggers us to buy, end caps make us consider additional purchases, "Sale!" stickers prompt us to buy things we might not otherwise.

The truth is that more and more of our daily lives are being triggered by others. Advertisers, online news outlets, political parties, websites, mobile apps—they are all learning how to capture our attention through cues. Of course, triggering is just a fact of the universe. It's not good or bad. Our human cognitive architecture is what it is—it's how we use this architecture that makes the difference. We in the learning space can use triggering to support our learners in learning—and performing. Indeed, it will be in partnership with technology that triggering will have its most power.

When these four forces come together—learning science, a performance focus, intimate technology, and triggering—we as workplace learning professionals will be much more effective than we are now. But here's a secret—you don't have to wait to start. You can begin to make big improvements today. Use the 6Ds as your meta-structure. Then incorporate wisdom from psychological science, much of which is already baked into 6Ds thinking. Finally, look for ways to support your efforts with technology that connects with your learners/performers—in terms of both learning and performance.

Of course, you will have to deal with one sticky wicket. The future of workplace learning and performance is imbued with new paradigms—new paradigms that will challenge old mental models and traditional ways of doing things. In some organizations, it's going to be a bloody mess. Resistance will be everywhere!

To be successful, you'll have to nurture a change management attitude within yourself and your colleagues. There's much to learn about how to champion change—certainly too much to detail in this space. Let me highlight a couple of points here. First, gather allies. Change takes time and perseverance. You'll need both ideational and social support. Change champions need others—not only to help get things done, but also to come up with innovations and to strengthen ideas and initiatives through reality-checking. Perhaps most often ignored is the importance of others in maintaining our resolve. We really do need each other—never more so than when we're slogging through the long journey of change.

Second, don't feel you need to reach nirvana all at once. Perfection is a fantasy world! Do what you can do now and prepare your stakeholders for changes that will come. The best way to do this is through "stealth messaging"—doing little things within our normal practices that send a message about what is important. This book highlights a number of ways to utilize stealth messages. For example, when people come to you asking you and your team to build a training course, don't forget to ask about other factors that are at play. When people are framing the finish line as the end-of-session smile sheet, remind them that the real goal is performance. Proselytizing can be counterproductive because it heightens mental filters and can stiffen resistance. Gently educate your stakeholders every once in a while, but don't rely on persuasive arguments. You're better off incorporating stealth messages within your practices.

Above all, remember that helping people learn and perform is a noble and worthy cause. We should hold that in our hearts. The cold logic of helping our organizations is a truism, but we humans often need more—more to be inspired, more to persevere, more to work cooperatively with each other, more to be innovative, more to exert our iron will to drive for change and improvement. In the final analysis, we are helping people in the work that we do.

The next step is yours.

REFERENCES

Addison, R., Haig, C., & Kearney, L. (2009). *Performance architecture: The art and science of improving organizations*. San Francisco, CA: Pfeiffer.

Allen, M., & Sites, R. (2012). *Leaving ADDIE for SAM: An agile model for developing the best learning experiences*. Alexandria, VA: ASTD Press.

Alliger, G., Tannenbaum, S., Bennett, W., Jr., Traver, H., & Shotland, A. (1997). A meta-analysis of the relations among training criteria. *Personnel Psychology, 50*(2), 341–358.

Amabile, T., & Kramer, S. (2011). *The progress principle: Using small wins to ignite joy, engagement, and creativity at work*. Boston, MA: Harvard Business Review Press.

American Express. (2007). The real ROI of leadership development: Comparing classroom vs. online vs. blended delivery. Retrieved from www.personneldecisions .com/uploadedfiles/Case_Studies/PDFs/AmericanExpress.pdf

American Society for Training and Development. (2011). *Developing results: Aligning learning's goals and outcomes with business performance measures* (ASTD Research Report No. 191106). Alexandria, VA: Author.

American Society for Training and Development. (2013). *2013 state of the industry*. Alexandria, VA: Author.

Anand, P. (2012). Branding the learning function. *T+D, 66*(9), 49–51.

Anderson, P. J. (2010). *Cognitive psychology and its implications* (7th ed.). New York: Worth Publishers.

Aperian Global. (2012). GlobeSmart. Retrieved September 10, 2014, from http://corp.aperianglobal.com/globesmartn

Ariely, D. (2010). *Predictably irrational: The hidden forces that shape our decisions*. New York: Harper Perennial.

Ariely, D. (2011). *The upside of irrationality: The unexpected benefits of defying logic.* New York: Harper Perennial.

ASTD Research. (2009). *The value of evaluation: Making training evaluations more effective.* Alexandria, VA: ASTD.

Babbie, E. R. (2012). *The practice of social research* (13th ed.). Belmont, CA: Cengage Learning.

Baker, M. (2014). 3 things a flat tire reminded me about how young people learn. Retrieved from http://phasetwolearning.wordpress.com/2014/08/13/3-things-a-flat-tire-reminded-me-about-how-young-people-learn/

Baldwin, T., & Ford, J. (1988). Transfer of training: A review and directions for future research. *Personnel Psychology, 41*(1), 63–105.

Baldwin, T., Pierce, J., Joines, R., & Farouk, S. (2011). The elusiveness of applied management knowledge: A critical challenge for management educators. *Academy of Management Learning & Education, 10*(4), 583–605.

Banerjee, S., Wahdat, T., & Cherian, A. (2014). How we turned a "feel good" training program into a successful business transformation. In R. Pollock, A. Jefferson, & C. W. Wick, *The field guide to the 6Ds* (pp. 285–292). San Francisco, CA: Pfeiffer.

Banks, B. (2014). How we fostered a proactive approach to leader development. In R. Pollock, A. Jefferson, & R. Pollock, *The field guide to the 6Ds* (pp. 411–415). San Francisco, CA: Pfeiffer.

Barnett, K., & Vance, D. (2012). *Talent development reporting principles* (whitepaper) (p. 55). Windsor, CO: Center for Talent Reporting.

Bartlett, R. (2014). How we implemented a low-cost, low-effort follow-up. In R. Pollock, A. Jefferson, & C. W. Wick, *The field guide to the 6Ds* (pp. 431–433). San Francisco, CA: Pfeiffer.

Basarab, D. (2011). *Predictive evaluation: Ensuring training delivers business and organizational results.* San Francisco, CA: Berrett-Koehler.

Baumeister, R., Bratslavsky, E., Muraven, M., & Tice, D. (1998). Ego depletion: Is the active self a limited resource? *Journal of Personality and Social Psychology, 74*(5), 1252–1265.

Bell, L. (2008). Raising expectations for concrete results: Leadership development at Holcim. In T. Mooney & R. Brinkerhoff (Eds.), *Courageous training: Bold actions for business results* (pp. 175–193). San Francisco, CA: Berrett-Koehler.

Bersin, J. (2008). *The training measurement book: Best practices, proven methodologies, and practical approaches.* San Francisco, CA: Pfeiffer.

Betoff, E. (2007, September). *Profile of the chief learning officer: Executive program in work-based learning leadership.* Paper presented at the Fort Hill Best Practices Summit, Mendenhall, Pennsylvania.

Binder, C. (2010). Measurement, evaluation, and research: feedback for decision making. In J. Moseley & J. Dessinger (Eds.), *Handbook of improving performance in the workplace: Volume 3, Measurement and evaluation.* San Francisco, CA: Pfeiffer.

Bingham, T., & Galagan, P. (2008). No small change. *T+D, 62*(11), 32–37.

Blanchard, K. (2004). Foreword. In S. Blanchard & M. Homan, *Leverage your best, ditch the rest: The coaching secrets top executives depend on* (pp. ix–xii). New York: HarperCollins.

Blanchard, K., Meyer, P., & Ruhe, D. (2007). *Know can do! Put your know-how into action.* San Francisco, CA: Berrett-Koehler.

Boehle, S. (2006). Are you too nice to train? *Training, 43*(8), 16–22.

Bordonaro, F. (2005). What to do. In M. Dulworth & F. Bordonaro (Eds.), *Corporate learning: Proven and practical guides for building a sustainable learning strategy* (pp. 123–232). San Francisco, CA: Pfeiffer.

Bossidy, L., Charan, R., & Burck, C. (2002). *Execution: The discipline of getting things done.* Princeton, NJ: Crown Business.

Boyd, S. (2005). *Using job aids.* Alexandria, VA: ASTD.

Brafman, O., & Brafman, R. (2009). *Sway: The irresistible pull of irrational behavior.* New York: Broadway Books.

Brinkerhoff, R. O. (1987). *Achieving results from training.* San Francisco, CA: Jossey-Bass.

Brinkerhoff, R. O. (2003). *The success case method: Find out quickly what's working and what's not.* San Francisco, CA: Berrett-Koehler.

Brinkerhoff, R. O. (2006). *Telling training's story: Evaluation made simple, credible, and effective.* San Francisco, CA: Berrett-Koehler.

Brinkerhoff, R. O., & Apking, A. M. (2001). *High impact learning: Strategies for leveraging performance and business results from training investments.* Cambridge, MA: Perseus Publishing.

Brinkerhoff, R. O., & Montesino, M. (1995). Partnerships for learning transfer: Lessons from a corporate study. *Human Resource Development Quarterly, 6*(3), 263–274.

Broad, M. (2005). *Beyond transfer of training: Engaging systems to improve performance.* San Francisco, CA: Pfeiffer.

Broad, M., & Newstrom, J. (1992). *Transfer of training: Action-packed strategies to ensure high payoff from training investments.* Cambridge, MA: Perseus Books.

Brown, P., Roediger, H., III, & McDaniel, M. (2014). *Make it stick: The science of successful learning.* Cambridge, MA: Belknap Press.

Burke, L., & Hutchins, H. (2007, September). Training transfer: An integrative literature review. *Human Resource Development Review, 6*, 263–296.

Burke, M., Sarpy, S., Smith-Crowe, K., Chan-Serafin, S., Salvador, R., & Islam, G. (2006). Relative effectiveness of worker safety and health training methods. *American Journal of Public Health, 96*(2), 315–324.

Burnett, S., & Connolly, M. (2003). Hewlett-Packard takes the waste out of leadership. *Journal of Organizational Excellence, 22*(4), 49–59.

Buzan, T., & Griffiths, C. (2013). *Mind maps for business: Using the ultimate thinking tool to revolutionize how you work* (2nd ed.). New York: FT Press.

Caffarella, R. S. (2009). *Planning programs for adult learners: A practical guide for educators, trainers, and staff developers* (2nd ed.). San Francisco, CA: Jossey-Bass.

Caffarella, R. S., & Daffron, S. (2013). *Planning programs for adult learners: A practical guide* (3rd ed.). San Francisco, CA: Jossey-Bass.

Center for Talent Reporting. (2013). *TDRp: Managing learning like a business to deliver greater impact, effectiveness, and efficiency.* Windsor, CO. Retrieved from www.centerfortalentreporting.org/communicating-tdrp-to-others/

Center for Talent Reporting. (2014). About us–Center for Talent Reporting Charter. Retrieved from www.centerfortalentreporting.org/about-us/

Charlton, K., & Osterweil, C. (2005, Autumn). Measuring return on investment in executive education: A quest to meet client needs or pursuit of the Holy Grail? *Ashridge Journal*, pp. 6–13.

Clark, R. C. (1986). Defining the D in ISD. Part I: Task-general instruction methods. *Performance and Instructional Journal*, *25*(3), 17–21.

Clark, R. C. (2015). *Evidence-based training methods* (2nd ed.). Alexandria, VA: ATD.

Clark, R. C., & Mayer, R. E. (2011). *e-Learning and the science of instruction: Proven guidelines for consumers and designers of multimedia learning* (3rd ed.). San Francisco, CA: Pfeiffer.

Colvin, G. (2006). What it takes to be great. *Fortune*, *154*(9), 88–96.

Colvin, G. (2008). *Talent is overrated: What really separates world-class performers from everybody else*. New York: Penguin Group.

Conklin, T. (2012). *Pre-accident investigations: An introduction to organizational safety*. Burlington, VT: Ashgate Publishing.

Corporate Executive Board. (2009). *Refocusing L&D on business results: Bridging the gap between learning and performance*. Washington, DC: Corporate Executive Board.

Covey, S. (2004). *The 7 habits of highly effective people: Powerful lessons in personal change* (2nd ed.). New York: Simon & Schuster.

Coyle, D. (2009). *The talent code: Greatness isn't born. It's grown. Here's how*. New York: Bantam Dell.

CrossKnowledge. (2014). The C-suite imperative: Workforce development and business outcomes. Retrieved from www.crossknowledge.com/en_GB/elearning /media-center/publications/workforce-development-the-economist/s.html

Crozier, R. A. (2011). *The engagement manifesto: A systemic approach to organizational success*. Bloomington, IN: AuthorHouse.

Csikszentmihalyi, M. (2008). *Flow: The psychology of optimal experience*. New York: Harper & Row.

Darling, M., & Parry, C. (2001). After-action reviews: Linking reflection and planning in a learning practice. *Reflections*, *3*(2), 64–72.

Davachi, L., & Dobbins, I. (2008). Declarative memory. *Current Directions Psychological Sciences*, *17*(2), 112–118.

Davachi, L., Kiefer, T., Rock, D., & Rock, L. (2010). Learning that lasts through AGES. *NeuroLeadership Journal*, *1*(3), 53–63.

De Geus, A. (2002). *The living company*. Boston, MA: Harvard Business Review Press.

Deming, W. E. (1986). *Out of the crisis*. Cambridge, MA: MIT Press.

Denning, S. (2011). *The leader's guide to storytelling: Mastering the art and discipline of business narrative* (2nd ed.). San Francisco, CA: Jossey-Bass.

DeSmet, A., McGurk, M., & Swartz, E. (2010, October). Getting more from your training programs. *McKinsey Quarterly*.

Deutschman, A. (2005, May). Making change. *Fast Company*, pp. 52–62.

DiClemente, C., & Prochaska, J. (1998). Toward a comprehensive, trans-theoretical model of change. In W. Miller & N. Heather (Eds.), *Treating addictive behaviours*. New York: Plenum Press.

Dirksen, J. (2012). *Design for how people learn*. Berkeley, CA: New Riders.

Dixon, N. (1990). The relationship between trainee responses on participation reaction forms and posttest scores. *Human Resource Development Quarterly*, *1*(2), 129–137.

Donohoe, J., Beech, P., Bell-Wright, K., Kirkpatrick, J., & Kirkpatrick, W. (2014). How we used measurement to drive "SOAR—service over and above the rest." In R. Pollock, A. Jefferson, & C. W. Wick, *The field guide to the 6Ds*. San Francisco, CA: Pfeiffer.

Dresner, M., & Lehman, L. (2009, Spring). The astounding value of learning brand. Corporate University Xchange. Retrieved from http://documents.corpu.com/research /CorpU_Astounding_Value_of_Learning_Brand.pdf

Drucker, P. (1974). *Management: Tasks, responsibilities, practices*. New York: Harper & Row.

Dugdale, K., & Lambert, D. (2007). *Smarter selling: Next generation sales strategies to meet your buyer's needs—every time*. Harlow, UK: Pearson Education.

Duhigg, C. (2012). *The power of habit: Why we do what we do in life and business*. New York: Random House.

Dulworth, M., & Forcillo, J. (2005). Achieving the developmental value of peer-to-peer networks. In M. Dulworth & F. Bordonaro (Eds.), *Corporate learning: Proven and practical guidelines for building a sustainable learning strategy* (pp. 107–121). San Francisco, CA: Pfeiffer.

Dweck, C. (2007). *Mindset: The new psychology of success*. New York: Ballantine Books.

Educase. (2012). 7 things you should know about flipped classrooms. Retrieved from http://net.educause.edu/ir/library/pdf/eli7081.pdf

Elkeles, T., & Phillips, J. J. (2007). *The chief learning officer: Driving value within a changing organization through learning and development*. Burlington, MA: Butterworth-Heinemann.

Ericsson, K. A., Krampe, R., & Tesch-Romer, C. (1993). The role of deliberate practice in the acquisition of expert performance. *Psychological Review, 100*(3), 363–406.

Feldstein, H., & Boothman, T. (1997). Success factors in technology training (pp. 19–33). In J. J. Phillips & M. L. Broad (Eds.), *Transferring learning to the workplace*. Alexandria, VA: ASTD.

Fitz-enz, J. (2000). *The ROI of human capital*. New York: AMACOM.

Frechtling, J. A. (2007). *Logic modeling methods in program evaluation*. San Francisco, CA: Jossey-Bass.

Frielick, S. (2004). Beyond constructivism: An ecological approach to e-learning. In R. Atkinson, C. McBeath, D. Jonas-Dwyer, & R. Phillips (Eds.), *Beyond the comfort zone: Proceedings of the 21st ASCILITE conference* (pp. 328–332). Perth, 5–8 December. www.ascilite.org.au/conferences/perth04/procs/frielick.html

Gaffney, P. (2007). Mind of the manager. In M. Hammer, The seven deadly sins of performance management. *MIT Sloan Management Review, 48*(3), 24.

Gagné, R., Wager, W., Golas, K., & Keller, J. (2004). *Principles of instructional design* (5th ed.). Independence, KY: Cengage Learning.

Gawande, A. (2008). *The checklist manifesto: How to get things right*. New York: Metropolitan Books.

Georgenson, D. L. (1982). The problem of transfer calls for partnership. *Training and Development Journal, 36*(10), 75–78.

George Washington University. (2014). The Evaluators' Institute. Retrieved from http://tei.gwu.edu/

Gilbert, T. (1978). *Human competence: Engineering worthy performance*. New York: McGraw-Hill.

Gilley, J., & Hoekstra, E. (2003). Creating a climate for learning transfer. In E. F. Holton III & T. T. Baldwin (Eds.), *Improving learning transfer in organizations*. San Francisco, CA: Jossey-Bass.

Gladwell, M. (2008). *Outliers: The story of success*. New York: Little, Brown and Company.

Godden, D., & Baddeley, A. (1975). Context dependency in two natural environments: On land and underwater. *British Journal of Psychology, 66*(3), 325–331.

Goh, C. S. K. (2014). How we enhanced and stretched our first-level managers' learning experience. In R. Pollock, A. Jefferson, & C. W. Wick, *The field guide to the 6Ds* (pp. 337–343). San Francisco, CA: Pfeiffer.

Goldsmith, M., & Morgan, H. (2004). Leadership is a contact sport: The follow-up factor in management development. *Strategy + Business,* (36), 71–79.

Goldsmith, M., Morgan, H., & Effron, M. (2013). Change leadership behavior: The impact of co-workers and the impact of coaches. In L. Carter, R. Sullivan, M. Goldsmith, D. Ulrich, & N. Smallwood (Eds.), *The change champion's field guide* (2nd ed., pp. 236–245). San Francisco, CA: Pfeiffer.

Goodrich, H. (1997). Understanding rubrics. *Educational Leadership, 54*(4), 14–17.

Gottfredson, C., & Mosher, B. (2011). *Innovative performance support: Strategies and practices for learning in the workflow*. New York: McGraw-Hill.

Gottfredson, C., & Mosher, B. (2014). "We're lost, but we're making good time": Performance support to the rescue. Retrieved from www.learningsolutionsmag .com/articles/934/were-lost-but-were-making-good-time-performance-support-to -the-rescue

Govaerts, N., & Dochy, F. (2014, June). Disentangling the role of the supervisor in transfer of training. *Educational Research Review, 12,* 77–93.

Gregory, P., & Akram, S. (2014). How we moved from order takers to business partners. In R. Pollock, A. Jefferson, & C. W. Wick, *The field guide to the 6Ds* (pp. 281–284). San Francisco, CA: Pfeiffer.

Grenny, J., Patterson, K., Maxfield, D., McMillan, R., & Switzler, A. (2013). *Influencer: The new science of leading change* (2nd ed.). New York: McGraw-Hill.

Grigorova, M., & Moffett, R. (2014). How we created a high impact Mars University brand. In R. Pollock, A. Jefferson, & C. W. Wick, *The field guide to the 6Ds* (pp. 523–526). San Francisco, CA: Pfeiffer.

Gupta, K. (1999). *A practical guide to needs assessment*. San Francisco, CA: Pfeiffer.

Haddad, R. (2012, February 8). How to facilitate true learning transfer. Retrieved May 20, 2014, from www.clomedia.com/articles/how-to-facilitate-true-learning-transfer.

Hamdan, N., McKnight, K., & Arfstrom, K. (2013). Flipped Learning Network. Retrieved from www.flippedlearning.org/cms/lib07/VA01923112/Centricity/Domain /41/LitReview_FlippedLearning.pdf

Harburg, F. (2004). They're buying holes, not shovels. *Chief Learning Officer, 3*(3), 21.

Harless, J. (1989). Wasted behavior: A confession. *Training, 26*(5), 35–38.

Hattie, J. (2008). *Visible learning: A synthesis of over 800 meta-analyses relating to achievement*. New York: Routledge.

Hayes, W. (2014). How we use alumni to help set expectations for new program participants and their leaders. In R. Pollock, A. Jefferson, & C. W. Wick, *The field guide to the 6Ds* (pp. 319–324). San Francisco, CA: Pfeiffer.

Heath, C., & Heath, D. (2008). *Made to stick: Why some ideas survive and others die.* New York: Random House.

Hewertson, R. B. (2014). *Lead like it matters . . . .because it does: Practical leadership tools to inspire and engage your people and create great results.* New York: McGraw-Hill.

Hinton, D., Singos, M., & Grigsby, L. (2014). How we designed a complete experience to deliver business results. In R. Pollock, A. Jefferson, & C. W. Wick, *The field guide to the 6Ds.* San Francisco, CA: Pfeiffer.

Hodell, C. (2011). *ISD from the ground up: A no-nonsense approach to instructional design* (3rd ed.). Alexandria, VA: ASTD Press.

Holton, E. F., III. (2003). What's really wrong: Diagnosis for learning transfer system change. In E. F. Holton, III, & T. T. Baldwin (Eds.), *Improving learning transfer in organizations* (pp. 59–79). San Francisco, CA: Jossey-Bass.

Holton, E. F., III, & Baldwin, T. T. (2003). *Improving learning transfer in organizations.* San Francisco, CA: Jossey-Bass.

Holton, E. F., III, Bates, R., & Ruona, W. (2000). Development of a generalized learning transfer system inventory. *Human Resource Development Quarterly, 11*(4), 333–360.

Hughes, G. (2014). How we improved the signal-to-noise ratio to transform the presentation culture at KLA-Tencor. In R. Pollock, A. Jefferson, & C. W. Wick, *The field guide to the 6Ds* (pp. 375–386). San Francisco, CA: Pfeiffer.

Hume, S. (2014, March 20). McDonald's spent more than $988 million on advertising in 2013. Retrieved from www.csmonitor.com/Business/The-Bite/2014/0330/McDonald-s-spent-more-than-988-million-on-advertising-in-2013

Hunter, R. (2004). *Madeline Hunter's mastery teaching: Increasing instructional effectiveness in elementary and secondary schools.* Thousand Oaks, CA: Corwin.

Ibarra, H. (2004). Breakthrough ideas for 2004: The HBR list. *Harvard Business Review, 9*(2), 13–32.

Imai, M. (1986). *Kaizen: The key to Japan's competitive success.* New York: McGraw-Hill /Irwin.

Islam, K. (2006). *Developing and measuring training the six sigma way: A business approach to training and development.* San Francisco, CA: Pfeiffer.

Islam, K. (2013). *Agile methodology for developing & measuring learning: Training development for today's world.* Bloomington, IN: AuthorHouse.

Israelite, L. (Ed.). (2006). *Lies about learning: Leading executives separate truth from fiction in this $100 billion industry.* Alexandria, VA: ASTD Press.

Jaccaci, A., & Hackett, C. (2014). How we achieved lean improvements with learning transfer. In R. Pollock, A. Jefferson, & C. W. Wick, *The field guide to the 6Ds* (pp. 423–430). San Francisco, CA: Pfeiffer.

Jaenke, R. (2013). Identify the real reasons behind performance gaps. *T+D,* pp. 76–78.

Jefferson, A. McK., Pollock, R. V. H., & Wick, C. W. (2009). *Getting your money's worth from training and development: A guide to breakthrough learning for managers and participants.* San Francisco, CA: Pfeiffer.

Kahneman, D. (2013). *Thinking, fast and slow.* New York: Farrar, Straus and Giroux.

Kaplan, R., & Norton, D. (1992). The balanced scorecard—Measures that drive performance. *Harvard Business Review, 70*(1), 71–79.

Kapp, K. M., Blair, L., & Mesch, R. (2013). *The gamification of learning and instruction fieldbook: Ideas into practice.* San Francisco, CA: Pfeiffer.

Karpicke, J. (2012). Retrieval-based learning: Active retrieval promotes meaningful learning. *Current Directions in Psychological Science, 21*(3), 157–163.

Kaufman, R., & Guerra-López, I. (2013). *Needs assessment for organizational success.* Alexandria, VA: ASTD Press.

Kaye, B. (2005, September). Love it and use it. *Learning Alert,* 15. Wilmington, DE: The Fort Hill Company.

Keeton, J. (2014). How we moved the finish line for leadership development. In R. Pollock, A. Jefferson, & C. Wick, *The field guide to the 6Ds* (pp. 333–336). San Francisco, CA: Pfeiffer.

Keith, N., & Frese, M. (2008). Effectiveness of error management training: A meta-analysis. *Journal of Applied Psychology, 93*(1), 59–69.

Keller, G., & Papasan, J. (2013). *The ONE thing: The surprisingly simple truth behind extraordinary results.* Austin, TX: Bard Press.

Kelley, H. (1950). The warm-cold variable in first impressions of persons. *Journal of Personality, 18*(4), 431–439.

Kelly, D. (2014). The importance of adding performance support to the mix. Retrieved from http://twist.elearningguild.net/2014/07/the-importance-of-adding-performance-support-to-the-mix/

Kerfoot, B. (2013, November/December). Brain science provides new approach to patient safety training. *Patient Safety and Quality Healthcare.* Retrieved from www.psqh.com/november-december-2013/1794-brain-science-provides-new -approach-to-patient-safety-training

Kerfoot, B., & Baker, H. (2012). An online spaced-education game for global continuing medical education: A randomized trial. *Annals of Surgery, 256*(1), 33–38.

Kesner, I. (2003). Leadership development: Perk or priority? *Harvard Business Review, 81*(5), 29–38.

Kirkpatrick, D. L. (1998). *Evaluating training programs* (2nd ed.). San Francisco, CA: Berrett-Koehler.

Kirwan, C. (2009). *Improving learning transfer.* Burlington, VT: Ashgate Publishing.

Knowles, M., Holton, E. F., III, & Swanson, R. (2011). *The adult learner* (7th ed.). Boston, MA: Taylor & Francis.

Knudson, M. (2005). Executive coaching. In J. Bolt (Ed.), *The future of executive development* (pp. 40–53). San Francisco, CA: Executive Development Associates.

Konkle, T., Brady, T., Alverez, G., & Oliva, A. (2010). Scene memory is more detailed than you think: The role of categories in visual long-term memory. *Psychological Science, 21*(11), 1551–1556.

Kontra, S., Trainor, D., & Wick, C. W. (2007, September 12). *Leadership development at Pfizer: What happens after class.* Webinar presented at the CorpU. Retrieved from www.corpu.com

Korn Ferry. (2014, August). Learning agility: What LA is and is not. Retrieved from www.kornferryinstitute.com/institute-blog/2012-11-26/learning-agility-what-la -and-not

Kouzes, J. M., & Posner, B. Z. (1990). *The leadership challenge: How to get extraordinary things done in organizations*. San Francisco, CA: Jossey-Bass.

Kouzes, J. M., & Posner, B. Z. (2008). *The leadership challenge* (4th ed.). San Francisco, CA: Jossey-Bass.

Kuehner-Hebert, K. (2014). The art and science of proving learning value. *Chief Learning Officer, 13*(9), 42–45.

Kuhn, T. S. (2012). *The structure of scientific revolutions: 50th anniversary edition*. Chicago, IL: University of Chicago Press.

Lally, P., van Jaarsveld, C., Potts, H., & Wardle, J. (2010). How habits are formed: Modeling habit formation in the real world. *European Journal of Social Psychology, 40*(6), 998–1009.

Lancaster, S., Di Milia, L., & Cameron, R. (2013). Supervisor behaviors that facilitate training transfer. *Journal of Workplace Learning, 25*(1), 6–22.

Langley, G., Moen, R., Nolan, K., Nolan, T., Norman, C. L., & Provost, L. (2009). *The improvement guide: A practical approach to enhancing organizational performance* (2nd ed.). San Francisco, CA: Jossey-Bass.

Latham, A. (2013, October 2). Why training fails. Retrieved from www.astd.org/Publications/Blogs/Management-Blog/2013/10Why-Training-Fails.

Leimbach, M., & Emde, E. (2011). The 80/20 rule for learning transfer. *Chief Learning Officer, 10*(12), 64–67.

Leimbach, M., & Maringka, J. (2014). Impact of learning transfer on global effectiveness: Enhancing worldwide collaboration. Retrieved from www.wilsonlearning.com/wlw/research-paper/hr/global-effectiveness.

Lennox, D. (2014). How we used spaced learning and gamification to increase the effectiveness of product launch training. In R. Pollock, A. Jefferson, & C. W. Wick, *The field guide to the 6Ds* (pp. 435–441). San Francisco, CA: Pfeiffer.

Levinson, S., & Greider, P. (1998). *Following through: A revolutionary new model for finishing whatever you start*. New York: Kensington Books.

Liker, J. (2004). *The Toyota way: 14 management principles from the world's greatest manufacturer*. New York: McGraw-Hill.

Lombardo, M., & Eichinger, R. (1996). *The career architect development planner* (1st ed.). Minneapolis, MN: Lominger.

Lublin, J. (2014, January 10). Do you know your hidden work biases? *Wall Street Journal*, pp. 1, 4.

Maas, J., & Robbins, R. (2011). *Sleep for success! Everything you must know about sleep but are too tired to ask*. Bloomington, IN: AuthorHouse.

Mager, R., & Pipe, P. (1997). *Analyzing performance problems: Or, you really oughta wanna* (3rd ed.). Atlanta, GA: CEP Press.

Margolis, D. (2010). Special delivery: Learning at UPS. *Chief Learning Officer, 9*(3), 24–27.

Margolis, F., & Bell, C. (1986). *Instructing for results*. San Diego, CA: University Associates.

Mattox, J., II. (2010, Fall). Manager engagement: Reducing scrap learning. *Training Industry Quarterly*, pp. 29–33.

McCall, M. W., Jr., Lombardo, M. M., & Morrison, A. M. (1988). *The lessons of experience: How successful executives develop on the job*. Lexington, MA: Lexington Books.

McDonald, D., Wiczorek, M., & Walker, C. (2004). Factors affecting learning during health education sessions. *Clinical Nursing Research, 13*(2), 156–167.

Medina, J. (2014). *Brain rules: 12 principles for surviving and thriving at work, home, and school* (2nd ed.). Seattle, WA: Pear Press.

Mencken, H. L. (1917, November 16). The divine afflatus. *New York Evening Mail.*

MindGym (2013). *The bite-size revolution: How to make learning stick.* Retrieved from uk.themindgym.com/the-bite-size-revolution-how-to-make-learning-stick

Mok, P. (2014). How we use experiential learning to engage learners' hearts as well as minds. In R. Pollock, A. Jefferson, & C. W. Wick, *The field guide to the 6Ds* (pp. 367–374). San Francisco, CA: Pfeiffer.

Morris, C. D., Bransford, J., & Franks, J. (1977). Levels of processing versus transfer appropriate processing. *Journal of Verbal Learning and Verbal Behavior, 16*(5), 519–533.

Mosel, J. (1957). Why training programs fail to carry over. *Personnel, 34*(3), 56–64.

Mosher, B. (2014). Supporting performance: Helping make training stick. Webinar presented December 6, 2014. www.l-ten.org/webinararchives

National Research Council. (2000). *How people learn: Brain, mind, experience, and school.* Washington, DC: National Academies Press.

National Weight Control Registry. (n.d.). Research findings. Retrieved from www.nwcr.ws/Research/published%20research.htm

Newton, S. (2014). How we used NPS to track and improve leadership impact. In R. Pollock, A. Jefferson, & C. W. Wick, *The field guide to the 6Ds* (pp. 513–518). San Francisco, CA: Pfeiffer.

Nguyen, F. (2011). Insights from a thought leader: Dr. Frank Nguyen. In C. Gottfredson & B. Mosher, *Innovative performance support: Strategies and practices for learning in the workflow.* New York: McGraw-Hill.

Nguyen, F., & Klein, J. (2008). The effect of performance support and training as performance interventions. *Performance Improvement Quarterly, 21*(1), 95–114.

O'Driscoll, T. (1999). *Achieving desired business performance.* Silver Spring, MD: ISPI.

Pallarito, K. (2009, May 20). E-mailing your way to healthier habits. Retrieved from http://consumer.healthday.com/health-technology-information-18/misc -computer-health-news-150/e-mailing-your-way-to-healthier-habits-627207.html

Parskey, P. (2014). How we guide our clients to design with the end in mind. In R. Pollock, A. Jefferson, & C. W. Wick, *The field guide to the 6Ds* (pp. 495–502). San Francisco, CA: Pfeiffer.

Pasupathi, M. (2013). *How we learn.* The Great Courses. Chantilly, VA: The Teaching Company.

Patterson, K., Grenny, J., Maxfield, D., McMillan, R., & Switzler, A. (2008). *Influencer: The power to change anything.* New York: McGraw-Hill.

Patton, M. Q. (2008). *Utilization-focused evaluation* (4th ed.). Thousand Oaks, CA: Sage.

Pennebaker, R. (2009, August 30). The mediocre multitasker. *The New York Times,* p. WK5.

Petty, G. (2009). *Evidence-based teaching: A practical approach* (2nd ed.). Cheltenham, UK: Nelson Thornes Ltd.

Pfeffer, J., & Sutton, R. I. (2000). *The knowing-doing gap: How smart companies turn knowledge into action.* Boston, MA: Harvard Business School Press.

Phillips, J. J., & Phillips, P. P. (2002). 11 reasons why training & development fails ... and what you can do about it. *Training, 39*(9), 78–85.

Phillips, J. J., & Phillips, P. P. (2008). *Beyond learning objectives: Develop measurable objectives that link to the bottom line.* Alexandria, VA: ASTD Press.

Phillips, J. J., & Phillips, P. P. (2009). The real reasons we don't evaluate. *Chief Learning Officer, 8*(6), 18–23.

Phillips, P. P., Phillips, J. J., & Aaron, B. (2013). *Survey basics: A complete how-to guide to help you.* Alexandria, VA: ASTD Press.

Pink, D. H. (2006). *A whole new mind.* New York: Riverhead Books.

Pink, D. H. (2008). *Drive: The surprising truth about what motivates us.* New York: Riverhead Books.

Plotnikoff, R., McCargar, L., Wilson, P., & Loucaides, C. (2005). Efficacy of an e-mail intervention for the promotion of physical activity and nutrition behavior in the workplace context. *American Journal of Health Promotion, 19*(6), 422–429.

Pollock, R. (2013, May 9). Training is not a hammer. Retrieved from www.hci.org/blog/training-not-hammer

Pollock, R., & Jefferson, A. (2012). *Ensuring learning transfer.* Alexandria, VA: ASTD Press.

Pollock, R., Jefferson, A., & Wick, C. W. (2014). *The field guide to the 6Ds: How to use the six disciplines to transform training and development into business results.* San Francisco, CA: Pfeiffer.

Porter, M. E. (1996). What is strategy? *Harvard Business Review, 74*(6), 61–78.

Porter, M. E. (1998). *Competitive advantage: Creating and sustaining superior performance.* New York: The Free Press.

Prochaska, J., & DiClemente, C. (1983). Stages and processes of self-change in smoking: Toward an integrative model of change. *Journal of Consulting and Clinical Psychology, 51*(3), 390–395.

Prokopeak, M. (2009). Passion and precision. *Chief Learning Officer, 8*(6), 26–29.

Quinn, C. (2009). *Branding: Marketing Foundations Suite.* Online course. Durham, NC. Retrieved from http://imprintlearn.com/learn/e-learning/

Reichheld, F. F. (2003). The one number you need to grow. *Harvard Business Review, 81*(12), 46–54.

Ridge, J. B. (2013). *Evaluation techniques for difficult to measure programs: For education, nonprofit, grant funded, business and human service programs* (2nd ed.). Bloomington, IN: XLIBRIS.

Ries, A., & Trout, J. (2001). *Positioning: The battle for your mind: 20th anniversary edition.* New York: McGraw-Hill.

Rip, G. (2014). How we use proficiency coaching to improve performance. In R. Pollock, A. Jefferson, & C. W. Wick, *The field guide to the 6Ds* (pp. 475–479). San Francisco, CA: Pfeiffer.

Roam, D. (2013). *The back of the napkin: Solving problems and selling ideas with pictures.* New York: Portfolio Trade.

Robertson, D. (2014, May 12). 70:20:10: Seize the seventy. Retrieved from www.trainingzone.co.uk/feature/702010-seize-seventy/186936

Robinson, D., & Robinson, J. (2008). *Performance consulting: A practical guide for HR and learning professionals* (2nd ed.). San Francisco, CA: Berrett-Koehler.

Roche, T., & Wick, C. W. (2005). Agilent Technologies. In L. Carter, M. Sobol, P. Harkins, D. Giber, & M. Tarquino (Eds.), *Best practices in leading the global workforce: How the best global companies ensure success throughout their workforce* (pp. 1–23). Burlington, MA: Linkage Press.

Roche, T., Wick, C. W., & Stewart, M. (2005). Innovation in learning: Agilent Technologies thinks outside the box. *Journal of Organizational Excellence, 24*(4), 45–53.

Rosenbaum, S. (2014). How we bring employees up to speed in record time using the learning path methodology. In R. Pollock, A. Jefferson, & C. W. Wick, *The field guide to the 6Ds* (pp. 345–351). San Francisco, CA: Pfeiffer.

Rossett, A., & Schafer, L. (2006). *Job aids and performance support: Moving from knowledge in the classroom to knowledge everywhere* (2nd ed.). San Francisco, CA: Pfeiffer.

Rothwell, W. J., Lindholm, J., & Wallick, W. (2003). *What CEOs expect from corporate training: Building workplace learning and performance initiatives that advance organizational goals.* New York: AMACOM.

Rothwell, W., & Kazanas, H. (2008). *Mastering the instructional design process: A systematic approach* (4th ed.). San Francisco, CA: Pfeiffer.

Royer, J. M. (1979). Theories of the transfer of learning. *Educational Psychologist, 14*(1), 53–69.

Rummler, G. (2007). *Serious performance consulting according to Rummler.* San Francisco, CA: Pfeiffer.

Rummler, G. A., & Brache, A. (2012). *Improving performance: How to manage the white space on the organization chart* (3rd ed.). San Francisco, CA: Jossey-Bass.

Ruona, W., Leimbach, M., Holton. E. F. III, & Bates, R. (2002). The relationship between learner utility reactions and predicted learning transfer among trainees. *International Journal of Training and Development, 6*(4), 218–228.

Russ-Eft, D., & Preskill, H. (2009). *Evaluation in organizations: A systematic approach to enhancing learning, performance, and change* (2nd ed.). New York: Basic Books.

Ryan, T. P. (2007). *Modern experimental design.* Hoboken, NJ: Wiley-Interscience.

Saks, A., & Belcourt, M. (2006). An investigation of training activities and transfer of training in organizations. *Human Resources Management, 45*(4), 629–648.

Salas, E., Tannenbaum, S., Kraiger, K., & Smith-Jentsch, K. (2012). The science of training and development in organizations: What matters in practice. *Psychological Science in the Public Interest, 13*(2), 74–101.

Schmidt, G. (2013, Summer). Building a world-class training organization. *SPBT Focus, 23*(3), 20–22.

Schwartz, M. (2014). How we engage managers to acknowledge the achievements of leadership program participants. In R. Pollock, A. Jefferson, & C. W. Wick, *The field guide to the 6Ds* (pp. 449–452). San Francisco, CA: Pfeiffer.

Senge, P. M. (2006). *The fifth discipline: The art & practice of the learning organization.* New York: Doubleday.

Seppa, N. (2013, August 24). "Impactful distraction." *Science News, 184*(4), 20–24.

Shapiro, B., Rangan, V., & Sviokla, J. (1992). Staple yourself to an order. *Harvard Business Review, 70*(4), 113–122.

Sharkey, L. (2003). Leveraging HR: How to develop leaders in "real time." In M. Effron, R. Gandossy, & M. Goldsmith (Eds.), *Human resources in the 21st century* (pp. 67–78). San Francisco, CA: Jossey-Bass.

Short, P., & Plunkett-Gomez, M. (2014, Fall). The power of virtual coaching and mobile video. *SPBT Focus, 24*(4), 44–45.

Simons, D., & Chabris, C. (1999). Gorillas in our midst: Sustained inattentional blindness for dynamic events. *Perception, 28*(9), 1059–1074.

Sinek, S. (2009a). *Start with why: How great leaders inspire everyone to take action.* New York: Penguin.

Sinek, S. (2009b, September). How great leaders inspire action. Retrieved from https://www.ted.com/talks/simon_sinek_how_great_leaders_inspire_action

Smith, R. (2008). Aligning learning with business strategy. *T+D, 62*(11), 40–43.

Smith, R. (2010). *Strategic learning alignment: Making training a powerful business partner.* Alexandria, VA: ASTD Press.

Smith-Jentsch, K., Salas, E., & Baker, D. (1996). Training team performance-related assertiveness. *Personnel Psychology, 49*(4), 909–936.

Sousa, D. (2011). *How the brain learns.* Thousand Oaks, CA: Corwin.

Spitzer, D. (1984). Why training fails. *Performance and Instructional Journal, 23*(7), 6–10.

Stolovitch, H., & Keeps, E. (2004). *Training ain't performance.* Alexandria, VA: ASTD Press.

Subramaniam, K., Kounios, J., Parrish, T., & Jung-Beeman, M. (2009). A brain mechanism for facilitation of insight by positive affect. *Journal of Cognitive Neuroscience, 21*(3), 415–432.

Sullivan, J. (2005). Measuring the impact of executive development. In J. Bolt (Ed.), *The future of executive development* (pp. 260–284). New York: Executive Development Associates.

Tenner, A., & DeToro, I. (1997). *Process redesign: The implementation guide for managers.* Reading, MA: Addison-Wesley.

Thalheimer, W. (2006). Spacing learning events over time: What the research says. Retrieved from http://willthalheimer.typepad.com/files/spacing_learning_over_time_2006.pdf

Thalheimer, W. (2008). We are professionals, aren't we? What drives our performance? In M. Allen (Ed.), *Michael Allen's 2008 e-learning annual* (pp. 325–337). San Francisco, CA: Pfeiffer.

Thalheimer, W. (2009). *Aligning the learning and performance context: Creating spontaneous remembering.* Retrieved from www.work-learning.com/catalog.html

Tharenou, P. (2001). The relationship of training motivation to participation in training and development. *Journal of Occupational and Organizational Psychology, 74*(5), 599–621.

Thiagarajan, S. (2006). *Thiagi's 100 favorite games.* San Francisco, CA: Pfeiffer.

Thull, J. (2010). *Mastering the complex sale: How to compete and win when the stakes are high!* (2nd ed.). Hoboken, NJ: John Wiley & Sons.

Tobin, D. (2009). Corporate learning strategies. Retrieved from www.tobincls.com/5346/5367.html

Todd, S. (2009, October). *Branding learning and development.* Paper presented at the Fort Hill Best Practices Summit, Mendenhall, Pennsylvania.

Torrance, M. (2014, November). Agile and LLAMA for ISD project management. *TD at Work, 21*(1411), 1–16.

Tosti, D. (2009). Afterword. In R. Addison, C. Haig, & L. Kearney (Eds.), *Performance architecture* (p. 145). San Francisco, CA: Pfeiffer.

Trainor, D. (2004, February). *Using metrics to deliver business impact.* Presented at the Conference Board's 2004 Enterprise Learning Strategies Conference, New York.

Trolley, E. (2006). Lies about managing the learning function. In L. Israelite (Ed.), *Lies about learning* (pp. 101–126). Alexandria, VA: ASTD Press.

U.S. Coast Guard. (2009). Job aids. *In Standard Operating Procedures for the Coast Guard's Training System* (Vol. 4). Washington, DC: U.S. Coast Guard Headquarters. Retrieved from https://www.uscg.mil/forcecom/training/docs/training_SOP4_May09.pdf

Van Adelsberg, D., & Trolley, E. (1999). *Running training like a business: Delivering unmistakable value.* San Francisco, CA: Berrett-Koehler.

Vance, D. (2010). *The business of learning: How to manage corporate training to improve your bottom line.* Windsor, CO: Poudre River Press.

Van Tiem, D., Moseley, J., & Dessinger, J. (2012). *Fundamentals of performance improvement: Optimizing results through people, process, and organizations* (3rd ed.). San Francisco, CA: Pfeiffer.

Vroom, V. H. (1994). *Work and motivation.* San Francisco, CA: Jossey-Bass.

Waggl. (n.d.). Waggl: Get feedback and spark engagement one question at a time. Retrieved from www.waggl.it/

Washburn, K. D. (2010). *The architecture of learning: Designing instruction for the learning brain.* Pelham, AL: Clerestory Press.

Watkins, M. (2003). *The first 90 days: Critical success strategies for new leaders at all levels.* Boston. MA: Harvard Business School Press.

Weber, E. (2014a). How we turn learning into action. In R. Pollock, A. Jefferson, & C. W. Wick, *The field guide to the 6Ds* (pp. 459–468). San Francisco, CA: Pfeiffer.

Weber, E. (2014b). *Turning learning into action: A proven methodology for effective transfer of learning.* London: Kogan Page.

Welch, J., & Welch, S. (2005). *Winning.* New York: HarperCollins.

Wick, C. W., Pollock, R., & Jefferson, A. (2009). The new finish line for learning. *T+D, 63*(7), 64–69.

Wick, C.W., Pollock, R., & Jefferson, A. (2010). *The six disciplines of breakthrough learning: How to turn training and development into business results* (2nd ed.). San Francisco, CA: Pfeiffer.

Wick, C. W., Pollock, R., Jefferson, A., & Flanagan, R. (2006). *The six disciplines of breakthrough learning: How to turn training and development into business results* (1st ed.). San Francisco, CA: Pfeiffer.

Wik, T. (2014). How to run learning like a business. *Chief Learning Officer, 13*(6), 48–51, 60.

Wilde, K. (2006). Foreword. In C. W. Wick, R. Pollock, A. Jefferson, & R. Flanagan, *The six disciplines of breakthrough learning* (1st ed., pp. xv–xvi). San Francisco, CA: Pfeiffer.

Wilde, O. (1893). *Lady Windemere's fan.*

Willmore, J. (2006). *Job aids basics.* Alexandria, VA: ASTD Press.

Zenger, J., Folkman, J., & Sherman, R. (2005). The promise of phase 3. *Training and Development, 59*(1), 30–35.

NAME INDEX

SUBJECT INDEX

Page references followed by *fig* indicate an illustrated figure; followed by *t* indicate a table and followed by *e* indicate and exhibit.

ABOUT THE AUTHORS

Roy V.H. Pollock, **D.V.M.**, **Ph.D.**, is chief learning officer and co-founder of The 6Ds Company and co-author of *The Six Disciplines of Breakthrough Learning*, *The Field Guide to the 6Ds*, and *Getting Your Money's Worth from Training and Development*. Roy has a passion for helping individuals and teams succeed. He is a popular international speaker and consultant on improving the value created by training and development.

Roy has a unique blend of experience in business and education. He has served as chief learning officer for the Fort Hill Company; vice president, global strategic product development for SmithKline Beecham Animal Health; vice president, Companion Animal Division for Pfizer; and assistant dean for curriculum at Cornell's Veterinary College.

Roy received his B.A. from Williams College *cum laude* and his doctor of veterinary medicine and Ph.D. degrees from Cornell University. He studied medical education at the University of Illinois. Roy lives and teaches at Swamp College in Trumansburg, New York.

Andrew McK. Jefferson, **J.D.**, is co-founder and chief executive officer for The 6Ds Company. He is a co-author of *The Six Disciplines of Breakthrough Learning*, *The Field Guide to the 6Ds*, and of *Getting Your Money's Worth from Training and Development*.

Andy is a frequent and popular presenter and world-wide consultant who excels in helping companies maximize the value they realize from their investments in learning and development. He is also an accomplished business executive with deep line-management expertise.

Prior to founding The 6Ds Company, Andy served as the chief executive officer of The Fort Hill Company, CEO of Vital Home Services, and chief operating officer and general counsel of AmeriStar Technologies, Inc.

Andy is a graduate of the University of Delaware and graduated *Phi Kappa Phi* with honors from the Widener University School of Law, where he served on the school's board of overseers. Andy is a Trustee of The Unidel Foundation and serves on numerous boards. He and his family make their home in Wilmington, Delaware.

Calhoun W. Wick is the founder of the Fort Hill Company, co-author of *The Six Disciplines of Breakthrough Learning* and author of *Learning Edge: How Smart Managers and Smart Companies Stay Ahead.* Cal is internationally recognized for his work on improving the performance of managers and organizations. In 2006, he was named "Thought Leader of the Year" by ISA, the Association of Learning Providers.

Cal recognized the critical importance of learning transfer and the need for a scalable transfer solution. He was an early pioneer in the use of technology to support post-instruction transfer and application.

Cal earned his master's degree as an Alfred P. Sloan Fellow at MIT's Sloan School of Management.

About the 6Ds Company

The 6Ds Company was created to help organizations achieve even greater returns from their investments in learning and development. Roy, Andy, and their 6Ds-certified partners offer both open-enrollment and in-company 6Ds workshops and consulting services around the world. Since 2006, The 6Ds Company has partnered with John Wiley & Sons to bring the 6Ds to a global audience.

Additional information is available at: *www.the6Ds.com* or by writing info@the6Ds.com.